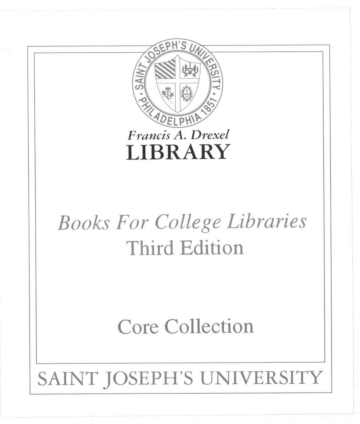

Francis A. Drexel
LIBRARY

Books For College Libraries
Third Edition

Core Collection

SAINT JOSEPH'S UNIVERSITY

**Industrial Relations and
Manpower in Construction**

The MIT Press
Cambridge, Massachusetts, and
London, England

**Industrial Relations and
Manpower in Construction**

Daniel Quinn Mills

196304

Copyright © 1972 by The Massachusetts
Institute of Technology

This book was designed by The MIT Press
Design Department. It was set in IBM
Univers by CCI Compositors, printed by
Halliday Lithograph Corp. and bound
by The Colonial Press Inc. in the United
States of America.

Library of Congress Cataloging in
Publication Data

Mills, Daniel Quinn.
    Industrial relations and manpower in
    construction.

    Bibliography: p.
    1. Construction workers — U.S.
2. Collective bargaining — Construction
industry — U.S.   3. Construction industry — U.S.   I. Title.   HD8039.B92U649
338.4'7'6240973   77-161850
ISBN 0-262-13078-5

Contents

This study is the first to bring together the large volume of new information for the 1960s on industrial relations, employment patterns, and manpower utilization and training in the building and construction industry. In the past decade the growing volume of statistical studies and public reports on the industry has been accompanied by greater awareness, if not understanding, of issues of inflation, seasonality, training, and civil rights.

The first census of construction since 1939 provides data for 1967; the report of the President's Committee on Urban Housing (the Kaiser Committee) was published in 1968; the first serious studies of seasonality since the 1920s were published in the late 1960s; new sources of data on racial composition of the work force have grown with governmental equal employment programs; the activities of the Construction Industry Collective Bargaining Commission and the Federal Mediation and Conciliation Service have generated new data on the structure of collective bargaining and labor disputes. While many of these studies and sources of data leave much to be desired, they represent a quantum jump in information over that available for the previous decades. Mr. Mills has been actively associated with this process of data development and improvement.

But the principal merit of the study is that it begins to provide a coherent explanation and understanding of construction industry developments in recent years. Consider, as one illustration, the very important question as to why construction wage rates rose so rapidly in the period 1966–1970, much more rapidly than manufacturing wages. By 1970, construction settlements were running at an average of 15 to 18 percent a year, while manufacturing settlements were no more than half that rate.

The popular explanations for these developments, to which many economists have seemed to subscribe, have laid the blame at the door of union hiring halls, the union role in apprenticeship programs, alleged exclusionary racial policies, the Davis-Bacon Act, inefficient work practices, weak contractors' organizations, or the inequality of bargaining power said to be fostered by the Taft-Hartley law. These views naturally dictated particular "solutions" to the inflation problem in terms of legislative and administrative actions to undermine what was construed to be excessive union power. Such popular "analysis" and remedies represent a faulty understanding of the structure and problems of the industry.

Mr. Mills appropriately finds the source of the inflation difficulty in other circumstances. There is a great deal of annual flow in manpower between construction and other industries. While average employment is around 3 million workers, something like 6 million work in the industry in the course of the year. The high employment of 1966–1968 in industry generally, rather than a large increase in construction employment, reduced the normal flow to construction and attracted workers out of construction. Tight labor markets, rather than developments in construction, were responsible for shortages. Within construction, a boom in industrial construction, particularly in the areas of the north-central states, was responsible for setting in motion substantial wage rate increases. Once under way in some mechanical crafts in these localities, the structure of bargaining in the industry, combined with the generally greater independence of rank-and-file workers in the period, spread the pattern of increases. The bargaining structure in these circumstances contributed to accelerated increases among rival craft bargainers. The tempo increased each year through 1970 and would, no doubt, have continued into 1971 except for public intervention through Executive Order 11588, issued by the President on March 29, 1971.

Mr. Mills provides a comparable understanding for issues of manpower supply, training, and equal employment opportunities, which have loomed large in public comments on the industry.

This volume will be of considerable interest to all those, whether students or practitioners alike, who are concerned with construction, industrial relations, and public policy related to employment.

John T. Dunlop
Cambridge, Massachusetts
October 1971

Preface

Several years ago under the auspices of the U.S. Bureau of Labor Statistics and the Construction Industry Joint Conference (an organization of national unions and contractors' associations), I began to study the problems of manpower in construction. There had been no single, comprehensive study of industrial relations and the labor market in construction since the 1920s. What was needed, however, was not only a more current work but one that would explain the behavior of the construction industry in the hectic period of full employment in the late 1960s. The importance of understanding what had led to the inflationary spiral in construction costs was underscored by the failure of two federal administrations to control inflation without resort to formal wage and price controls. Inflation in construction, and in several other key sectors, was a prime factor in the President's decision to move the national economy away from full employment in 1969 and to impose controls in 1971. Much of this book is devoted to exploring the sources of inflationary pressures in construction and the means of reducing them. If this and other sectors can be made more stable in the future, perhaps full employment can become a consistent feature of our economy.

It is unfortunate but unavoidable that a study of economic and industrial relations experience cannot be fully up to date. An author must choose some point in time at which his document ceases to explore new data or emerging events. This study ended in early 1971. However, an effort has been made in the text to stress fundamental aspects of the labor market in construction which are not likely to be modified significantly in the near future.

There was also no way to make this study completely comprehensive. The construction industry is too large, too complex, and too decentralized to allow an encyclopedic treatment, especially within the scope of a single volume. In consequence, many readers will find aspects of the industry's structure and performance discussed too briefly or not at all. I have tried, however, to reflect accurately the variousness of the industry and the relationships between contractors and their employees, and to avoid unqualified generalizations where conditions differ. But it was often necessary to allude only in passing to interesting arrangements that are local in nature or specific to a branch of the industry or a single trade. Many studies, more detailed than this one, are required to do justice to these special situations.

This book is divided into four parts. The first describes collective bargaining in the industry, including the special problems that developed during the inflation of the late 1960s. The second discusses manpower utilization in construction, involving the seasonality of work, other causes of employment intermittency, and the problems of racial imbalance. The third part is concerned exclusively with training, especially apprenticeship. The fourth addresses the problems of public policy in the industry and the special problems of residential construction.

Finally, I must express a great debt to many persons in the construction industry, in civil rights groups, and in the government of the United States who have been unsparing of their time over many years to assist me in the preparation of this book. I owe a special debt to Dr. Howard Rosen, Director of the Office of Manpower Research, Manpower Administration, U.S. Department of Labor, for the financial support of much of this research; to Miss Gail Coleman for her research assistance; to Mr. Joe Russell of the Department of Labor and Professor John T. Dunlop of Harvard University for their very extensive aid; and to my wife, Joyce, for her patience. I remain, of course, solely responsible for all errors and omissions in the text.

Construction and Collective Bargaining

1 The Construction Industry in the United States

Introduction

Construction merits close study by persons interested in the American economy generally and in industrial relations in particular. The industry is of great
importance to the overall functioning of the economy, in part because the
volume of construction expenditures constitutes a major element of private
and public investment. Variations in the level and rate of investment have
long been recognized by economists to be particularly significant in generat-
ing fluctuations in the activity of the economy as a whole. The behavior of
the construction industry is by this mechanism directly related to the economic well-being of the entire nation. Characteristics of construction that
are sometimes causes and sometimes results of the instability of total investments are a major subject of this book. In the long run, the volume of investment in buildings, roads, dams, and other construction largely determines
the capacity of our national economy to produce and distribute goods and
services for consumers.

Construction is an unusual sector of the national economy. The nature of
the production process, which generally involves fabrication and assembly
of specially designed products at a special location determined by the cus-
tomer, is much different from that found in manufacturing, service, or transportation industries. Firms, labor markets, and industrial relations in construction are specialized to meet the industry's requirements. Thus it is not
possible to acquire an understanding of the institutions and procedures of
industrial relations and manpower training in construction from studies of a
general nature, which in this country are normally based on the experience of
manufacturing industries.

Two aspects in particular of the construction industry are the source of
its influence on industrial relations in other sectors of the economy. The
first is the geographic dispersion of the industry. Virtually every community
in the nation has firms and labor organizations active in construction, unlike
many industries that are concentrated in one or a few geographic areas. The
second aspect is the employment in construction of workers whose skills are
widely used in other industries. Building and construction tradesmen are
employed in large numbers by nonconstruction firms and government
agencies on new construction work.[1] There are substantial flows of workers

[1] The employment of building tradesmen in new construction by public agencies and
nonconstruction firms for projects that these agencies or firms will own (that is, projects
built neither by contract nor for sale) is referred to as force-account construction and

between construction and other industries, reflecting differing wages and working conditions and fluctuations in the availability of jobs. Further, workers employed in construction and maintenance generally are aware of wages and conditions paid to persons of similar skills in other industries. Through the processes of mobility and comparison of wages and conditions, industrial relations in construction and other industries interact continually with each other.

General Description of Construction

Construction may be defined as a group of interrelated production activities involving the erection, maintenance, and repair of physical structures, including buildings, highways, earthworks, and so on. The value of materials, labor, and other inputs to the construction process in recent years has constituted 13 to 14 percent of the total gross national product.[2] The industry employs some 5 to 6 percent of the nation's labor force. A large proportion of these workers is skilled, so that craftsmen employed in construction generally constitute some 15 percent of the nation's skilled blue-collar workers.

Most construction is undertaken by private parties, but new construction expenditures by public authorities are roughly one-third of total construction volume, most of which is spent for projects owned by state and local governments (though much of the work is given financial assistance by the federal government). Residential construction expenditures constitute about one-third of total new construction, with nonresidential building and nonbuilding construction the remainder.

Construction contractors provided more than 3.4 million yearlong jobs in 1970[3] and, because of turnover, employed more than 6 million persons at one time or another during the year.[4] During any given month, construction

---

involves the employment of some 15 to 30 percent of all building tradesmen (data from U.S. Bureau of Labor Statistics).

[2] See current issues of *Construction Review* (monthly of U.S. Department of Commerce, Business and Defense Services Administration).

[3] Annual average employment estimates from *Employment and Earnings* (monthly issued by the U.S. Bureau of Labor Statistics). Annual average employment figures are best interpreted as measures of yearlong jobs, since they are derived by averaging monthly estimates of names on payrolls and are unaffected by turnover. See David A. Farber, "Apprenticeship in the United States: Labor Market Forces and Social Policy," *Journal of Human Resources* 2 (Winter 1969): 70–90. These estimates do not include the self-employed.

[4] Unpublished Social Security data.

(including the self-employed) employs roughly 7 to 10 percent of the male labor force in the United States, with seasonal shifts in the demand for labor largely accounting for the variance. In terms of employment, it is the largest single industry (or closely related group of industries) in the American economy.[5]

Associated with construction is a large group of ancillary industries, including among others the manufacture of structural clay products (such as brick), lumber and wood products, paints, iron and steel materials, and heating, plumbing, and electrical products. Total expenditures estimates for all construction activity (the value put-in-place measure) include, of course, the value of the products of supplying industries. In 1968, for example, total new construction value put-in-place was some $85 billion, including $36 billion in income that originated in contract construction.[6]

There are a great many firms in construction, and they are normally specialized by branch of the industry (for example, highway construction) or by trade (for example, carpentry). The 1967 census of construction, the first since 1939, showed that 349,363 establishments with a payroll (that is, with any employees) were operating as contractors or as operative builders during that year.[7] Other data indicate that there were also several hundred thousand self-employed persons in the industry.[8] The Standard Industrial Classification lists contractors by branch of the industry and by trade in a rough intermingling of the two systems of classification. Most establishments in the in-

[5] "Closely related" is meant to imply fairly great mobility of firms and employees from one branch of the industry to another and the existence of somewhat similar production processes.

[6] Value put-in-place is value of construction at a site during a given period. Income originating in construction excludes value of materials and equipment installed. (Both figures in the text are current dollar estimates.) The two sets of data are largely but not completely comparable. Total new construction value put-in-place includes construction by contract and also that done by the work force of the owner (force-account construction). Furthermore, some maintenance and repair work is done on contract. In 1967, 89 percent of contractors' receipts were from new construction; see U.S. Bureau of the Census, *1967 Census of Construction Industries* (Washington, D.C., 1970). For data on income by industry, see *Survey of Current Business* (monthly issued by the U.S. Department of Commerce, Office of Business Economics).

[7] "Operative" builders are firms that do construction not by contract but for sale or lease to others.

[8] For example, the Internal Revenue Service reported 856,000 businesses in construction in 1964; however, in *County Business Patterns,* the Census Bureau's Business Division, using Social Security data, reported only 313,000 establishments with employees in contract construction during the same year. See Peter J. Cassimates, *Economics of the Construction Industry,* National Industrial Conference Board Studies in Business Economics no. 111 (New York, 1969), pp. 26–28.

dustry are special trade contractors (for example, electrical and plumbing contractors). However, no individual sector of the special trades includes as many firms as general contracting (more than 90,000 firms in 1967).

During the 1950s and 1960s, total construction activity slowly expanded. Annual average employment increased by 22 percent from 1961 through 1969, while employment in all nonagricultural establishments expanded more than 29 percent. The slow overall growth of the industry masked significant variations in the volume of activity in particular branches. For example, private new residential construction was depressed during much of the 1960s and fell as a proportion of total new construction from 39 percent in 1961 to 33 percent in 1969. However, new private nonresidential building construction expanded from 20 percent of all new construction in 1961 to 24 percent in 1969.[9] Private nonresidential building construction may be considered the heart of the construction industry — in many ways the most sophisticated technologically and the most completely organized (that is, unionized) sector. The impact of expansion in this sector on collective bargaining is a major theme of the chapters that follow.

The Characteristics of Firms and Sectors of the Industry

The particular range of specialization in construction firms is to a large degree technologically determined, but specialization serves major economic functions as well. A specialized firm is best able to adapt to the changing demands of construction and to retain the flexibility necessary for successful operation in a highly unstable product market. Because construction projects vary considerably in structural characteristics, location, and size, a single firm attempting to perform all elements of each job would find itself constantly expanding and contracting. Flexibility is best realized by separating functions into different firms; when a building is to be erected, a group of firms are assembled through contractual relationships.[10]

The Standard Industrial Classification lists twenty types of construction firms. General building contractors, heavy and highway contractors, and

---

[9] More striking, perhaps, is another comparison. From 1961 through 1969, expenditures on private nonresidential building construction doubled, while expenditures on new residential construction rose only 40 percent.

[10] See Robinson Newcomb and Miles L. Colean, *Stabilizing Construction: The Record and the Potential* (New York: McGraw-Hill, 1952), especially Chapter 6, "The Organization of the Construction Industry."

special trade contractors constitute the three major divisions of the industry. In all, seventeen sectors in the three divisions are explicitly identified, along with a residual group of special trade contractors not classified elsewhere. The Construction Census for 1967 provides considerable information regarding each sector of the industry, by type of contractor. A brief review of certain characteristics of firms in the different sectors will illustrate the complexity of the industry's structure.

In some specialties the firm is largely a labor-only contractor, with receipts to the firm including very little other than its wage bill. In others the firm provides materials as well as labor, and in still others payments for the use of machinery constitute an important element of total billings. For example, in 1967 value-added[11] as a percent of total receipts averaged more then 90 percent for wrecking contractors but only 48 percent for plumbing, heating, and air-conditioning contractors (because of the importance of materials purchases by the contractor for installation) and 29 percent for general contractors (because of materials installed and subcontracting). Receipts from sale of materials (or fixtures) are of great importance to the plumbing firm,[12] leading both contractors and labor to try to protect the contractor's role as a supplier to the general contractor or owner. In wrecking work there is no such concern. The general contractor, in contrast to both of the foregoing, is in many respects a financial manager for a job, subcontracting most of it. General contractors are understandably concerned to retain their position as overall manager of the job by controlling the flow of project funds to subcontractors.

Capital expenditures and rental payments (largely for equipment rentals) constitute a significant element of total firm receipts in only a few sectors. Highway, heavy, and excavating contractors use considerable quantities of earthmoving, paving, and other equipment; wrecking and structural steel erection contractors also have significant capital costs. For other firms, capital and rental expenses rarely exceed 2 percent of total receipts.

Construction firms are generally small. No firm does more then 1 percent by volume of receipts of the work in the industry nationally. The bigger firms by receipts are general and heavy and highway contractors,[13] but a large por-

---

[11]"Value-added" is defined as equal to total receipts less land receipts, payments for construction work subcontracted to others, and payments for materials, components, and supplies.

[12]See Martin Segal, *The Rise of the United Association* (plumbers and pipefitters) (Cambridge: Harvard University Press, 1969).

[13]*Engineering News-Record* publishes each year a list of the 400 largest contractors, their volume (by value of contracts received), and the characteristics of their operation.

tion of their receipts are subcontracted.[14] In 1967, the average construction establishment with employees had between 9 and 10 men (the average number throughout the year). Heavy and highway contractors tend to be the largest group in terms of employees, while specialty contractors tend to be much smaller. For example, in 1967 the average painting contractor employed fewer than 5 men, the average masonry contractor 7 men, and the average electrical contractor 9 men.[15]

Finally, most construction firms are localized in operation. This is particularly the case with small firms, but it is true of many large ones as well. In 1967, receipts from the home state of a firm constituted some 88 percent of total receipts of all construction firms. In no sector of the industry were home state receipts less than 89 percent of total sector receipts except in heavy (nonhighway) work (62 percent). Even highway contracting is a largely home-state industry (91 percent of total receipts are from the home states). Localization in the industry reflects in some cases the small size of firms, in others the importance of close business or political relationships in obtaining jobs.[16]

The census unfortunately provides no published information on specialization of firms by branch of the industry. There are data, however, indicating the importance in total receipts to a sector of the industry from work performed in the different branches. In 1967, nonresidential building construction accounted for 56 percent of the construction receipts of plumbing, heating, and air-conditioning contractors, but only 36 percent of receipts for painting contractors.[17] Maintenance or repair work is of much greater importance to some types of contractors than to others. For example, repainting takes up a much larger portion of the work of painting contractors than rewiring or replumbing does for electrical or plumbing contractors.

The relative importance of different branches of the industry to the several types of contractors has major economic implications, because the characteristics of construction demand are not the same for each branch. For example, effective demand for residential work is highly responsive to changes in credit

[14]Subcontracting accounts for a larger portion of the receipts of general building contractors than of heavy and highway contractors.
[15]*1967 Census of Construction Industries.*
[16]Despite the general localization of firms, there is a limited number of companies that are national in scope or operate at different times in several areas of the country. These firms have historically had a great influence on industrial relations in construction.
[17]Highway and street construction provided only 32 percent of the receipts of highway and street contractors. The classification of contractors by type and branch becomes a little confusing at this point.

conditions. Nonresidential building is much less subject to such changes. The specialties that rely on residential work (including floor laying, tiling, painting, concrete slab placement, and carpentry) have experienced considerably different economic fortunes in recent years than those in which residential work is insignificant. In consequence, contractors who depend on residential work have had to attempt to adjust prices and wages both to the unfavorable situation in residential markets (owing to high interest rates) and to the expanding nonresidential market. The trades in which nonresidential building plays a dominant role (including electrical, steel erection, boilermaking, elevator construction, sheet metal, plumbing, and mechanical contracting) have had generally favorable economic conditions in recent years. Similarly, sectors of the industry that rely on maintenance work are often in a different economic position than those doing only new construction.

Construction expenditures for public ownership are not subject to the same influences as private work, and they constitute a largely separate market. Public expenditures made up 31 percent of all construction receipts by contractors in 1967 but were of considerably less importance to some sectors than to others. For example, highway and street contractors received 78 percent of total receipts from construction of publicly owned projects; other heavy contractors received 41 percent of receipts from public sources. Conversely, public funds made up only 25 percent of receipts by general contractors, plumbing and mechanical contractors, and electrical contractors. In those sectors in which residential work is most important, public funds were practically insignificant (for example, operative builders — largely homebuilders — received only 3 percent of total receipts from publicly owned jobs; carpentry subcontractors received 7 percent of receipts from publicly owned jobs).

Contractual and subcontractual relationships in construction are very complex. Typically an owner hires a general contractor to erect a building according to a set of specifications. The general contractor then subcontracts the elements of the job he does not wish to perform himself. But there are wide variations from this practice. In some cases an owner signs independent (prime) contracts with a different firm for each phase of a job. Under legislation in some states covering public work, several prime contracts are awarded on a single job, and the general contractor is simply one of three or four firms holding contracts directly with the state or other government agency. Furthermore, subcontractors may subcontract elements of a job themselves. In all, the 1967 census reported that 44 percent of gross construction receipts were subcontracted,[18] with general contractors subcontracting 63 percent of receipts and specialty contractors 15 percent.

The contractual relationships among contractors and subcontractors, especially between generals and their subcontractors, are a constant source of divisiveness among employers in construction.[19] The precise nature of the obligations assumed by the different firms in their contractual relationships often determine the profitability of jobs for the firms. There is a constant struggle between employers in the courts, in the legislatures, and even on the jobsites as to the nature of contractual responsibilities and their fulfillment. Since these disputes often involve large sums of money, the associations of general and specialty contractors (and in some cases the unions) often become engaged in the struggle.[20]

The relationship between general and specialty contractors has changed over time, both on the job and in terms of the relative importance of each in the industry. In 1939 general contractors accounted for 26 percent of total net receipts in all construction, in 1967 for 36 percent. The share of specialty trade contractors was correspondingly reduced, from 44.3 percent in 1939 to 34.3 percent in 1967 (see Table 1). The situation with respect to employment is the reverse. From 1939 to 1967 the proportion of yearlong jobs in construction provided by general contractors fell from 28.4 percent to 25.7 percent; the proportion provided by the specialty trades rose from 42.1 percent to 46.7 percent. (A decline in employment by highway contractors was largely offset by increased employment by heavy contractors.) These data suggest that certain elements of nonresidential building construction (that branch of the industry in which general contracting is most prevalent) have shown high rates of productivity growth since 1939. The increasing importance of general contractors in the total volume of construction and their decreasing significance in employment have contributed in recent years to bitter disputes among employers in the industry as to the relative role of general and specialty contractors in determining and implementing industrial relations policies.

[18]The estimates of total receipts subcontracted are based on a special survey included in the census. All other figures for receipts by sectors of the industry cited are *net* of subcontracts (the census reports the net figures).
[19]Disputes among contractors are a not infrequent cause of jurisdictional disputes. See John T. Dunlop, "Jurisdictional Disputes: 10 Types," *Constructor* (journal of the Associated General Contractors), July 1953, p. 165.
[20]See, for example, Richard H. Clough, *Construction Contracting* (New York: John Wiley & Sons, 1969); see also Henry A. Cohen, *Public Construction Contracts and the Law* (New York: F. W. Dodge, 1961).

Contractors' Associations

Contractors are organized by sector of the industry into trade associations, although not all contractors are members of an association. The associations normally have local, regional, and national bodies, with the national organization chartering local chapters.[21] Often, however, national staffs are small and financing is limited, so that the associations are most active and vital at the local level.

The local associations perform a wide variety of functions for their members, including public relations, lobbying, legal advice, labor relations activities, and members' benefits (such as group life insurance for contractors or types of liability insurance), and they deal with architects, owners, suppliers, and others. The national office of the association also conducts lobbying and public relations and provides legal and industrial relations advice. It often publishes periodicals carrying trade news, innovations, legislative reports, and analyses of the national scene as it affects members' concerns. Each national association normally holds a national convention and may sponsor trade shows as well.

The staffing of contractors' associations is generally sparse. Larger local associations may employ an executive director, and sometimes assistants for him, who may draw full- or part-time salaries. At the national level there is usually a full-time executive director, normally with only a small supporting staff. The Associated General Contractors, the National Association of Home Builders, and the National Electrical Contractors Association are unusual in having fairly extensive national staffs. Most of the activities of the associations at the local and national level are conducted by committees composed of and chaired by contractor members who are not compensated for their time, so that the operations of most associations depend on the voluntary efforts of individual businessmen.

[21] Major associations include the Associated General Contractors of America (AGC), the National Constructors Association, the Mason Contractors Association, the National Electrical Contractors Association, the Mechanical Contractors Association, the Painting and Decorating Contractors Association, the Sheet Metal and Air Conditioning Contractors Association, the Roofing Contractors Association, the National (Steel) Erectors Association, the International Association of Wall and Ceiling Constructors, the Lathing Contractors Association, and the National Association of Home Builders. AGC chapters are often either heavy and highway or building chapters. They include both union and nonunion contractors. There is also an association of nonunion contractors, the American Building Contractors (ABC), which includes both general and specialty contractors.

For a description of the Associated General Contractors, see Booth Mooney, *Builders for Progress* (New York: McGraw-Hill, 1965).

Table 1.   Value of Work Performed and Employment as a Percentage of Total, 1939 and 1967

	Value of Work Performed		Employment	
	1939	1967	1939	1967
General building contractors	26.0	36.0	28.4	25.7
Heavy contractors, total	27.3	25.3	27.6	25.6
Highway and street	13.1	9.6	15.0	9.0
Heavy, except highway and street	14.2	15.7	12.6	16.6
Special trade contractors, total	44.2	34.3	42.1	46.7
Plumbing, heating, air-conditioning	13.5	10.8		10.9
Painting, paperhanging, decorating	5.0	1.9		4.1
Electrical work	4.9	5.8		7.1
Masonry and other stonework	2.2	2.1		4.2
Plastering and lathing	2.0	0.8		1.4
Terrazzo, tile, marble, mosaic work	1.1	0.6		0.9
Carpentry	2.9	1.3	n.a.	2.4
Floor laying and floor work, n.e.c.[a]	0.8	0.8		1.1
Roofing and sheet-metal work	4.2	2.6		3.9
Concrete work	1.2	1.5		2.4
Water well drilling		0.4		0.4
Structural steel erection	1.8	0.8		1.2
Ornamental metalwork		0.1		0.1
Glass and glazing work	n.a.	0.3		0.4
Excavating and foundation work	0.7	1.2		1.5
Wrecking and demolition work	n.a.	0.2		0.3
Installing building equipment, n.e.c.	1.0	0.6		0.6
Special trade contractors, n.e.c.	3.1	2.5		3.7
Operative builders	2.4	4.4	1.9	2.0
Total	100.0	100.0	100.0	100.0

Source for Table 1 on the opposite page: U.S. Bureau of the Census, *1967 Census of Construction Industries* (Washington, D.C., 1970), and *1939 Census of Construction.*
[a]n.e.c. = not elsewhere classified.

The size of an association's staff, and thus the degree of professionalism in its administration, is largely a function of financing. Both local and national chapter staff must be paid from the funds of the association. Funds are raised from contractor members as dues, although the methods of obtaining funds and their level vary widely. The availability of funds to support a sizable national staff contributes strongly to the influence of certain associations on the actions of the industry as a whole.

The contractors' associations at the local level conduct labor negotiations and sign and administer collective bargaining agreements. A committee of contractors usually determines the industrial relations policies of the association, and they are approved by the membership. Negotiations are conducted by a team involving, variously, contractors, legal counsel, and association staff (if any). The national office of the association normally provides the local chapter with no more than information and advice on industrial relations.

As mentioned previously, a contractor need not be a member of a local association. Furthermore, he can be a member without being bound by the collective bargaining agreement negotiated by the association, or by its labor relations policies. Legally, an employer is included in a multiemployer bargaining unit (that is, an association) if he unequivocally intends to be bound by joint action rather than by individual bargaining. The employer's intention to be bound may be indicated by the fact of membership in an association that bargains for its members, or by written authorization.[22] Independent

---

[22]In addition to the material summarized in the text, the following aspects of the relationship between a firm and the multiemployer unit are important. Frequently an employer not a member of a bargaining association simply goes along with the association, intending to be bound by the agreement that is negotiated. If, upon joining an association, an employer states unequivocally that he will not be bound by the joint negotiations, he cannot be bound. Further, an employer may withdraw from a multiemployer unit at his own discretion on appropriate notice, except that he cannot withdraw after negotiations have begun (except by joint consent or in unusual economic circumstances). If he attempts to withdraw, he will still be legally bound by the association's agreement. There is one major exception, however. If the union involved in the negotiations agrees to the withdrawal of the employer from the association's bargaining unit, then the employer may withdraw at *any* time. The contractor cannot make his participation in multiemployer negotiations contingent upon a desirable outcome of the negotiations. Finally,

contractors (those not included in an association for bargaining purposes) are an important aspect of the industrial relations process in construction. While it is uncommon for a union to agree to different contractual terms with independents and an association, separate negotiations among a union, an association, and independents occur often and give the union an opportunity to divide the employers as a method of seeking an improved contract.

The Labor Force and Unionization

The Labor Force

The building construction labor force is composed of more than twenty crafts and many more specialties. Many contractors hire directly only one or two of these crafts. The numbers of persons and crafts hired directly will depend on the type of work and geographic area in which the contractor operates. Different branches of the industry require a different combination of crafts in the production process. Nonresidential building construction (including office, commercial, and religious buildings, but excluding industrial facilities) employs perhaps the widest range of trades. Subcontracting is also most intensely developed in this branch of the industry, reflecting the high degree of specialization of firms. The general building contractor normally hires the basic trades (carpenters, operating engineers, laborers, teamsters, and bricklayers), with subcontractors hiring the journeymen in their specialties. There is of course considerable variation in this pattern, depending on the nature of the project, its size and location, the practices of different geographic areas, and the methods of operation of different firms. Heavy and highway construction requires five trades (carpenters, laborers, operating engineers, cement masons, and teamsters), usually hired by the general contractor. Residential building construction requires fewer trades than nonresidential, although more than heavy and highway work, but it also involves specialties not found in nonresidential building. The work is generally nonunion, and jurisdictional lines among the trades are correspondingly less pronounced. Other branches of the industry require a relatively large proportion of men in specific trades. Pipeline construction, for example, requires primarily laborers, operating engineers, and pipefitters. Construction of indus-

in the event that some contractors withdraw from the association during negotiations with union consent, other members of the association remain bound by an agreement reached by the association. (The preceding is a summary of NLRB and court policy and decisions regarding the relationship of an individual employer to a multiemployer bargaining unit.)

trial plants may require many pipefitters, often with special qualifications to do the complex piping work involved. Since each branch of the industry has its own labor requirements, the trades are confronted with different combinations of employment opportunities in the different branches. On the one hand, the industry is characterized by specialization of the labor force among its various branches; on the other, it is an incomplete specialization that creates a substantial pattern of interdependence as well.

The unpredictable nature of construction has important consequences for the labor force. The volume of construction in process fluctuates in part because some types of construction work are seasonal, but also because of market demand. Sometimes large projects are built in an area that has seen very little major construction for years before and will see very little for years after. Other areas, especially large cities, experience a large and continuing volume of work. But even there, some types of work may be declining in importance while others are increasing. In an unstable economic environment, employers greatly value flexibility of operations — the ability to hire and lay off men as job conditions demand it. Equally important is the ability to hire men at a predetermined wage scale, so that the profit on a job is not eaten up by wage changes negotiated after the bid price has been established. The flexibility that the contractor requires for profitable operation, however, is sometimes translated into insecurity for the workingman. Labor organizations attempt to limit the effects on the employee of the changing conditions in which he and the contractor must operate.

Union Organization in Construction
The peculiar economic conditions and characteristics of employment in construction dictate that employers and unions are placed in a much more intimate relationship than in many other industries. Construction projects are normally of short duration, and the employment relationship itself is weak. Collective bargaining agreements, however, are areawide; they cover the contractor whenever and wherever he works in the area. The agreement provides a continuing relationship between the union and the employer. Because employers are generally small and employment intermittent, training is normally done on an areawide, multiemployer basis. Contractors and unions therefore negotiate not only wages and working conditions but also training and hiring practices. In an unstable industry, the development and retention of a skilled labor force require that employers and unions agree to practices that preserve the job opportunities of craftsmen. The problem, of course, is to adopt policies that are effective in protecting employment opportunities without either

unduly restricting needed expansion of the labor force or promoting uneco-
nomic practices.

Not all crafts, sectors of the industry, or geographic areas are unionized,
and some are less unionized than others. But all contractors, union or nonunion, are influenced by the prevailing labor relations policies. Wages in the
union sector influence what nonunion contractors must pay. Frequently,
nonunion scales are below union scales, but union men are often considered
better mechanics. The various statistical studies bearing on degree of union
organization and union-nonunion wage differentials are surveyed in the note
that follows. The material is technical in nature, and the general reader may
wish to read only the summarizing paragraph at the end.

Technical note: Unionization in construction The degree of union organization in construction is subject to considerable statistical confusion. There are
no continuous data reporting degree of organization for the industry as a
whole or for its branches. There have been, however, several one-time surveys
of parts of the industry that offer some insight into organization. Perhaps
most useful is the Census Bureau's special Survey of Economic Opportunity
in 1967, taken from a sample of 30,000 households. The survey reported
union membership or nonmembership (and annual earnings in 1966) based
on occupation of longest job. It showed that 53.7 percent of construction
craftsmen (private wage and salary workers) were union members and 30.4
percent of construction laborers. However, on an annual average, only some
70 percent of construction craftsmen are employed in the construction
industry.[23] Because craftsmen employed in construction are almost certainly more fully organized than those in other industries, these estimates of
organization are probably lower limits. Estimates prepared from membership
data provided by the international unions suggest that in 1967 an average of
63 percent of carpenters employed in construction itself were organized.[24]
For all crafts combined, census estimates based on a 1967 survey show 44
percent of those employed in construction (as major source of earnings) in
1966 were union members. Another special survey that dealt only with
general building contractors for 1965 reported that 45 percent of workers

[23]See D. Q. Mills, "Manpower in Construction: New Methods and Measures," in Industrial Relations Research Association, *Proceedings of the Twentieth Annual Winter Meeting: The Development and Use of Manpower* (Madison, Wisc., 1967), p. 270.
[24]Estimates made by Mr. Joe Russell.

(without regard to craft) were working in firms with collective bargaining contracts covering a majority of the firm's workers.[25]

Evaluating the degree of organization in the industry is complicated by the fact that employment is both seasonal and casual. The international unions report that their membership in construction (they have varying magnitudes of nonconstruction membership) varies less through the seasons than employment in the industry generally. Depending, therefore, on the distribution of unemployment among union and nonunion workers, union membership may form a higher percentage of the work force in the winter than in the summer. Finally, many persons who are not union members work for brief periods in the peak of the construction season under union contracts. Any particular estimates of the degree of organization in construction must therefore be treated carefully.

Certainly some branches of the industry are more fully organized than others. Residential construction, accounting for perhaps a third of total construction employment (though this figure varies both seasonally and annually and must be estimated from expenditure data for lack of direct surveys), is probably the least organized; perhaps 80 percent of the workers are nonunion.[26] Nonresidential building is probably the most fully organized branch of the industry, with heavy and highway work following. Geographically, union organization is greatest in major cities, least in suburban and rural areas and the South. Finally, what little evidence is available suggests that union organization in construction was not markedly greater in the mid-1960s than in 1936, when a Bureau of Labor Statistics study indicated that 68 percent of construction workers employed by general contractors or their subcontractors were union members.[27]

Hourly wage scales and annual earnings are probably greater in the unionized sector than in nonunion construction, but again data regarding the size of the differentials are incomplete and often ambiguous. The 1965 survey of general

[25] U.S. Bureau of Labor Statistics, *Building Construction, 1965,* Report no. 335-9 (Washington, D.C., 1968).

[26] A 1969 survey by the National Association of Home Builders of its membership found that while 18.6 percent of firms reported that they were unionized in all crafts, 36.1 percent reported that they were unionized in *no* craft. Firms reporting that they were unionized were also asked if they operated open or union shop; 52 percent said they operated open shop. See Michael Sumichrast and Sara A. Frankel, *Profile of the Builder and His Industry* (Washington, D.C.: National Association of Home Builders, 1970), p. 200.

[27] U.S. Bureau of Labor Statistics, *Compensation in the Construction Industry,* Bulletin no. 1656 (Washington, D.C., 1970), p. 10.

contractors reported that average compensation of construction workers in companies where the majority of workers were covered by collective bargaining was 52 percent higher than in other firms.[28] Unfortunately, these data are not standardized in any way for differences in the distribution of workers among occupations. The 1967 survey of economic opportunity suggested that annual earnings in 1966 of males whose longest job was in construction and who were union members exceeded those of nonunion members by 71 percent.[29] But these earnings data again include all occupations and total annual earnings from all sources. Some additional information for limited geographic areas on union and nonunion wages is included in a survey done of home-builders in the Columbus, Ohio, metropolitan area. The survey found that 2.5 percent of the homebuilders interviewed were paying above union scale in at least one craft, about 8 percent were paying the union scale with fringe benefits, 13 percent were paying the union scale without fringe benefits, and 60 percent were paying below the union scale. (Fourteen percent of the home-builders reported using union carpenters; 13 percent, union bricklayers; 22 percent, union electricians; 21 percent, union plumbers; 12 percent, union painters; and 9 percent, union laborers.)[30]

In summary, union organization varies by branch of the industry, by geographic area, and by trade. Organization also varies both seasonally and over periods of years. No dramatic changes in the general level of organization have been visible since the 1930s, but in the late 1960s a variety of indicators suggested that union organization in many branches of the industry was lessening.[31] Also, wage scales tend on the average to be higher in the unionized sectors of the industry and may considerably exceed those in nonunion construction in many areas. These wage differentials may reflect not only the bargaining power of the unions but also differences in skill levels and product market conditions.

The Building and Construction Trades Unions

The role of jurisdiction Construction workers are largely organized into nine-

---

[28]U.S. Bureau of Labor Statistics, *Building Construction, 1965.*
[29]Data from U.S. Bureau of Labor Statistics.
[30]Battelle Memorial Institute, "Final Report on a Study of Recent Developments in the Residential Construction Industry," prepared by Edward E. Laitila et.al. for the Small Business Administration (Columbus, Ohio, 1969), pp. 47 ff. See also John T. Dunlop and D. Q. Mills, "Manpower in Construction," in *Report of the President's Committee on Urban Housing: Technical Studies,* vol. 2 (Washington, D.C., 1968), pp. 286–287, for a list of geographic areas in which the Secretary of State issued Davis-Bacon determinations for housing construction that were below the areas' union scales.
[31]See Chapter 3.

Table 2. Affiliates of the Building and Construction Trades Department, AFL-CIO, 1967

National Union	Total Membership	Percentage in Contract Construction
Asbestos workers	12,500	95
Boilermakers	140,000	n.a.
Bricklayers	149,000	100
Carpenters	800,000	75
Electrical workers (IBEW)	875,000	19
Elevator constructors	14,450	100
Engineers, operating	330,000	75
Granite cutters	2843	n.a.
Ironworkers	162,006	74
Laborers	474,529	84
Lathers	15,500	100
Marble polishers	8659	83
Painters	200,569	n.a.
Plasterers	68,000	99
Plumbers	284,707	85
Roofers	22,811	100
Sheet metal workers	100,000	n.a.
Stonecutters	1900	n.a.

Source: U.S. Bureau of Labor Statistics, *Directory of National and International Labor Unions in the United States, 1967,* Bulletin no. 1596 (Washington, D.C., 1968).

teen international unions, eighteen of which are affiliated with the Building and Construction Trades Department of the AFL-CIO. Table 2 includes a list of the AFL-CIO affiliates (the Teamsters are former affiliates), 1967 membership of the international union, and the proportion of the membership estimated to be in contract construction.[32]

The building and construction trades unions are organized, for the most part, on a craft or craft-industrial basis. Craft unions (for example, the carpenters and bricklayers) are the result of the association in the union of persons doing a particular type of work, often involving a particular material (such as wood or masonry). With the historical growth of the union, related specialties were often absorbed into the international, in some cases through mergers or absorption of other national unions. Furthermore, as new materials replaced the traditional materials used by the craft (such as metal for wood or cinder block

[32]Several other unions also have construction membership, including the International Union of District 50 (formerly a district of the United Mine Workers) and the Allied Industrial Workers. These unions have relatively small representation in the industry and are largely confined to certain limited geographic regions. They are self-proclaimed industrial unions rather than craft or craft-industrial unions.

for brick), the jurisdiction of the union was extended to cover work with the new materials.[33] Craft-industrial unions are organized as much around an industry as an occupation and generally include several work specialties. For example, the electricians and the pipe trades have work jurisdictions that apply to the electrical contracting industry and to the plumbing and pipe-fitting industry, respectively. In the case of the pipe trades, the industry orientation of the union is especially clear, for steamfitters and plumbers were organized into separate international unions until 1911-1913, when the United Association absorbed the steam fitters and was granted a charter by the American Federation of Labor as the only international union in the plumbing and pipe-fitting industry.[34]

The concept of exclusive work jurisdiction is fundamental to unionism in the building and construction trades.[35] At some point in its history, each international union received a charter from the AFL, granting it exclusive jurisdiction over specific work operations; as stated previously, these might involve either manual operations, designated materials, or designated industries. Each union asserts the right to control its work jurisdiction by obtaining recognition as the source of manpower for employers doing the work or by obtaining the affiliation of employees assigned to the work. Because of changes in materials, technology, and other aspects of construction, the jurisdictional claims of different unions often conflict and may become the source of disputes at the jobsite.[36] Jurisdictional disputes are a major source of friction in the industrial relations of the construction industry. Strikes over jurisdiction are common, even though collective bargaining agreements and federal

[33] For a description of this process in the carpenters' trade, see Robert A. Christie, *Empire in Wood: A History of the Carpenters Union* (Ithaca, N.Y.: Cornell University Press, 1956).

[34] See Segal, *Rise of the United Association.*

[35] See Philip Taft, *The AFL in the Time of Gompers* (New York: Harper & Brothers, 1957), pp. 185–210. For interpretations of the underlying reasons for the dependence of the American labor movement in general, and the building trades in particular, on the principle of exclusive work jurisdiction, see Selig Perlman, *A Theory of the Labor Movement* (New York: Macmillan, 1928), and Nathaniel R. Whitney, "Jurisdiction in American Building Trades Unions," Johns Hopkins University Studies in Historical and Political Science no. 1 (Baltimore, 1914).

[36] There were, on the average, 350 jurisdictional strikes in construction each year in the 1960s (1960–1967), involving the loss of some 250,000 workdays. Jurisdictional strikes constituted 40 percent of all work stoppages in construction between 1960 and 1968, but they were generally of short duration, contributing only 8 percent of man-days lost due to strikes in the industry. See Bureau of Labor Statistics, *Compensation in the Construction Industry,* p. 28.

law prohibit them. Jurisdictional disputes arise when two or more unions claim the assignment of men to a particular task. They are inevitable in an industry in which wage rates and other conditions of employment differ by occupation, in which mechanics are organized into labor unions on craft lines, and in which production processes and materials are continually changing.[37] Because work jurisdiction is central to industrial relations in construction, it is unlikely that disputes can ever be eliminated. Rather, the objective of the industry has been to develop means of resolving them in such a way as to minimize the disruption of production.[38]

The most important mechanisms for voluntary adjustment are the National Joint Board for the Settlement of Jurisdictional Disputes and the National Appeals Board. Most collective bargaining contracts in construction specify that disputes over work assignment are to be submitted for resolution to the National Joint Board. The board is made up of representatives both of contractors (general and specialty) and of unions and is chaired by an impartial umpire (a neutral).[39]

Structure and administration of the unions The international unions are associations of American and Canadian local unions. Groups of locals in various trades participated in the foundation of internationals some eighty to one hundred years ago in order to prevent the standards of the organized sectors of the trade from being undercut by the unorganized sectors. The local unions that participated in the founding of the internationals gave them the power to issue and remove charters and to organize and combine locals. The early period was marked by bitter struggles, which in some cases have continued to

[37]See Dunlop, "Jurisdictional Disputes: 10 Types." See also Kenneth T. Strand, *Jurisdictional Disputes in Construction* (n.p.: Washington State University Press, 1961).
[38]Jurisdictional strikes were made an unfair labor practice under the Taft-Hartley Act in 1947, and procedures for the handling of such cases by the National Labor Relations Board were spelled out in Section 10(k) of the act. Section 10(l) provides injunctive relief and opens the way for damage suits in federal courts. In adjusting a jurisdictional dispute, the NLRB is required to make a positive assignment of work to a particular craft. Unfortunately, the NLRB has little expertise in dealing with competing jurisdictional claims, and its procedures are lengthy and cumbersome. As a result, contractors and unions have sought to establish voluntary machinery internal to the industry to adjust these disputes. Federal law explicitly recognizes the value of private dispute settlement and allows the NLRB to dismiss unfair labor practice charges when voluntary adjustment is attempted.
[39]The National Joint Board has undergone alteration from time to time, often with changes in membership and procedures, because of dissatisfaction on the part of contractors' associations and international unions with its methods of settling disputes and its inability in some cases to achieve enforcement of its awards.

this date, between international union officers and larger locals over their respective roles.[40]

An international union is normally headed by a general president and a general executive board. Regional vice-presidents or executive board members and the general president are elected by the convention of the labor organization meeting at intervals of two to five years. The international organization is governed by a constitution adopted and amended by the convention (which is the supreme body of the international union).[41] Between conventions, the general president runs the labor organization, subject to the approval of the general executive board, which is made up of general vice-presidents normally selected to represent the various regions of the country. General presidents rarely take part in collective bargaining except when national agreements are being developed and rarely intervene in the operation of local unions unless matters of general policy are in question. In many cases such authority is used with great circumspection by international presidents, who are well aware of the political danger of alienating local unions (whose representatives must reelect the general president in the national convention).

In many international unions there exists an intermediate structure, consisting of regional vice-presidents and perhaps regional councils, as well as district councils in metropolitan areas, which may exercise authority in the affairs of the local unions. In some trades and in some areas regional or district councils exercise the collective bargaining functions and other prerogatives that usually rest with the local unions. Representatives of the international unions are stationed in the regions to represent the international officers and to assist locals in collective bargaining and other functions. The international representatives are ordinarily appointed by the general president of the international union and report to him. They visit local unions and district councils in their regions regularly. Some unions maintain staffs of international organizers, as well as other representatives.[42]

Each local union owes its existence to a charter from the international union, despite the fact that many of them antedate the formation of the international. The charter defines both a geographic and work jurisdiction for

[40]See Lloyd Ulman, *The Rise of the National Trade Union,* 2nd ed. (Cambridge: Harvard University Press, 1966).
[41]Some internationals require in addition a ratification vote by the membership to approve constitutional amendments.
[42]For a discussion of the administration of the Laborers' International Union, see Derek C. Bok and John T. Dunlop, *Labor and the American Community* (New York: Simon & Schuster, 1970), pp. 140–150.

the local. In some of the larger cities, for example, a single international union will have chartered several locals with distinctive work jurisdictions.

In the building trades, local unions have for the most part preserved a considerable degree of autonomy in the conduct of their affairs. The negotiation of collective bargaining agreements, their provisions, and their enforcement are largely matters of local authority, subject only to general supervision from the international union. There are, of course, exceptions to this rule, some of which will be discussed later.

Locals in the building trades vary in size from very large organizations composed of thousands of members and with extensive geographic jurisdictions to groupings of only a few members and a geographic jurisdiction of a few square miles. Locals tend to be larger in the trades in which the geographic mobility of contractors and workers is greatest. In some crafts, small local unions in the same geographic area have been organized into district councils for collective bargaining and other purposes.

Normally the local union elects a president, vice-president, and other officers, some of whom are salaried, and one or more business agents (or business managers), who are almost always full-time salaried representatives. In the case of very large unions, there may be a general agent and several business managers.[43] The role of the president and vice-president of the local union is often restricted to internal matters that are less important to industrial relations than the role of the business agent. Though business agents are full-time salaried officials of the local, they must stand for election either at one-, two-, or three-year intervals. Most business agents do not work with the tools of the trade, although they have worked as journeymen themselves and are familiar with jobsite conditions. The functions of the business agent are as many as one would expect of a representative of an institution in the labor market. The business agent, along with other officers or an elected committee, represents the labor organization in negotiations with employers and their representatives. He represents the labor organization before legislative bodies and public officials of all sorts and assists legal counsel in the courts. He handles grievances on the jobsite, representing the views of his membership and the interests of the labor organization. He directs strikes, boycotts, or whatever concerted activities are undertaken by the local; he defends its jurisdiction from encroachment by other labor organizations or by employers. Business agents attend the international union convention and are to a large extent the

[43] One western local of the Operating Engineers, for example, elects a general agent who then appoints some seventy business agents.

constituency of the general president and executive board of the international union.

As an elected official of the local union, the business agent is a political figure in what is essentially a political office. Often he has offices or other favors with which to support his position. Business agents may be voted out of office. Opponents of an agent in the local union will watch him carefully and may bring before the membership at the election alleged deficiencies in his leadership. Generally, an agent who is out of touch with the views of his membership does not remain an agent long.

In many respects, the most important function of business agents, as well as international union officials and representatives, is what may be called policing the trade. Once agreements, practices, and customs of the trade are established, both by general agreement among the union membership and by explicit or tacit agreement with employers, the process of enforcing these arrangements begins. Enforcement of agreements and regulations in construction is often a difficult task. The industry is characterized by dispersed work sites that are continually shifting and by very rapid turnover both of employees and of employers. There may at any time be a large number of visiting contractors working within the local's jurisdiction, and it may also have a number of men working temporarily as nonmembers on permit. It may even deal with a number of employers who are working union in some trades and nonunion in others. In this complex and shifting environment, business agents and representatives seek to maintain the standards provided in the collective bargaining agreement.

2

The Structure of
Collective Bargaining
in Construction

Introduction

Both the organization of labor unions and collective bargaining between
workers and employers have a long history in construction. Organized labor
and bargaining evolved as a decentralized structure based on craft and geographic locality. The passage of federal labor legislation (the National Labor
Relations Act of 1935 and its successors) establishing procedures for
union organization and collective negotiations with employers affected construction very little. On the contrary, provisions were made in the text and
administration of the law to accommodate the special circumstances of
construction.

During the more than one hundred years since collective bargaining began
in construction, a great many changes have occurred in the industry. Many of
them have been incorporated into the procedures for bargaining. Among the
most significant changes in the industry have been the emergence of new
forms of specialization, among both employers and workers; the vast growth
of the industry and the emergence of a group of firms operating on an extended geographic basis, often nationwide; and the emergence of many new
technological processes and methods. In some instances the modifications of
bargaining resulting from changes in the industry have had the effect of merg-
ing labor organizations or separate bargaining arrangements, but more often
special arrangements have been added to those already in existence, adding to
the complexity of the relationships.

In the full-employment economy of the late 1960s there arose in construction a range of problems associated with collective bargaining. The most sa-
lient ones were rapidly rising labor costs and extensive work stoppages. Collective bargaining was not the sole source of these problems, but it was without
doubt a major factor contributing to the problems of collective bargaining.[1]

[1] Labor costs were not the only input costs that rose rapidly in the 1960s. Increases in
land values, interest charges, and some materials prices all exceeded the rate of increase
in labor costs for several years. By late 1970, interest charges and wholesale materials
price increases were declining, and the inflation in land values was slowing down. Negotiated wage scales, however, were climbing at the highest rate in our history. Thus, the
problem of wage increases may be usefully separated from other inputs. In any case,
this and the following chapter are concerned only with the structure of collective bargaining and the determination of wages in construction. For a discussion of labor costs
and other input costs in housing construction, see Nathaniel Goldfinger, "The Myth of
Housing Costs," *American Federationist* (journal of the AFL-CIO) 76 (December 1969):
1–6.
   Project delays and cost overruns, which became endemic in the late 1960s, were
as much the result of poor design and poor project management as of labor relations

There are , of course, no generally accepted standards by which to measure how high wages should be,[2] or how many strikes are too many. But in the late 1960s construction experienced rates of wage increase without precedent in our economy in this century, and a greater frequency of strikes than at any time since the Korean War. These circumstances created serious difficulties for all parties involved in the industry: labor, employers, government, and the public. Rising construction wages contributed importantly to rising construction costs, which in turn helped to keep alive an inflationary spiral in the economy generally. In attempting to control the rate of cost increase, the federal government and private owners cut back on construction expenditures. Strikes disrupted the industry seriously in many areas, leaving many construction mechanics unemployed for long periods, driving many contractors into bankruptcy, and causing losses to the purchasers of new buildings. Turmoil in the union sector contributed to a general expansion of non-union construction in branches of the industry previously the exclusive preserve of union contractors. Finally, the federal government, strongly concerned with inflation in construction and several other sectors (including food processing and distribution, and medicine), applied such strong fiscal and monetary restraints that a recession occurred in 1970. The excesses associated with full employment had led to falling demand and rising unemployment.[3] Few sectors felt the consequences more immediately than construction.

Many observers linked the problems of construction with collective bargaining, and those of the collective bargaining process with the bargaining structure itself.[4] Certainly, the experience of full employment placed sub-

---

difficulties. But the problems of project design and management must be the subject of another study.

[2] Many arguments may be offered to justify rapidly increasing wage scales in construction, including the hazardous and unpleasant nature of much of the work, the likelihood of unemployment, the absence of job security provisions, and the skill required for many tasks. Still further justifications might be offered in particular cases, including catching up with other crafts or other areas and specially unfavorable circumstances on certain jobs.

[3] The unemployment rate for construction workers rose from 6 percent in 1969 to approximately 11 percent in 1970. Annual average employment in contract construction declined some 8 percent from 1969 to 1970.

[4] See, for example. U.S. Chamber of Commerce, *Chaos in the Construction Industry* (Washington, D.C., 1969); Thomas O'Hanlon, "The Stranglehold of the Building Trades," *Fortune* 78 (December 1968): 102ff., and "The Case against the Unions," *ibid.* 77 (January 1968): 170ff. The President, in Executive Order no. 11242 (issued September 22, 1969) establishing the Construction Industry Collective Bargaining Commission, spoke of "the pressing problems" of the industry and related them in part to the bargaining structure.

stantial strains on the bargaining structure, leading to prolonged strikes and exacerbating inflationary tendencies. The successful operation of a full-employment economy in the future will apparently require an ability to prevent full employment in construction from being accompanied by rapidly rising labor costs and industrial unrest.

The bargaining structure should be understood here to include the following aspects of industrial relations: (1) centralization: issues negotiated centrally rather than negotiated locally; also, issues bargained on an industry-wide rather than on a sector basis; (2) the parties: the parties at the bargaining table and any others bound by the agreement (in construction, this might also include employers who accept the terms of the agreement without necessarily signing it); (3) the scope: the subjects of negotiation; (4) procedures: the rules by which the collective bargaining process is conducted, including the sequence of negotiations, the authority of the negotiators, the process of ratification of the agreement, and the establishment of patterns in the settlements.

Bargaining in Perspective

The structure of industrial relations in construction is suited to the conditions of the industry in that it reflects the organization of the product market. Specialization of contracting firms is dictated by economic advantage;[5] however, it requires flexibility in the operation of the firm. Flexibility is of critical importance, for a firm may have to expand or contract rapidly as market conditions change or move great distances in search of work. The craft union supports the specialization of production by performing functions that stabilize the industry. It enforces standards of work and compensation, participates in formal training, and refers men to work at the contractor's request. At the same time, it allows the direct employment relationship (between the individual employer and employee) to remain casual. Thus the craft union structure may be said to allow exceedingly flexible employ-

[5] Consider, for example, the structure of construction enterprises under centrally planned economies, in which contracting by specialized enterprises has been retained as the most economically sensible organization of the industry. See Kang Chao, *The Construction Industry in Communist China* (Chicago: Aldine, 1968), and Joseph S. Berliner, "The USSR Construction Industry," report prepared for the Council for Economic and Industrial Research (Washington, D.C., 1955). For the historical development of specialized firms in this country, see William Haber, *Industrial Relations in the Building Industry* (Cambridge: Harvard University Press, 1930).

ment relationships to exist for a skilled work force while maintaining stability in the labor market as a whole.

Collective bargaining agreements in construction are normally negotiated between a local union in a single craft and an association of contractors who employ men of that craft. The agreement normally covers a geographic area (the geographic jurisdiction of the local) and specific types of work operations (the work jurisdiction of the craft). Wage scales, fringe benefits, and working conditions are established for the term of the agreement (generally two or three years), although wages may be increased in steps during this period. Because the agreement establishes uniform conditions that apply to all union contractors in the geographic area, it serves to regulate competition among firms with respect to wages and working conditions. Labor costs remain a major aspect of price competition among firms,[6] but only in relation to the efficiency of the builder in his use of the labor force, not by virtue of differing wages and conditions of work.

The psychological relationship between employers and unions is complex and requires brief comment. Attitudes on both sides are so ambivalent that one side may express a group of seemingly contradictory beliefs about the other. This ambivalence extends even to factual discussions and proposals for change, so that many persons unfamiliar with the industry have been misled as to its character and operation. Essentially, the employer recognizes that the unions (1) provide a measure of stability in a highly competitive industry; (2) perform an important manpower allocation function; and (3) represent the wishes and welfare of the workingman (with whom the employer may sympathize). Conversely, however, the union may interfere with the employer's prerogatives as a businessman, restricting his range of operations and thus his chance to make a profit on a job. The union can be either friend or enemy to the employer. The union leadership and the workers are similarly divided in their attitudes toward management. On the one hand, the contractor provides the work; he gives the worker a livelihood. Usually he is personally known to the leadership and may actually be a member or past member of the union. In construction, there is little of the social distance that exists in other industries between employers and the workingman. On the other

---

[6] Pricing in construction is a very complex process with many variations. In work financed by public funds, jobs are normally awarded by competitive bidding among contractors based upon a finished set of architectural and engineering specifications. The low bidder is normally selected. In private work, prices are often negotiated between the owner and the general contractor, and between the general and his subcontractors.

hand, the contractor is also viewed as an employer who tries at every turn to limit the gains of labor in the interest of his own profit.

Conditions in the industry determine the relative strength of favorable or unfavorable attitudes held by either party toward the other. For example, in a full-employment economy the initiative rests most often with labor, and the attitudes of contractors toward the unions are generally negative. The classic pattern of bargaining is for each side to exact its demands from the other when conditions permit, then to try to hang on to its gains as conditions change. The ambivalence of personal attitudes and relationships in such a context is easy to understand.

The technology of the industry has changed over the years, but the fundamentals of the industrial relations structure have hardly altered in this century. The view that unions have recently obtained a stranglehold[7] over industrial relations in construction is erroneous. The relative strength of unions in the building trades has been recognized for years. In 1930 William Haber wrote that in construction "the preponderance of power on the part of organized labor in many cities has made relations with the employers arbitrary and dictatorial." If anything, real collective bargaining has come to the industry only since 1930, for Haber added that "the collective agreement has only in a few instances been the result of a deliberate proceeding where the demands and counter-demands were discussed and weighted by equals. On the contrary, in too many cases...the agreement has resembled a union ultimatum."[8] Yet there have been repeated attempts, some successful, by employers to break up the unions. In 1900, employers in Chicago locked out the unions with the intent of forcing the Building Trades Council to dissolve. On April 26, 1901, the council voted to disband. "The unions were thoroughly defeated and discouraged; their closed-shop monopoly was broken, their funds exhausted and their membership defeated." But by 1907 the council was restored, the unions were reorganized individually, and the secretary of the Contractors' Council wrote, " 'The recuperative powers of the defeated unions are certainly marvelous.' "[9] In the aftermath of World War I, the unions experienced similar patterns of struggle, defeat, and reorganization in many areas, and the Depression saw the process repeated. The favorable economic and legal climate since the 1930s, with the development of a national

---

[7] See O'Hanlon, "The Stranglehold of the Building Trades" and "The Case against the Unions."
[8] Haber, *Industrial Relations in the Building Industry,* pp. 512, 513.
[9] *Ibid.,* pp. 376-378.

labor policy encouraging collective bargaining,[10] has enabled the unions to make considerable gains, but their strength is not a recent development in construction.

The contractors have nonetheless been able to retain a considerable range of prerogatives in the face of the unions. For example, the employers launched the lockout of 1900 in Chicago in order to defend six cardinal principles, none of which has been abandoned some seventy years later: two have been won, and the other four settled by compromise.[11] Recently a study was made of the contract provisions of the Associated General Contractors' agreement with the basic trades in the San Francisco area.[12] The detailed evidence in the report suggests relatively little interference and no appreciable change in management's right to manage over the period 1947–1969. The contractors, despite occasional public statements to the contrary, have successfully preserved many of the prerogatives needed to retain flexibility in a variable market.[13] In this context, the contractor's side of the bargaining table has had its own long record of success in negotiations with the building trades.[14]

[10]Unlike the industrial unions, however, the building and construction trades have made very little use of the National Labor Relations Board to establish bargaining relationships based on elections or to gain control over employment practices.

[11]Haber, *Industrial Relations in the Building Industry,* pp. 374–375. The principles and their current status follow: (1) no restrictions on the use of machinery (restrictions exist today regarding *how* machinery is used); (2) no restriction on the use of any manufactured article except prison-made goods (the union label limits use of nonunion-made goods today); (3) no limitations on the amount of work a man should perform during his working day (for the most part formally nonexistent today); (4) denial of the right of any person to interfere with workmen during working hours (except stewards and business agents, whose rights are limited); (5) denial of the right of the unions to prohibit the employment of apprentices (programs are now jointly administered); (5) elimination of the sympathetic strike (contracts now include no-strike clauses).

[12]Raymond K. Rowley and J. Sabbatini, "Labor Unions' Encroachment on Contractors' Right to Manage," Stanford University, Department of Civil Engineering, Construction Institute Technological Memo no. 1 (Stanford, Calif., 1969).

[13]Employers' prerogatives are not ordinarily written into collective bargaining agreements in construction. However, the Boston Model Cities training agreement specified them, at least in part, for virtually all branches of the industry in the area: "The determination of the size of the work force, the allocation of work to employees, establishment of quality standards and judgment of workmanship required, and the maintenance of discipline shall be the responsibility of the employing general or specialty contractor." Agreement among the Building and Construction Trades Council of Boston, the Associated General Contractors of Massachusetts, Inc., and the Building Trades Employers Association of Eastern Massachusetts, Inc., October 11, 1968.

[14]Perhaps one reason why bargaining appears so unilateral in construction is that normally the unions restrict the scope of the issues discussed within understood limits. For example, demands for job security are rarely raised by the union with the individual firm (a potentially disastrous issue for contractors). Were the unions more apt to challenge basic fea-

Current Structure of Bargaining

Local and Regional Bargaining
Collective bargaining agreements in construction are characteristically negotiated between a local union (or district council) in a single craft and the employers of that craft as represented by an association.[15] The agreements
apply within the geographic jurisdiction of the local union (or district council) and apply to its work jurisdiction. Local negotiations are prevalent in
building construction, but there are many exceptions. In some branches of
the industry, nationwide agreements exist (especially those dealing with pipelines, sprinkler systems, and elevator construction). In others, regional agreements embracing many states have been established (for example, those
covering boilermakers, operating engineers on dredging work, and electricians on transmission lines). In some states, local unions are so large that
entire states are covered by a single contract with a single local. The structure
of bargaining also varies greatly in the different regions of the country. In the
West, bargaining on a regional or metropolitan-area basis has become the
standard for most crafts. In the rest of the country, local bargaining is still
the rule. In some cases, special geographic areas have been established for
coverage of pension plans, medical care, and work jurisdiction.

Contractor associations with collective bargaining responsibilities vary
widely in composition and structure. In some areas of the Northeast, negotiations are conducted by a building trades employers' association in a metropolitan area, or by a builders' exchange. Negotiations with each craft are
carried out by a committee including contractors or representatives of the
trade association (for example, if negotiations are with the painters, the local
association of the painting and decorating contractors will be included) and
representatives of the building trades employers' association (BTEA) or the
builders' exchange. The BTEA plays a central coordinating role when several
negotiations are in progress at once or follow one another closely. In the
remainder of the country, negotiations usually are limited to the individual
trades and their employers, but the general contractors' associations (espe-

---

tures of the industrial relations system in the industry, there would certainly be a more
visible response from the contractors.

[15]See John T. Dunlop, "The Industrial Relations System in Construction," in Arnold R.
Weber, ed., *The Structure of Collective Bargaining* (Chicago: University of Chicago Graduate
School of Business, 1961), pp. 255–278, for a very useful and extensive analysis and
description of bargaining structure in construction.

cially the AGC on the local level) will often attempt to provide some central leadership and negotiate their own contracts with the trades they employ.

Coordination of negotiations involving several trades in an area may take place formally at the bargaining table (through representatives of all the trades and employers' associations), informally through separate negotiations, or not at all, although there is always considerable interest in what each trade is doing or is going to do. In some cities, the building trades council and the BTEA traditionally hold formal negotiations for many trades at the same time. In others, unusual economic or other circumstances have led the unions to coordinate the negotiations themselves. Employers' associations sometimes do the same. Coordination of the bargaining among trades, when it succeeds, often avoids the succession of work stoppages that may occur as one trade after another negotiates a contract. However, the attempt by one side to impose formal coordinated bargaining where the other objects may lead to strikes or lockouts.

Another form of coordination of negotiations occurs when contract dates for several trades expire simultaneously, or nearly so. In this situation, the local building trades council and employers associations often try to settle any disputes that may arise without disruptive effects on the industry. Common expiration dates are not an unusual feature of bargaining structure in some cities, and they appear to have contributed to industrial relations stability in many instances.

The role of national union and contractor representatives in local collective bargaining is limited. For the most part, wages and conditions of work are negotiated without their participation, although they may become involved when work stoppages threaten. Currently, most of the eighteen international unions have authority under their constitutions to approve local strikes (and thus the issues over which strikes may occur), but in many unions such authority can be exercised only when strike benefits are requested.[16] Repre-

---

[16] For example, the Constitution of the United Association (plumbers and pipefitters) provides (Section 202) that

"all strike and lockout applications shall be referred to the General Organizer in the district, who shall be required to make a thorough investigation and report to the General Executive Board for their approval or disapproval. They, in conjunction with the General Secretary-Treasurer, shall carefully consider such applications with regard to chances of success in the proposed strike or lockout, justice of demands, and finances liable to be involved."

On the other hand, the Bricklayers Constitution provides (Article XXIII, Section 4) that

"a subordinate union, affiliated for one year or longer with this International Union, and *requiring assistance in indicating the rights and privileges guaranteed by this*

sentatives of the international are frequently sent into local negotiations to assist the local, or they may enter union-employer disputes to settle strikes. However, the willingness of national union leadership to intervene in local disputes is often limited, partly because of internal political reasons, but also because Title I of the Landrum-Griffin Act has generated lawsuits by local unions and their membership opposing intervention by international officers. National contractors' associations have no power to intervene in local disputes and are too poorly staffed to do so. In consequence, the national authorities are rarely able to inject their concern for the broader context of a bargaining situation into negotiations on the local level. This is particularly the case in the absence of a dispute between the local union and the local employers' association, although their agreement may be inconsistent with national objectives.

The multiemployer nature of the collective bargaining agreement and the competitive nature of the industry give rise to the special problem of the independent (nonassociation) contractor. Both the union and union contractors have a particular interest in the position taken by independents. The union must try to prevent nonunion employers, or employers who have agreements with other crafts, from undermining its agreement with an association of contractors. In order to preserve union standards (and to retain the work jurisdiction of the bargaining unit), subcontracting clauses are customarily included in collective bargaining agreements. These clauses prohibit employers who are signatories from subcontracting work to firms that fail to comply with the standards of the union agreement.[17] Union employers want to be certain that other employers do not receive better conditions from the union, for lesser wage scales or other provisions granted to an independent contractor might give him a competitive advantage over association members. The agreement of an association with the union extends the same provisions

---

Constitution, shall transmit to the Executive Board a clear, concise and comprehensive statement in writing of all the facts and circumstances connected with the pending trouble of cause of dissatisfaction." (Emphasis added.)

[17]Considerable litigation surrounds these clauses. The proviso to Section 8 (c) of the Taft-Hartley Act exempts clauses regulating contracting or subcontracting at the jobsite in the construction industry from the "hot-cargo" prohibition. Apparently the NLRB has now adopted the position that construction unions may picket or strike to obtain subcontracting clauses but may not picket or strike for enforcement purposes. The continuing litigation recently saw the NLRB strike down the subcontracting clause developed by the IBEW for insertion in local collective bargaining agreements, in part because the clause appeared to the NLRB to require recognition of the union by the subcontractor, as well as compliance with union standards. Local 437, IBEW, 180 NLRB No. 32 (1969).

to all participating employers. Independent contractors are normally required by the union to become signatories. In many cases, either formally or informally, the union agrees that any more favorable provisions granted to independent contractors will be extended to association members.[18]

Special problems relating to the choice of representatives exist on the employers' side of the bargaining table. In many areas, either the Associated General Contractors or another organization of general or specialty contractors (such as a builders' exchange or a building trades employers' association) negotiates agreements with several crafts. Where an organization of this kind sets overall bargaining policy, the employers may present a more united front than would otherwise be the case. On the other hand, the problem of relative wages and conditions for different trades and branches often plagues this arrangement. In other areas, each craft union bargains with its own employers individually or with an association. In the larger cities, in which numerous specialty contractors may exist in each branch of the industry, bargaining is likely to be quite decentralized. In some areas, there is so much movement of contractors in and out and the volume of work done by local builders is so small compared to that done by outside contractors that the employers' side of the table must be virtually reassembled at each negotiation. In such situations, the union side enjoys much greater continuity of organization and representation than the employers.

The structure of bargaining in construction reflects economic conditions in several ways. In slack periods, the unions will sometimes agree to negotiate as a group or to follow a pattern set by a joint negotiating committee. In better times, each local tends to pursue its own advantage independently of the others. In fact, the structure of bargaining among crafts in a local context can be remarkably flexible. When the economy is weak, the unions take shelter under the protective wing of the local building and construction trades council.[19] When the economy is strong, they seek to split up the correspond-

---

[18] An NLRB trial examiner has recently held that it is an unfair labor practice for a union to require that an independent contractor execute a contract identical to the union's agreement with a contractors' association. Electrical Workers (IBEW), NLRB Cases Nos. 9-CB-1445, 1493, and 9-CC-450 (January 2, 1970). More commonly, the union begins by insisting on better conditions from the independent contractor and then modifies its position in accordance with the provisions of the association agreement.

[19] In Detroit, for example, as economic conditions worsened in the winter and spring of 1970, twenty-four unions, bargaining for the first time on a multiunion basis, negotiated a two-year master labor agreement with contractor associations. See "Multi-Trade Bargaining Sets Wage Scales," *Engineering News-Record*, March 5, 1970, p. 52.

ing employers' joint groups and to bargain individually with the association of their own employers.[20]

The National Agreement

The structure of bargaining is further complicated by the existence of the national agreement. Most international unions have either negotiated or adopted a standardized agreement for the visiting contractor. Normally these agreements are short documents providing that the contractor will do union work, subcontract all work union, and meet the local wages, fringes, and other working conditions. In return, the contractor is given assistance from the international union in manning his job and in settling any disputes that arise in the course of it. Agreements of this type are to be distinguished from those establishing conditions in branches of the industry, such as pipeline construction, in which there is no local bargaining.[21] The national agreement is much more important in some branches of the industry than in others. In the construction of industrial plants, the National Constructors Association (NCA) and the United Association of Plumbers and Pipefitters (UA) have an agreement that establishes terms and conditions of work on a national basis, but wages and fringe benefits are negotiated locally. Where no locally negotiated wage scales are applicable, the contractor and the international union negotiate the rates to be paid on the project.[22]

The national agreement may be used in several different types of situations by the international union. It is often used as a method of organizing the large contractor whose area of operation covers much of the country. The problems of the large contractor existed at the origin of the national contract

---

[20] For example, a multicraft bargaining pattern established in Cleveland in 1947 broke up under the impact of the high-employment economy of the 1960s.

[21] In the elevator construction branch of the industry, a national agreement applies (under which local wage rates are determined by a formula related to the hourly rates of other building trades unions), but New York City has a separate arrangement. Boilermakers' agreements are normally on a multistate, regional basis that involves the national representatives in bargaining. See pp. 38 ff. for a discussion of the structure of bargaining in different branches of the industry.

[22] It is difficult to estimate the employment of mechanics under national agreements, but it is undoubtedly a large proportion of the total work force. At the Ironworkers Convention in 1964, a union official commented that NCA contractors (all operating under national agreements) were "the largest contractors' association in the United States — (1) operating 100% union and (2) largest for the direct employment of building trades unions." *The Iron Worker* (journal of the International Association of Bridge, Structural and Ornamental Iron Workers) 64 (November 1964): 8. President Schoemann of the UA announced to his 1961 convention that contractors under the national agreement "at any given time. . . are responsible for the employment of some 25 to 50 percent of our members." "UA 28th Convention Proceedings," *United Association Journal* 76 (November 1961): 36.

some forty years ago, and meeting them remains its major function.[23] Another use of the agreement is to organize contractors and their employees who perform specialties (which often involve new and unusual processes), within the work jurisdiction of a union.[24]

There have been three major sources of dissatisfaction with the national agreement. While its most outspoken critics have been local contractors' associations, local unions have been hardly less bitter in some cases. The dissatisfaction of local contractors' associations is caused by the fact that the national agreement normally binds the national contractor to the conditions of the local agreement but not to the local contractors' association or bargaining unit. In consequence, contractors with national agreements often work through local strikes or lockouts and may appear in other ways to undermine the position of local contractors' associations.[25] Ironically, large local unions often feel that the national contract, by binding the large contractor to the local agreement, deprives the local of the chance to extract concessions from him that it could not obtain from local builders. It is not uncommon to have resolutions from strong locals introduced at national conventions challenging the authority of the general president to negotiate national agreements or modifying this authority.[26] Responding to such a

[23] For the origin of the national agreement, see Haber, *Industrial Relations in the Building Industry,* p. 288.

[24] The Painters, for example, have negotiated a national agreement covering priming, painting, coating, and preparatory work for water storage systems and general storage tanks. The national agreement is with the National Tank Fabricating and Erector Contractors and a number of independent contractors who do most of the work on tank towers, reservoirs, standpipes, chemical plant penstocks, surge tanks, and ground storage tanks. See Brotherhood of Painters, Decorators and Paperhangers of America, *22nd General Convention: Reports of General Officers* (1969), p. 12. See also "Painters Win National Pact on Tank Jobs," *AFL-CIO News,* July 25, 1970, p. 3.

[25] In 1970, the Associated General Contractors' national body adopted a policy under which it will ask for the resignation of any member firm whose labor policy requires it to work during a contract negotiation strike or lockout involving a local AGC chapter.

[26] The following resolution was submitted by Local Union 816, Paducah, Kentucky, to the 1966 convention of the IBEW and was *not* adopted:

"In Article IV, Section 3, Paragraph 12 Powers of the I.P. 'to enter into, or authorize and I.V.P., representatives, or assistant to enter into, agreements with any national or international labor organization or association of employers, or with any company, corporation, or firm doing an inter-state, or inter-provincial business in electrical work, to cover the entire jurisdiction of the IBEW.'

"This resolution is to add to this paragraph 'Employees covered by said agreements shall elect by popular vote every two years, the representatives negotiating said agreements.'

"The purpose of this resolution is to guarantee every member a right to vote for his representative. It is not directed at any representative, nor do we have any gripe against any representative. These rights have been guaranteed by Federal law and we feel should apply to everyone."

challenge at his 1961 convention, President Schoemann of the UA replied,

Now what I am suggesting is, that by means of the National Construction Agreement we have been able to get something we wanted and needed very badly — the unionization of large national construction firms which at one time operated non-union everyplace. If it had been possible to organize these contractors by means of local agreements, the national agreement would never have come into being.

When most of these contractors were organized, there was no Taft-Hartley and no Landrum-Griffin, no Denver Building Trades rule and no mandatory injunction. Even in those good old days, our local unions acting alone could not organize the national contractors. How on earth are you going to get the job done today?

But let's assume that your local union is a big strong local union, one that thinks it can best take care of its business its own way. Sometimes, for the right answer to our problems, we have to go back to the most fundamental principles. The union mechanic who works on commercial and industrial jobs cannot say to the non-union mechanic who works on residential jobs: I have no need for you. In time, that non-union mechanic will acquire skill. His non-union contractor will acquire a pool of skilled non-union men, and he will be able to underbid the fair contractor on commercial work, and he will get that work.[27]

That the national agreement does protect the national contractor from the exactions of strong locals is particularly clear in the case of the Operating Engineers. There are serious problems with the national agreement, President Wharton reported to his convention in 1969, because of

. . .the conditions that many local unions impose upon the National contractors which they are unable to secure in their local contracts with the local contractors association. This makes for many problems of enforcement and breeds discontent in the local union and distrust for the local unions and the International which sign the agreement. The attempt to impose conditions beyond those provided for in the local with work stoppages to insure such demands have caused these agreements to lose favor among the contractors and the owners with the result that many projects that would otherwise have been built are now in the nonunion category, likewise, many contractors formerly union are now nonunion and rarely ever return to the fold.[28]

In summary, the national agreement does tend to undercut local contractors during a strike. But it also prevents the local unions from exacting concessions from visiting contractors that local contractors would refuse to grant (a situation to which the local contractors are likely to be willing witnesses). By protecting the visiting contractor from local resistance, the national agree-

---

International Brotherhood of Electrical Workers, *Proceedings of the 20th Convention* (1966), p. 311.

[27]"U.A. 28th Convention Proceedings," p. 37.

[28]International Union of Operating Engineers, *Officers' Report to the 28th Convention* (1968), p. 30.

ment tends to preserve competition in the industry. Finally, it helps local and national unions to organize contractors who might otherwise be non-union.

Special Arrangements for Certain Branches of Construction

The mainstream of construction is the nonresidential building sector. Histori-cally, this sector has been the most strongly organized and has established the highest wage rates and best working conditions. It is the sector in which local collective bargaining is most prevalent. Other branches of the industry are often covered by different collective bargaining agreements or by differ-ent conditions negotiated in a single agreement, primarily designed for building construction. Separately negotiated provisions are most important for heavy and highway construction, pipeline construction, gas distribution, contract maintenance, homebuilding (in some instances), and, most recently, prefabricated residential building construction. Heavy and highway construc-tion assumed considerable importance in the 1920s and 1930s, and it was during these decades that employers' associations developed in this branch of the industry. Employers in heavy and highway construction strongly resisted the imposition of building construction work rules and wage rates on their industry. Organization of these contractors was undertaken in the 1950s by several crafts simultaneously through the negotiation of specific agreements for heavy and highway work, often on a statewide basis.[29]

Pipeline construction was largely unorganized in the late 1940s, but a joint campaign by the four crafts most involved in pipeline work signed up most of the contractors in this branch of the industry by 1952. Initially, heavy and highway rates and conditions were applied to pipeline work, but in the early 1960s the pipeline contractors obtained separate agreements. The pipeline agreements specify wage rates by geographic zones, fringes, working condi-tions and special crew composition, and travel pay arrangements.[30] Recently, the UA and the Laborers have developed national gas distribution agreements that are separate from those in other branches of the industry.[31]

---

[29] For a historical description of the organization of heavy and highway work, includ-ing the role of the National Joint Heavy and Highway Construction Committee, see Garth Mangum, *The Operating Engineers: The Economic History of a Trade Union* (Cambridge: Harvard University Press, 1964). For a more recent description of the activities of the re-formed committee, see Bricklayers, Masons and Plasterers Inter-national Union of America, *25th Biennial and 77th Report of the President. . .* (1968), p. 10.

[30] See Mangum, *Operating Engineers,* for a history of the pipeline agreements.

[31] See the discussion of gas distribution agreements by President Wharton, Internation-

In the late 1950s, thirteen of the international building trades unions established the General Presidents' Committee on Contract Maintenance. This committee has sole authority to negotiate and administer project agreements. A contractor with a maintenance contract may apply to the committee for a project agreement, which may be granted if he and the job meet certain conditions. Under the agreement, the contractor commits himself to paying the regular building trades hourly rates in the area (building construction rates) in return for several concessions on other working conditions. Such an agreement might include, for example, maintenance by contract in an oil refinery.[32]

Separate agreements for homebuilding have never been common, although crafts sometimes negotiate special rates for homebuilding. Generally, nonresidential building rates and conditions are applied to homebuilding by the union, and homebuilders are represented on employers' negotiating committees in some crafts.[33] Finally, special agreements for prefabricated home manufacturers and erectors are now being negotiated under various guises.

Some branches of the industry have special mechanisms for settling disputes. The Council on Industrial Relations for the Electrical Contracting Industry is a national joint body that since 1921 has arbitrated disputes submitted to it by local parties when a strike threatened. The arbitration awards of the CIR extend to wage rates and other proposed changes in collective bargaining agreements.[34] Since most local unions are bound to decisions of the CIR as a means of resolving disputes short of strikes, the electrical branch of the industry has for years been almost strike-free.

Since 1950, the pipe industry has developed its own industrial relations council, modeled after the CIR. In recent years, escalating wages, labor shortages, and other problems often resulting in strikes have caused employers in

---

al Union of Operating Engineers, *Officers' Report to the 28th Convention* (1968), p. 44.

[32] By 1970 there were 92 maintenance-by-contract agreements nationally. Problems with these agreements included disputes with in-plant industrial unions who sought to obtain maintenance work for themselves from their employers and continued jurisdictional disputes among the building trades themselves. See the report of Carpenters' Vice-President Skinner, *The Carpenter* 90 (October 1970): 39, 45; also Mangum, *Operating Engineers,* p. 268.

[33] Much homebuilding is nonunion, and even where work is wholly or partially union, the commercial agreement is difficult for the unions to enforce.

[34] See Council on Industrial Relations for the Electrical Contracting Industry, *Rules and Procedures,* 9th ed. (Washington, D.C., 1968).

the pipe trades to seek to expand the council's activities.[35] The sheet metal industry has followed suit. The tilesetters have had for many years another form of dispute settlement machinery. Local unions, intent on protecting their capacity to obtain improved agreements without national union intervention, have resisted arbitration. In 1961, the National Constructors' Association and the Building and Construction Trades Department of the AFL-CIO entered into a National Disputes Adjustment Plan the purpose of which was to reduce the frequency of work stoppages. The plan provides for prejob conferences to deal with disputes before work is started, and it provides machinery (involving the international union) to settle disputes without stoppages.[36] Attempts to establish similar machinery for dispute settlements between the AGC and the basic trades at the national level have thus far been unsuccessful.

Project agreements For large projects involving a considerable volume of construction at a single site (or interrelated group of sites) over a period of years, a special agreement will sometimes be negotiated. It may involve the owner of the project as well as his contractors, or it may be sought by the contractor at the owner's insistence. These agreements normally attempt to guarantee the progress of the work without interruption by strikes and to establish special mechanisms for dispute settlement; sometimes they provide means for determining wages and conditions at the projects. While project agreements may be negotiated independently at the national level, at other times they are negotiated with the full cooperation of local parties.

Two Examples of Bargaining Structure

Fragmented bargaining in New York State The bargaining structure of New York State is a good example of the fragmented bargaining characteristic of the eastern United States.[37] It is extremely complex, involving at least 720 local unions representing some 21 crafts. These locals bargain with no fewer

[35]See, for example, the speech of President Anthony L. Cherne of the Mechanical Contractors Association of America to the convention of the UA in 1966, "Special UA 29th Convention Issue," *United Association Journal* 78 (December 1966). See also the speech of President Robert L. Horovitz of the National Association of Plumbing, Heating, and Cooling Contractors, *ibid.,* p. 136.

[36]See National Constructors Association and AFL-CIO Building and Construction Trades Department, *National Disputes Adjustment Plan,* rev. ed. (Washington, D.C., 1968).

[37]The following description of bargaining structure was prepared by the U.S. Department of Labor in the summer of 1970.

than 160 different employer associations. There are about 400 agreements covering both building and heavy and highway construction.[38]

The number of local unions in each craft ranges from 3 for the sprinkler-fitters (of the United Association) to 139 building locals for the carpenters. The carpenters and several other crafts have grouped local unions in some areas into district councils for collective bargaining. There are 16 carpenters' district councils in the state. The number of separate agreements for each craft ranges from 1 for the sprinklerfitters to 46 for the plumbers (see Table 3). The crafts may bargain with a single employer association or with as many as 37 different associations to produce the agreements covering the state's work force (some 100,000 employees).

Geographic jurisdictions of the locals vary from a single township to the entire state. Local jurisdiction normally follows county lines, and in some instances township lines. In at least 4 crafts — bricklayers, lathers, plumbers, and teamsters — the geographic jurisdiction of at least one local covers two or more noncontiguous areas. In most crafts that have both building and heavy and highway branches, the heavy and highway agreements involve much broader geographic jurisdictions.

Generally, there is no uniformity among crafts within the geographic boundaries of bargaining units, whether they are local unions or district councils. Some crafts have a few units in an area where others have many. Furthermore, even where areas of about the same size are included in bargaining units, their boundaries rarely coincide. Rather, there is a complex pattern of overlapping jurisdictions.

Because local unions were established before improvements in transportation, and around cities or towns that later grew greatly, many crafts have separate geographic jurisdictions (and separate collective bargaining contracts) within single labor market areas. To demonstrate the lack of uniformity among crafts and to highlight the complexity of the various jurisdictions, Table 4 shows the number of locals or district councils within 25- and 50-mile radii of 5 cities in upper New York State. (The 5 selected cities are spaced at intervals across the center of the state.)

There is an average of 69 local unions within a 25-mile radius of these 5 cities and an average of 160 local unions within a 50-mile radius. Bargaining

---

[38] This section and the next describe bargaining structure as it applies to building and heavy and highway construction. They exclude branches of the industry (such as pipeline construction) to which separate national arrangements apply.

Table 3. Number of Local Unions, Number of Associations Involved in Bargaining, and Number of Agreements by Construction Craft, New York State, Summer 1970

Craft	No. of Locals	No. of Associations Involved in Bargaining	No. of Agreements
Asbestos workers	6	6	6
Boilermakers	4	3	3
Bricklayers	56	21	41
Carpenters (building)	139 l (16 dc)	35	23
Carpenters (h and h)	100	16	16
Cement masons (h and h)	56	n.a.	8
Electricians (inside)	28	25	28
Electricians (linemen)	4	4	4
Elevator constructors	7	n.a.	1 (several wage zones)
Glaziers	10	n.a.	10
Ironworkers	15	7	12
Laborers (building)	36	37	26
Laborers (h and h)	26	n.a.	9
Lathers	20	14	20
Operating engineers (building)	10	23	13
Operating engineers (h and h)	12	11	8
Painters	26	25	25
Pile drivers (building)	6 l + 4 dc		
Pile drivers (h and h)	6 l + 4 dc	16	10
Plasterers	49	10	41
Plumbers	50	33	46
Roofers	12	10	12
Sheet metal workers	11	13	11
Sprinklerfitters	3	1	1
Steamfitters	n.a.	n.a.	n.a.
Teamsters (building)	16	16	17
Teamsters (h and h)	16	3	3

Source: Data assembled from collective bargaining agreements by the Construction Industry Collective Bargaining Commission.
Note: h and h = heavy and highway; l = local unions; dc = district councils.

Table 4. Number of Local Unions or District Councils with Bargaining Jurisdiction within 25 and 50 Miles of 5 Selected Cities in New York State, Summer 1970

Craft	Buffalo		Rochester		Syracuse		Utica		Albany	
	25 mi.	50 mi.	25 mi.	50 mi.	25 mi.	50 mi.	25 mi.	50 mi.	25 mi.	50 mi.
Asbestos workers	1	2	1	3	1	3	1	2	1	3
Boilermakers	1	1	1	2	1	3	2	2	1	2
Bricklayers	6	10	4	8	6	13	5	12	4	10
Carpenters (building)	4	6	2	6	4	7	3	7	2	5
Carpenters (h and h)	2	5	2	4	3	6	3	6	2	6
Cement masons (h and h)	5	9	3	7	6	13	5	13	1	6
Electricians (inside)	2	7	3	7	4	8	3	7	3	6
Electricians (linemen)	1	1	1	1	1	1	1	1	1	1
Elevator constructors	2	3	3	5	3	8	4	7	3	6
Glaziers	1	2	2	4	1	5	2	6	1	3
Ironworkers	2	4	1	5	1	8	2	4	1	4
Laborers (building)	4	5	2	7	5	11	3	9	3	8
Laborers (h and h)	4	7	2	6	5	10	3	10	4	9
Lathers	3	4	2	7	4	8	2	5	2	5
Operating engineers (building)	2	5	2	5	2	6	3	5	1	2
Operating engineers (h and h)	3	4	2	5	1	3	2	3	4	5
Painters	2	5	3	4	4	9	5	10	5	11
Piledrivers (building)	1	3	2	4	4	7	2	6	2	5
Piledrivers (h and h)	1	2	2	3	3	6	2	6	2	6
Plasterers	5	10	4	8	7	14	5	14	1	7
Plumbers	2	6	3	10	5	13	3	9	4	10
Roofers	1	3	2	5	1	4	2	3	1	3
Sheet metal workers	2	4	2	5	1	3	1	2	1	3
Sprinklerfitters	2	2	1	1	1	1	1	1	1	1
Steamfitters	2	6	3	9	3	10	4	11	6	12
Teamsters (building)	2	4	2	6	4	7	3	7	1	4
Teamsters (h and h)	1	3	2	5	4	7	3	5	1	5
Totals	64	123	59	142	85	196	76	180	59	148

Source: Data assembled from collective bargaining agreements by the Construction Industry Collective Bargaining Commission.
Note: h and h = heavy and highway.

in building construction is most fragmented among bricklayers, carpenters, electricians, laborers, painters, plasterers, plumbers, and steamfitters. To select a single instance, there are an average of 5 bricklayers locals within a 25-mile radius of each city, and 11 within 50 miles. Examples of extreme fragmentation are shown by the 14 plasterers locals and 13 bricklayers, cement masons, and plumbers locals (respectively) within a 50-mile radius of Rochester, and the 12 steamfitters, 11 painters, and 10 bricklayers and plumbers locals (respectively) within a 50-mile radius of Albany.

It should not be inferred from these data that the bargaining structure in New York State is more complex now than it was in the past. On the contrary, in most crafts local unions have been merged and district councils created in order to reduce the fragmentation of bargaining units. The merger of local unions is not a simple process for an international union, however, for many locals prize their separate jurisdiction highly. Mergers very often create distinct political problems for the international union and sometimes provoke employer opposition as well.

In most crafts doing both building and heavy and highway work, the geographic jurisdiction of the local union or district council is also the bargaining jurisdiction for the building branch, while the heavy and highway branch usually combines several locals for bargaining purposes. For example, the 16 carpenters district councils negotiate 23 building agreements but only 16 heavy and highway agreements; building laborers work under 26 agreements, heavy and highway laborers under only 9; operating engineers have 13 building agreements but only 8 heavy and highway agreements.[39] There are fewer agreements in heavy and highway work, and the heavy and highway agreements provide a common expiration date and uniform working conditions for signatory local unions and contractors' associations. Wage rates are often bargained on a local basis; one agreement may provide a uniform total wage and fringe package, but allocation of the package to wages and fringes varies from local to local.

New York City constitutes a largely separate area of industrial relations from the upstate region. The structure of bargaining in the city reflects both the interdependency of firms and crafts in this small but densely populated geographic area and their intense specialization, which is probably more pro-

[39]The less fragmented bargaining structure in heavy and highway work reflects the greater mobility of contractors in this branch.

nounced here than anywhere else in the United States.[40] For example, the bricklayers international union (BMPIU) has 6 locals in the New York City area without any bricklayer membership; instead, members are waterproofers, tile-setters, marble setters, and cement block layers. The 7 BMPIU locals in the city that include bricklayers bargain jointly through an executive (i.e., district) council with 3 employers' associations; the specialty locals bargain separately with associations of their own contractors. The New York City District Council of Carpenters represents 27 local unions in negotiations with employers. These locals include carpenters, dock builders, millwrights, pile drivers, and soft floor layers. Three other local unions representing mill-wrights, pile drivers, dock builders, and timbermen bargain separately. The laborers have 21 separate local unions in New York, most of which are general building locals, the others specialty locals. One local union in the city bargains with 7 separate employer associations. The ironworkers have 5 local unions, 2 of which are structural ironworkers (i.e., steel erectors), one a riggers and machinery movers local, another an ornamental ironworkers local, and another a local of stone derrickmen. Despite this diversity, the ironworkers in New York City lack jurisdiction over the placing of reinforcing iron rods in concrete, a jurisdiction they have everywhere else in the nation. Instead, reinforcing ironwork is in the jurisdiction of the metallic lathers. Similar specialization of the work force exists in other trades.

New York City possesses its own board for jurisdictional awards, and an industry-wide mechanism for consultation regarding disputes at the termination of contracts through the Building and Construction Trades Council (BCTC) and the Building Trades Employers' Association (BTEA), both of metropolitan New York. In 1950, the BCTC and the BTEA began to conduct multitrade bargaining for several of the basic trades. Two contracts were negotiated before the arrangement broke up in 1953-1954, mainly because some of the participants felt that nonparticipating trades (especially the mechanicals) were obtaining better settlements.

Regional bargaining in California During the 1940s and 1950s, regional bargaining was adopted by the basic trades[41] and by most special trades in Cali-

---

[40]The high degree of specialization in New York City construction is made possible by the volume of work in the area, the proximity of work sites, the availability of internal transportation, and an historic policy of excluding out-of-city contractors and workmen.

[41]Traditionally, trades employed directly by the general contractor, including carpen-

fornia to replace a form of localized bargaining resembling that of upper New York State. While regional bargaining by craft appears to have been largely successful in California, a simultaneous effort at multicraft bargaining has failed. The results of regional bargaining have been mixed but probably involve less friction and a more stable system of industrial relations than in New York.

Bargaining structure in construction is less fragmented in California than in New York, but it is complex all the same. In 1963, 3 national agreements applied (covering the sprinklerfitters, pipeline construction, and elevator construction), 2 multistate agreements, 2 statewide agreements, separate regional agreements for northern and southern California in the basic and pipe trades, 7 metropolitan agreements for various cities and trades, and primarily local agreements for 3 trades (electricians, sheet metal workers, and bricklayers). There were 483 local unions of 19 international unions, with jurisdiction over 27 separate crafts in addition to building laborers and helpers. Some 335,000 workers employed by 33,000 contractors were involved.[42]

The regional agreements in the basic trades are noteworthy. In northern California, an Associated General Contractors chapter is the collective bargaining representative for 4 employer associations, which are signatories to most of the agreements involving the basic trades. Agreements cover all 46 counties of northern California for 4 trades but until 1971 excluded the San Francisco Bay area (4 counties) for carpenters. The southern California basic trades agreements cover 11 counties in all cases and are negotiated by a joint committee representing 4 contractors' associations. Homebuilder associations are signatory to the agreements in both the northern and southern regions.[43]

Regional bargaining in California came about in part because of the difficulties of union organization in many parts of the state. California has not always been a hospitable climate for the building trades. From 1921 to 1935, collective bargaining in the basic trades was effectively suspended by the Industrial Association (an organization of contractors, owners, banks, and material suppliers), which imposed the so-called "American Plan," or open shop, on many sectors of construction.[44] Collective bargaining resumed in

ters, cement masons, operating engineers, laborers, and teamsters. These are also the trades most involved in heavy and highway construction.

[42] See Gordon W. Bertram, *Consolidated Bargaining in California Construction* (Los Angeles: University of California Institute of Industrial Relations, 1966), pp. 6, 8. Bertram describes the structure of bargaining as of 1963.

[43] *Ibid.,* p. 11.

[44] See Frederick L. Ryan, *Industrial Relations and the San Francisco Building Trades* (Norman: University of Oklahoma Press, 1936).

the late 1930s, but many locals were still unable to obtain formal agreements. In 1941, regional agreements with most of the basic trades were signed in both northern and southern California, providing the unions with areawide organization and contracts, and employers with more uniform conditions and greater industrial relations stability.[45]

The importance of organization campaigns to the structure of collective bargaining in the industry in California is underlined by the negotiation in 1941 of the Southern California Master Labor Agreement.[46] It provided for organization by the basic trades in an area long weakly and incompletely organized. The Master Labor Agreement was between the southern California chapter of the AGC and all the building trades unions and 9 building trades councils; other employers' associations later joined with the AGC in negotiating it. One set of negotiations established wage scales for the 6 basic trades, while the special trades negotiated separately with their own contractors. However, the agreement influenced negotiations in the special trades through the local building trades councils on the one hand, and through the general contractors in their relations with special trade subcontractors on the other.[47] The Master Labor Agreement collapsed in early 1950, when first the carpenters, then the operating engineers, and then the ironworkers withdrew. By this date, apparently, the industry was well organized, and the trades wished to be free to pursue their interests independently.[48] In later years, groups of the basic trades sometimes negotiated jointly with the employers, for a time renewing the multitrade pattern of the past, but the Master Labor Agreement has not been formally revived.

The development of regional bargaining in California was paralleled by its emergence in other western states. In general, it is true that the bargaining structure in many trades in the Far West is now less fragmented and that agreements cover much broader geographic areas than in the remainder of the country.[49] But regional bargaining in the West including California[50] has clearly been facilitated by a relative absence of large, almost contiguous urban areas — a circumstance not found in most of the remainder of the country.

[45] Bertram, *Consolidated Bargaining in California Construction*, pp. 14–22.
[46] See Frank Pierson, "Master Labor Plan," *Monthly Labor Review* 70 (January 1950): 14–18.
[47] Bertram, *Consolidated Bargaining in California Construction*, pp. 34–38.
[48] Bertram suggests that disputes over work jurisdiction and wage differentials were important to the breakup of the multitrade arrangement. *Ibid.,* p. 37.
[49] See Kenneth M. McCaffree, "Regional Labor Agreements in the Construction Industry," *Industrial and Labor Relations Review* 9 (July 1956): 595–609.
[50] See Bertram, *Consolidated Bargaining in California Construction*, p. 195.

Regional bargaining has had the effect of reducing geographic differentials in wages and working conditions within crafts and of facilitating the mobility of contractors and workers. It has contributed to industrial peace by reducing the likelihood of a multitude of disputes at contract terminations. It has provided a means by which the general interests of contractors and mechanics in a wide geographic area can have a direct influence on the determination of wages and conditions for small areas. And, perhaps most important, it has given stability to industrial relations in the West by removing the occasion for many localized disputes over union organization. Regional bargaining has not eliminated the disruptive effect of wage competition among different crafts, nor did it result in more moderate wage increases during the inflation of the late 1960s than in other areas of the country.[51] Finally, it should be recalled that localized bargaining remains the rule in several important specialty trades.[52]

Problems of Bargaining in Construction

Work Stoppages

Construction is a strike-prone industry. Rarely is there a year when the proportion of estimated working time lost due to stoppages in construction fails to exceed the national all-industry average, and it usually doubles or triples it.[53] Many stoppages occur over jurisdictional disputes, but they are usually

[51] For example, average union scales in the building trades rose somewhat more rapidly in the West than they did in the remainder of the country during the 1950s and 1960s. See U.S. Bureau of Labor Statistics, *Union Wages and Hours in the Building Trades* (annual bulletins).

[52] The reader should be cautioned against using the West Coast experience to make false generalizations about the possible results of a trend toward regional bargaining in the remainder of the country. The highly organized, highly fragmented bargaining structure that characterizes most of the country is not comparable to the weakly organized California construction industry existing before regional bargaining. A reform of bargaining structure in the East may have a rationalizing effect on industrial relations in construction not observed in California because of different original conditions. Regional bargaining in the East is also less likely to evolve as it did in the West without legislation or other external influences because lack of organization is not a motivating factor for unions and union contractors in the East.

[53] See U.S. Bureau of Labor Statistics, *Handbook of Labor Statistics, 1969*, Bulletin no. 1630 (Washington, D.C., 1969), Table 144. From 1957 to 1967, annual time lost in contract construction by work stoppages averaged 0.5 percent of total estimated working time. However, time lost due to seasonality and other aspects of the production process far exceeds that caused by strikes. See "Seasonal Unemployment in the Construction Industry: Report and Recommendations of the Secretary of Labor and Secretary of Commerce to the President and Congress," mimeo (Washington, D.C., 1969). See also U.S. Bureau of Labor Statistics, *Work Stoppages in Contract Construction,* Report no. 346 (Washington, D.C., 1968).

brief and involve few workers.[54] Strikes at the termination of a contract, however, are often long and involve many workers.[55] The interdependence of the production process is such that after a few weeks a strike by a single trade will often cause other crafts to halt work, so that the striking crafts may represent only a small proportion of the time lost.[56] Picketing by striking trades is not common in construction unless other trades are believed to be doing their work. Picketing, of course, tends to deprive all trades of their work on the project, since union men generally honor the pickets of any trade.

The bargaining structure has helped in two ways to make the industry strike-prone. First, contract termination dates of the several crafts are normally scattered throughout the winter, spring, and summer, so that strike may follow strike in succession. Second, exceptionally bitter strikes sometimes occur over the structure of bargaining itself. Thus, in Cleveland in 1965 a series of strikes accompanied the withdrawal of several crafts from what had been a joint bargaining structure first established in 1947. For the most part, a succession of strikes is the more common problem in construction, and one that disrupts the industry in many localities each year.[57]

The Imbalance between the Geographic Area of Bargaining and Mobility
The geographic scope of agreements in construction (and more importantly of wages and conditions) is typically narrower than the relevant product or labor markets. Bargaining units have often existed wherever there were centers of population, even very small ones. While many small locals have disappeared into larger bargaining units over the years, the distances that contractors and mechanics commonly travel have expanded much more rap-

---

[54]See Chapter 1.

[55]Strikes are an historic problem in construction, as well as a current one, and there have been adjustments in the conduct of collective bargaining to lessen their impact. For example, some seasons are more favorable to one party in negotiations than to the other. The period just before peak activity is most favorable to the labor organization, for a strike at that time is most crippling to employers and least likely to result in a net loss of work to the union (since the press of uncompleted contracts and the inflexibility of construction techniques in the short run tend to create an inelastic demand schedule for labor). Conversely, the slack season of the year is generally most favorable for the employers. Over many years a form of compromise has evolved in which negotiations occur just before the start of the season, a relatively neutral period of the year. For a full discussion, see Lloyd Ulman, *The Rise of the National Trade Union* (Cambridge: Harvard University Press, 1955), pp. 440–453.

[56]When jobs are kept operating despite the absence of one or more trades, contractors' costs tend to rise because of the difficulty of working around the unfinished jobs of striking trades.

[57]See, for example, "Kansas City Hurt by 196-Day Strike," *New York Times,* October 17, 1970, p. 54.

idly. Thus it is not unusual today to find many separate geographic jurisdictions within a single market area in certain regions of the country. These many jurisdictions sometimes put strong obstacles in the way of mobility of workers and contractors. It is not unusual, for example, for a contractor to bid a job in an area whose established working conditions are not well known to him. Considerable difficulties may arise on a job when costly and unexpected local conditions are imposed on such a contractor. Alternatively, contractors may hesitate to bid in areas in which conditions differ from their home area, or in which they have had previous labor difficulties.

The Exclusion of Wider Interests from Local Bargaining

The present geographic scope of bargaining often fails to provide for sufficient consideration of wider (state and national) interests in local bargaining. The very number and diversity of local agreements makes it difficult to impose the national policies of unions and contractors on local affiliates. Too often, local agreements are limited to reflecting local interests. Over the years, the national unions have established the primacy of national policy in certain areas of union activity (such as work jurisdiction, aspects of apprenticeship training, some pension plans, and provisions regarding traveling journeymen), but most aspects of collective bargaining agreements, including the economic package, remain in the jurisdiction of highly decentralized local bodies.

The Impact of Bargaining Structure on Wage Differentials

Collective bargaining by craft and area, as is common in construction, leads to major resistance to certain types of economic change. Once wage differentials between crafts and areas have been established, they are difficult to alter. There exist no industry-level mechanisms by which adjustments in differentials required by changes in demand and technology can be achieved. Rather, the crafts in which circumstances favor higher wages negotiate large settlements, and other crafts seek to catch up in order to maintain historic differentials. The mainspring of the process of catching up is clearly the individual union member. Often members are unwilling to accept lesser increases than those given other crafts, even though the desired increases will clearly affect employment in their craft.[58] Yet over longer periods of time

---

[58] Increasing wages in the painters' work jurisdiction, for example, have contributed to a situation in which a great deal of painting is done at the factory, before on-site installation. In response to this shift of work off-site, the painters are attempting, among other things, to diversify their membership and increase productivity by improving training. A similar example could have been chosen from several crafts, such as plastering and lathing, or from specialties within crafts.

the impact of economic forces cannot be resisted, and wage differentials do adjust to changing conditions.

In fact, wage differentials among trades should be expected to change even over the short run. If they do not, considerable disequilibrium in the labor markets may arise. Where relative prices are inflexible, rationing or underutilization of resources will result. Rationing of manpower involves delays in production and probable declines in productivity and quality of output. In consequence, the degree of flexibility in wage differentials is important not only to the process of wage determination but also to the efficient allocation and development of manpower resources.

The short-run rigidity of wage differentials has an important influence on the process of wage determination in construction. It is especially significant during periods of rapid inflation. The next chapter discusses the impact of bargaining structure and the rigidity of wage differentials on wage escalation in construction. It is not possible to test quantitatively and directly the effect of rate comparisons among the building trades on behavior in wage negotiations. However, a descriptive study of wage differentials and their variation over time and among regions is instructive.

Technical note: Patterns and changes in wage differentials The following pages summarize analyses that have been prepared of wage differentials and changes for selected building trades in construction and other industries. The patterns of wage increases during inflationary periods since World War II have also been investigated. No attempt has been made here to explain the sources of the observed variation in the differentials. The focus is on the extent to which differentials have varied and the patterns of variation.[59] Since data

[59] This analysis is based mainly on two sets of data: (1) the Bureau of Labor Statistics' annual survey of union rates in the building trades; and (2) the bureau's periodic surveys of wages and related benefits by occupation in nonconstruction industries located in major metropolitan areas. The survey of union wages in the building trades is conducted by mailed questionnaires and covers trades in 68 cities with a population of 100,000 or more. Data refer to scale and fringes as of July 1 of each year. Craft and regional averages were prepared by weighting the membership reported in the most recent survey (1967 in most cases). The occupational wage survey in metropolitan areas is conducted annually, partly by personal visits and partly by mail. Survey data are obtained from representative establishments in 6 major industry divisions, of which 2 (manufacturing and transportation, communication and public utilities) include the majority of building trades occupations in maintenance. (Force-account construction workers are excluded from the survey.) The average straight-time hourly earnings data provided exclude premium pay for overtime, weekend work, holidays, and late-night shifts. The two sources of data are not precisely comparable, in that building trades data are either the union scale or the scale plus fringes, while nonconstruction

regarding wage scales in the building trades are voluminous, it is necessary to be selective. For this study, wage differentials in a group of the nation's largest cities and among the larger crafts were prepared. Efforts were made to select representative crafts and areas, in order to obtain a wide spectrum of coverage. Unfortunately, the data were sometimes spotty, so that the base of comparison often differs for different topics.[60]

Building trades wage data are subject to a major shortcoming. Reporting of fringe benefits began in 1957; before that year data are available only for the basic hourly scale. This discontinuity in the data is serious. By 1957, some 17.6 percent of all workers under contracts in the building trades were covered by employer-financed pensions. In the previous year, for which fringes were not reported, 15.9 percent were covered. The situation is worse regarding coverage by employer-financed health and welfare funds. In 1957, 66.9 percent of workers were covered by such funds; in 1956, for which fringes were not reported, 63.6 percent were covered. In 1953, the earliest year for which estimates are available, 8.8 percent of workers were covered by pensions and 53.9 percent by health and welfare funds. Although the unavailability of fringe data for the years before 1957 means that differentials among the trades are biased in an unknown manner for the early 1950s, it is clear that in many areas fringes were less widespread and were lower as a percentage of total compensation than they are now.

The following list shows the results of a limited analysis of changes in wage differentials in construction and other industries (the analysis employed rank correlation coefficients and tested the significance of variance of means):

1.

Since World War II, a shift in wage leadership has occurred among the building trades in the major cities. The leadership position in the hourly scale has shifted from the bricklayer toward the mechanical trades.

2.

In major cities, wage and fringe differentials among the crafts in construction are very wide and tend to exceed the differentials among the same occupations in nonconstruction industries.

3.

Until recently, there was little year-to-year variation in wage differentials among

data are average earnings data. However, both exclude premium pay, so that conceptually the average hourly earnings estimates are very close to the construction wage scale for a single group of workers.
[60] A detailed list of crafts, areas, and time periods covered may be obtained from the author on request.

construction crafts within local geographic areas. Variation in wage differentials among a group of larger trades in selected major cities was gradual and in general very small.

4.

Since World War II, wage differentials in construction, in terms of the rankings of several crafts, appear to have been equally if not more flexible than those in nonconstruction industries. The ranking of several building trades by hourly wage scale exhibited greater flexibility than the ranking of the same crafts in nonconstruction industries. In the 1960s, however, flexibility in construction rankings decreased.

5.

The internal wage structure among the building trades in different industries varies a great deal by city and by year. A rational wage structure for a city might be expected to include identical wage rankings among occupations in different industries. In fact, these rankings differ considerably. Presumably, local economic and industrial relations influences (including bargaining power) are responsible for the variations in wage structure.

6.

Wage scales for the same craft vary greatly among regions and cities of the same size. Normally, differentials among cities are highest for laborers and for carpenters. For all five crafts studied, and in all but the largest cities (population of a million or more), differentials among cities have been widening since the early 1950s. Regional intracraft differentials in the wage rate (excluding fringes) are generally less than those among cities of the same size.

7.

Perhaps the most striking change that has occurred in wage differentials in construction antedates World War II. There has been a substantial compression of the spread between wage rates of journeymen and laborers and helpers. From 1907 on, the percentage differential between the journeyman and laborer-helper rates has generally risen when economic conditions were slow but narrowed during high-employment periods. Since the mid-1930s, the differentials have narrowed steadily, from an index of 194 (ratio of national average of journeyman scales to those of helpers and laborers) in 1933 to 133 in 1968. The decline has been less rapid since World War II, but still significant. From 1947 to 1968, the index fell 19 points, while the absolute cents per hour differential rose from $0.70 to $1.34.[61] The com-

[61] Arthur M. Ross, "Wage Differentials in the Building Trades," *Monthly Labor Review* 92 (October 1969): 14–17.

pression of these differentials has been due to several influences, including (1) the impact of high-employment conditions in wartime and in the postwar economy; (2) the increasing organization of unskilled workers in construction into the Laborers International Union; and (3) considerable increases in the productivity of labor, owing to mechanization, and in the skill content of some elements of the laborers' work jurisdiction.

In general, there has been a complex pattern of shifting wage differentials among crafts and areas, with some compression of the wage structure and some expansion. Most of these changes before 1968 were gradual. They have been aided by a variety of factors, including shifts in construction demand, variations in labor market conditions, and changing patterns of seasonality and intermittency of work in some crafts. Short-run changes in differentials among the crafts within limited geographic areas have been much less pronounced, although there is no reason to believe that long-run changes in construction labor market conditions (involving the supply and demand for labor) are any more dramatic than those that occur locally in the short run — in fact, the opposite is closer to the truth.[62] Yet the resistance of wage differentials to change in the short run appears very strong.

Conclusion

This chapter has demonstrated the complexity of collective bargaining structure in construction. Negotiated wage rates, wage differentials, working conditions, and to a lesser degree the structure of bargaining are each an adaptation by contractors and unions to the economic circumstances of a group of interrelated product markets. The product markets are differentiated by the type of structure involved, the nature of the production process, and the owner, size, and location of the job. The parties attempt to modify the terms of collective bargaining agreements, and even the process of negotiation in order to make the most out of a complex and shifting product market environment. Wages and working conditions may alter more rapidly than bargaining structure, though differentials among crafts and areas have their own degree of resistance to change. The bargaining structure is less variable and has an effect on settlements independent of economic circumstances. Conditions of the product markets, especially new developments, exert a pervasive influence on all aspects of industrial relations in construction, but these product market

[62]See D. Q. Mills, "Factors Affecting Patterns of Employment and Unemployment in the Construction Industry" (Ph.D. thesis, Harvard University, 1967).

influences are so complex, change so rapidly, and vary so much from one craft or area to another that analyzing them requires considerable understanding and experience and cannot be adequately described here.[63] Many circumstances are sui generis and can only be dealt with on an ad hoc basis. The analyses of bargaining structure in this chapter and of wage determination in the following one are no more than a preliminary lesson for the reader who intends to involve himself in the practicalities of these matters.

[63]See Dunlop, "The Industrial Relations System in Construction," for a theoretical analysis of the interrelationships of product market and labor market structures in collective bargaining. For an interesting case study in wage bargaining in construction, see William Hoskings, "A Study of Area Wage Structure and Wage Determination in the Building and Construction Industry of Central New York State, 1942–51" (Ph.D. thesis, Cornell University, 1955).

3

Introduction

During the inflation of the late 1960s and early 1970s, wages in construction rose very rapidly compared to those in most other industries. This was a departure from the role the industry had previously played in our economy. During the other inflationary periods following World War II, construction earnings increases had lagged behind those in certain other sectors, especially durable goods manufacturing. Since 1965, however, wage increases in construction have exceeded those obtained by other skilled workers, and settlements the size of those negotiated in construction have become an objective of workers in other industries. The effect of higher settlements in construction has been to widen differentials in earnings and wage rates with other workers. Thus, by 1970, average hourly earnings in contract construction exceeded those in all manufacturing by 55 percent, the greatest differential since 1947 and an increase in the differential of 19 points since 1960 (see Table 5).[1] Wage differentials among building tradesmen in contract construction and among those employed in maintenance or new construction by employers engaged in other industries also widened.[2] As a further example, wage rates paid to building tradesmen in contract construction rose relative to those paid to workers in the same occupations in basic steel after many years of general stability (see Table 6).

As the rate of increase in construction wage rates began to exert a destabilizing influence on the American economy,[3] observers offered a number

---

[1] Because of the intermittency of work, rising hourly wage scales are not always translated into higher annual incomes for construction workers. Statistical evidence is spotty, but while average hourly earnings in construction in 1964 exceeded those in primary metals manufacturing by 14 percent, annual earnings in construction were lower than in primary metals. See U.S. Bureau of Labor Statistics, *Seasonality and Manpower in Construction,* Bulletin no. 1642 (Washington, D.C., 1970), p. 55. By 1967, average hourly earnings in contract construction exceeded those in primary metals manufacturing by 23 percent, but annual earnings in primary metals continued to be higher. See U.S. Bureau of Labor Statistics, *Compensation in the Construction Industry,* Bulletin no. 1656 (Washington, D.C., 1970), p. 76. (Comparisons of wages and annual compensation among industries must always be carefully evaluated because of the different relative mix of skill levels in obtaining average earnings data.)

[2] Because it is difficult to obtain comparisons of wage rates in construction and other industries employing building trades workers, a special study of rates over several years in basic steel and construction was made.

[3] During 1970, the average negotiated wage and fringe benefit increase in 932 settlements reported to the Department of Labor was 15.4 percent for the life of the contract and 18 percent for first-year-only increases (data from Construction Industry Collective Bargaining Commission). Negotiated increases of $1.00 per hour per year were common and in many cases were exceeded. As recently as 1964, increases averaged less than $.25 per hour and less than 5 percent per year. See U.S. Bureau of Labor Statistics, *Compensation in the Construction Industry.*

of explanations. It was widely believed that the situation in construction was primarily a result of the monopoly power of the building trades unions. This view was stated most succinctly by the editors of *Fortune:*

> The eighteen unions that boss the building trades have been able to do so well by their three million members because of their tight control of the labor supply. Exempt from antitrust laws, they have created an artificial manpower shortage by restricting the number of union apprentices and subjecting them to ridiculously long training periods. Absolute power has permitted the unions to indulge in a fabulous variety of featherbedding and make-work practices.[4]

But this explanation is unsatisfactory for two major reasons. First, there is no indication that the control of the building trades unions over the construction work force increased along with the acceleration in the size of wage settlements in the late 1960s. If anything, the unions' control declined. And even if the unions had maintained their control over the work force, some further explanation would be needed to account for the much higher wage settlements. In fact, membership in the unions lagged behind the increase in construction employment during the 1960s, and unionization decreased in major sectors of the industry, including housing and industrial construction. By the early 1970s a vigorous movement among nonunion contractors had developed and was spreading across the nation from its first foothold in the mid-Atlantic states. A further symptom of the unions' growing difficulties, widely noted in the industry, was the emergence in 1969 of a nonunion industrial contractor as the largest contractor by volume in the United States.[5]

---

[4] 32 (October 1970): 2. See also Richard Hobart, "Nixon Sets a New Economic Course," *Washington Post,* January 22, 1971

[5] The existence of the nonunion sector of construction requires that the role of labor supply restriction be interpreted carefully. Economists have often asserted the theoretical identity, in a partial equilibrium model, of control of the supply of labor and control of the wage rate. See, for example, Henry Simons, "Some Reflections on Syndicalism," *Journal of Political Economy* 52 (March 1944): 1–19. "It is not commonly recognized, however, that control of wage rates *is* control of entry. . . ," Simons noted. Fritz Machlup, *The Political Economy of Monopoly* (Baltimore: Johns Hopkins Press, 1952), pp. 410–417, discusses at length the impact of wage determination on supply conditions and cites J. R. Hicks, *The Theory of Wages,* 2nd ed. (New York: St. Martin's Press, 1964), p. 166, " 'A man ignorant of economics nearly always feels the regulations of prices to be more justifiable than the limitation of supply — although they come to the same thing.' " However, where supply cannot be controlled but it is possible to influence the wage rate, secondary markets are likely to exist. This is particularly true in construction, where entry of firms is relatively easy (annual rates of entry by firms into contract construction are the highest among major industry divisions and in the 1960s have been greater than 125 per 1000) and where many building trades skills are widely distributed among the labor force. The secondary market must be kept at a rate of operation that is not threatening to the union, which may require either rates of compensation that do not diverge too greatly from the competitive market equilibrium or actual devices of supply restriction. Control over the price (that is, wage scale) alone is not sufficient.

Table 5. Average Hourly Earnings and Relative Earnings of Construction and Production Workers in Contract Construction and Selected Industries, United States, 1947–1970

Year	Average Hourly Earnings ($)					Relative Earnings: Construction to			
	Contract Constr.	Nonagr. Inds.	Manuf.	Basic Steel	Motor Vehicles	Nonagr. Inds.	Manuf.	Basic Steel	Motor Vehicles
1947–1951	1.79	1.28	1.38	1.66	1.69	1.39	1.29	1.07	1.06
1952–1956	2.36	1.66	1.80	2.27	2.21	1.43	1.32	1.05	1.07
1957–1961	2.95	2.02	2.19	2.97	2.68	1.46	1.35	0.99	1.10
1962–1966	3.57	2.37	2.54	3.37	3.22	1.50	1.40	1.06	1.11
1967–1970	4.63	2.95	3.10	3.88	3.94	1.57	1.49	1.19	1.17
1967	4.11	2.68	2.83	3.57	3.55	1.53	1.45	1.15	1.15
1968	4.41	2.85	3.01	3.76	3.89	1.54	1.46	1.17	1.13
1969	4.78	3.04	3.19	4.02	4.10	1.57	1.50	1.19	1.17
1970[a]	5.22	3.22	3.36	4.16	4.23	1.62	1.55	1.25	1.23

Source: U.S. Bureau of Labor Statistics, *Employment and Earnings Statistics for the United States, 1967–68*, Bulletin no. 1312-6 (Washington, D.C., 1968), and *Employment and Earnings* (monthly issued by the Bureau of Labor Statistics).

[a]Preliminary data.

Table 6. Wage Relatives[a] for Building Tradesmen in Contract Construction and Basic Steel, Basic Rates Only, United States and Chicago,[b] 1947–1970

July 1	Boilermakers U.S.	Chi.	Bricklayers U.S.	Chi.	Carpenters U.S.	Chi.	Electricians U.S.	Chi.	Painters U.S.	Chi.	Pipefitters U.S.	Chi.	Sheet Metal Workers U.S.	Chi.
1947–1951	1.32	1.38	1.48	1.39	1.32	1.53	1.32	1.34	1.36	1.46	1.41	1.42	1.26	n.a.
1952–1956	1.30	1.37	1.42	1.43	1.28	1.40	1.27	1.33	1.31	1.42	1.37	1.39	1.24	1.32
1957–1961	1.31	1.30	1.36	1.37	1.26	1.32	1.26	1.32	1.27	1.34	1.39	1.39	1.24	1.29
1962–1966	1.45	1.54	1.46	1.52	1.41	1.50	1.41	1.48	1.39	1.42	1.49	1.57	1.39	1.50
1967–1970	1.56	n.a.	1.59	1.71	1.58	1.68	1.56	1.62	1.54	1.63	1.69	1.73	1.56	n.a.
1967	1.51	1.67	1.52	1.59	1.50	1.63	1.47	1.46	1.48	1.55	1.60	1.69	1.48	1.69
1968	1.56	1.76	1.58	1.76	1.56	1.68	1.53	1.48	1.53	1.62	1.67	1.73	1.54	1.65
1969	1.54	1.79	1.58	1.70	1.57	1.64	1.56	1.71	1.53	1.60	1.68	1.70	1.54	1.61
1970[c]	1.62	n.a.	1.69	1.80	1.67	1.78	1.66	1.81	1.62	1.73	1.80	1.80	1.68	n.a.

Source: U.S. Bureau of Labor Statistics, *Union Wage and Hours: The Building Trades* (annual bulletins); American Iron and Steel Institute; and "Agreement Between United States Steel Corporation and the United States Steel Workers of America, Production and Maintenance Employees."

[a]The construction rate divided by the steel rate.

[b]Because basic steel production is more concentrated geographically than construction, national averages need to be supplemented by regional or local comparisons. The Chicago data show the changes in wage differentials in a narrow geographic area, but one that contains important elements of both industries.

[c]Preliminary data.

A second reason that union power is unsatisfactory as an explanation is the gradual erosion that has taken place in the unions' legal position. The Taft-Hartley Act outlawed the closed shop in construction and other industries in the late 1940s, but many of its features were continued in construction through the operation of exclusive hiring halls by the unions. In 1957, the Supreme Court established procedures by which a hall could not be used as a device to continue the closed shop. Rather, referrals from the hall had to be made on an objective basis that explicitly excluded union membership as a standard.[6] Finally, in the 1960s, selection procedures for apprenticeship, job referral, and union membership came under increasing federal surveillance, accompanied by considerable modifications in the methods of their operation, in an effort to ensure that there would be no racial discrimination in construction employment.[7] In summary, during the 1960s union control of the labor market in construction was being weakened, not strengthened.

Actually, high settlements in construction were the result of the interaction of two major factors. One was a set of favorable economic conditions. In the late 1960s, there occurred a large increase in the volume of private commercial and industrial work and public building work — sectors of the industry that are highly unionized, involve the more skilled mechanics and intricate work, are the domain of the larger contractors, and are the least price-elastic of all construction markets. Relative price changes among all construction inputs were favorable to more labor-intensive production, especially since interest rates (the price of elapsed time in completing a project) rose rapidly. These inflationary demand conditions were reinforced by a major drain-off of the labor supply available to construction, a result of the boom in other sectors of the economy. Aggregate construction employment grew only slowly in the 1960s, for the rapid growth of nonresidential building work was offset to a large extent by declining activity in residential and highway construction. It was rather the generally low unemployment of the late 1960s that, by putting pressure on labor markets generally, led to historically low unemployment rates in construction.[8]

Alternatively, in order for control over the wage rate to be equivalent to direct supply restriction, all transactions must occur at the specified rate. Labor organizations are limited in their control over actual wages paid and entry into the industry, and their influence in these areas varies over time and geographically according to the state of the labor market, the level and composition of construction demand, historic patterns of manpower development and allocation, and the economics of the operation of individual firms.
[6] See U.S. Department of Labor, Labor Management Services Administration, *Exclusive Union Work Referral Systems in the Building Trades* (Washington, D.C., 1970). The effectiveness of the federal regulations is in many instances subject to dispute.
[7] See Chapter 6.
[8] See Chapter 4.

The interaction of the economic factors just described with the collective bargaining structure in construction generated rapid wage increases. In times of economic expansion, the decentralized bargaining structure of the industry is conducive to high settlements. Leapfrogging of wage rates by craft and area creates a continued upward pressure on the level of wages. The militancy of union membership, together with the existing bargaining mechanisms, fueled the search for higher wage settlements,[9] and inflationary economic conditions generally sustained it. The following pages provide a more detailed description of the inflationary process in collective bargaining in construction. The final section of the chapter discusses the reforms that would be most effective in moderating the impact of future inflationary circumstances.

Determinants of the Size of Wage Settlements

The Composition of Demand

Total construction activity was moderately expansionary (in real terms) during the 1960s, but variations in the composition of construction were dramatic and had an important effect on the industry's wage behavior. Since construction is a large group of highly interrelated industries, variations in the rate of expansion of the different branches may affect manpower demand and supply in certain crafts and areas in ways that examination of the aggregate statistics does not reveal. Thus compositional changes in construction activity in the 1960s gave an inflationary bias, derived from economic conditions, to the cost behavior of the entire industry.

Nonresidential building construction was the most expansive segment of the construction market between 1960 and 1969 (see Table 7). The most plausible date for the start of the construction boom is 1964, since value put-in-place (expenditures)[10] on public building construction rose 56 percent from 1964 to 1969, while on private, nonresidential work they rose 70 percent. During the same period, total new construction expenditures rose 38 percent; nonresidential building work rose from 32 to 36 percent of total volume. Perhaps more significantly, the greatest rise in annual expenditures occurred in privately owned commercial and industrial building: an 84

---

[9] The role of the rank-and-file union member in the inflationary process should not be underestimated. Settlements proposed to the membership for ratification have been rejected many times as inadequate, even when they were comparable to other settlements in the area. Union officials rapidly get the message from the membership and push for whatever they can get, not only what seems appropriate or reasonable.

[10] Value put-in-place estimates are not the same measure as expenditures, but for expositional purposes they will be treated as such.

Table 7.   Changes in Construction Employment and Value Put-in-Place during the 1960s

	Percentage Change in Annual Estimates		
	1960–1969	1960-1964	1964–1969
Employment in contract construction	19.8	7.7	16.6
Value Put-in-Place			
Private ownership	64.9	20.5	36.9
Residential building	41.0	22.1	15.5
Nonresidential building	117.1	27.8	69.8
Industrial and commercial	134.8	27.4	84.3
Public Ownership	76.9	25.6	40.8
Nonresidential building	112.3	28.5	65.2
Heavy and highway	62.6	25.4	29.7
Total new construction	68.5	22.0	38.1

Source: *Construction Review* (monthly issued by Department of Commerce, Business and Defense Services Administration) 16 (December 1970) and U.S. Department of Commerce, Business and Defense Services Administration, *Construction Statistics, 1915–1964* (Washington, D.C., 1966).
Note: These estimates refer to increases in current dollar expenditures, not expenditures deflated for price increases. The serious difficulties of creating construction price deflators make a presentation of constant dollar estimates hazardous. See, for example, R. J. Gordon, "A New View of Real Investment in Structures, 1919–1966," *Review of Economics and Statistics* 50 (November 1968): 417–428, and "$45 Billion of U.S. Private Investment Has Been Mislaid," *American Economic Review* 112 (June 1969): 221–238.

percent increase, to 19 percent of the entire market, occurred between 1964, when the boom began, and 1969, when it slowed.[11]

The boom that developed in nonresidential building construction (involving construction of schools, public buildings, private office buildings, industrial plants, commercial facilities, and so on) in the 1960s was of great significance. Nonresidential building is a crucial sector of the contract construction industry. Labor is most fully organized in this sector, and the work is among the most technically sophisticated in construction. Commercial and industrial

[11] The percentage increases cited refer to current dollar expenditures (see note to Table 4). Current dollar increases are appropriate for studying the inflationary force of demand, but it should be understood that costs rose during the period and that the increases cited were in expenditures, not in the physical volume of work performed.

construction utilize the better-skilled craftsmen in each trade, as well as the trades requiring the longest periods of training. In consequence, rapid demand expansion in these sectors is particularily likely to generate pressure for high wage settlements, both because of a shrinking supply of the skilled men needed to do the work and because of the capacity of industrial and public owners to absorb cost increases.

Furthermore, industrial construction was especially expansive in certain geographic areas in which dramatic wage increases were negotiated in the early and mid-1960s. A pattern emerged from these increases that spread to the country as a whole. For example, building permits data from the 1960s show very large increases in the valuation of nonresidential construction permits authorized in the Gulf Coast states (especially Texas and Louisiana) and several states of the Upper Midwest (including Michigan, Ohio, and Illinois).[12] Much of the increase in nonresidential building in these states was accounted for by the plant expansion of chemical and manufacturing corporations. In both the Gulf Coast region and the Upper Midwest, expanding construction activity led to industrial unrest and rapidly rising labor costs.[13] Wage increases negotiated in Cleveland and Toledo in 1963-1964 were very high by the standards of the time and were soon equaled in other northern cities. The processes by which large negotiated wage increases spread throughout the industry are described later; the purpose of the present discussion is to identify the economic conditions that generated them initially.

The Drain-off of the Labor Force
Wage settlements in construction in the late 1960s also reflected the increasing tightness of the manpower supply. Construction is strongly dependent upon mobility of manpower among its various branches and to and from other industries in order to meet short-run increases in demand. Construction employment is generally casual, with contractors hiring or laying off men on

[12] See issues of *Construction Review*. In these states, nonresidential permit valuation more than doubled in the seven-year period 1963–1969.
[13] See Thomas O'Hanlon, "The Strangehold of the Building Trades," *Fortune* 78 (December 1968): 102 ff., and "The Case against the Unions," *ibid.* 77 (January 1968): 170 ff; also A. James Reichley, "The Big Shakedown in Baton Rouge," *ibid.* 80 (August 1969): 97 ff.; Don Sider, "The Big Boondoggle at Lordstown," *ibid.* (September 1969): 106 ff.; and Gilbert Burck, "The Building Trades versus the People," *ibid.* 82 (October 1970): 94 ff. The last three articles describe the labor problems accompanying the construction of the petrochemical complexes in the Baton Rouge, Louisiana, area; the building of a small-car manufacturing plant for General Motors at Lordstown, Ohio (in the Cleveland area); and the long strike of building trades workers in Kansas City in 1970. The reports in *Fortune* lack objectivity and are not always accurate, but they provide the flavor of these bitter disputes.

jobs in various stages of completion. The industry is dependent upon the availability of manpower for short-term, semiskilled employment when the level of construction activity is high.[14] During the late 1960s, traditional pools of semiskilled manpower evaporated as unemployment rates in the economy as a whole declined. In consequence, unemployment rates in several construction occupations were at very low levels by 1968.[15]

However, the reported annual average unemployment rate for the construction industry tends to be considerably higher than that in other industries, so that in the late 1960s construction experienced rapidly rising wages and high levels of unemployment simultaneously.[16] Though this situation might seem paradoxical, it was not. Nor does it indicate that rising wages were immediately translated into falling employment. Rather, employment continued to grow slowly. The juxtaposition of seemingly high industry unemployment rates and rising wages was a result of several factors. First, while the construction unemployment rate remained comparatively high, it had sunk to a low level by industry standards. Between 1961 and 1969, for example, the employment rate in construction for private wage and salary workers declined steadily from 15.7 percent to 6.0 percent. Second, the industry is so extensive geographically that averaging rates of unemployment

[14] A special Bureau of Labor Statistics study in 1961 showed that many of the several hundred thousand construction workers who changed jobs in 1961 went into other occupations and industries. Furthermore, 30 percent of those hired as construction craftsmen other than carpenters came from another occupational group; the figures for carpenters and construction laborers were 33 percent and 60 percent, respectively. Calculated from Gertrude Bancroft and Stuart Garfinkle, "Job Mobility in 1961," U.S. Bureau of Labor Statistics Special Labor Force Report no. 35 (Washington, D.C., 1963), reprinted from *Monthly Labor Review* 86 (August 1963): 897-906. In a similar but not directly comparable study of occupational mobility, construction carpenters and laborers were found to have relatively high rates of mobility, while those for construction craftsmen other than carpenters were somewhat lower. For example, 10.7 percent of those employed in any industry as carpenters in January 1965 had changed occupations by January 1966; for laborers and construction caftsmen, the figures were 15.1 percent and 6.6 percent. Samuel Saben, "Occupational Mobility of Employed Workers," U.S. Bureau of Labor Statistics Special Labor Force Report no. 84 (Washington, D.C., 1967), reprinted from *Monthly Labor Review* 90 (June 1967): 31-38. For a discussion on inter-industry mobility among construction workers, see D.Q. Mills, "Manpower in Construction: New Methods and Measures," in Industrial Relations Research Association, *Proceedings of the Twentieth Annual Winter Meeting: The Development and Use of Manpower* (Madison, Wisc., 1967), pp. 269-276; and U.S. Bureau of Labor Statistics, *Seasonality and Manpower in Construction,* pp. 62-67. Unfortunately, available data are not adequate to measure the impact of tightening labor markets on the flow of manpower to and from construction jobs.
[15] See Chapter 4.
[16] See Richard A. Lester, "Negotiated Wage Settlements, 1951-1967," *Review of Economics and Statistics* 50 (May 1968): 173-181.

nationally may disguise very tight labor markets in key areas. Third, unemployment rates specific to craft and area are largely nonexistent. At a given moment, labor shortages are usually more acute in some crafts than in others. Thus, labor market conditions may be tight with respect to the supply of men in certain crafts, though casual entrants swell the numbers employed or reported as unemployed in the industry as a whole. Local labor market conditions might result in rapid increases in wages which then spread in collective bargaining to other areas.

In general, therefore, the late 1960s saw a tightening of labor market conditions in construction because of increased demand (especially in certain key sectors of the industry) and because of a reduction in the available labor supply (owing mainly to increased employment in other industries).[17] Contractors, faced with the problems of manning jobs from a shrinking labor supply, were often willing to agree to large wage increases as a means of attracting additional labor. Furthermore, when temporary shortages of manpower required that the available labor force be paid for considerable overtime (at time and a half or double time), as often happened on industrial construction jobs, large increases in straight-time earnings could still be less expensive to the employer if they allowed him to obtain a larger work force.

Finally, collective bargaining is normally conducted in such a way that expectations regarding the future labor supply may affect the wage package agreed upon, especially in trades requiring extended periods of training. When a large volume of work and continued pressure on the supply of skilled laborers are anticipated, wage increases tend to be higher. This was, and is, the situation in many construction negotiations, with public authorities and academicians stressing the volume of construction that must be accomplished in the next decade in order to meet the nation's housing, urban redevelopment, and mechanical and electrical power goals.[18] As a consequence, the parties in the

[17]Because construction is an industry in which entry to many jobs is fairly casual, the unemployment rate follows the national unemployment rate very closely. (From 1947 to 1967, the simple correlation coefficient between the construction and all civilian worker unemployment rates was 0.9751.) Unemployment estimates by industry are based on the industry of the last job, which tends to inflate estimates for industries like construction that hire workers on a casual basis. Statistics based on work experience over a longer period, or on skills possessed, would provide a more useful view of labor supply conditions in the building trades.

[18]See, for example, U.S. President, *First Annual Report on National Housing Goals* (Washington, D.C., 1969). Also U.S. Congress, Joint Economic Committee, Subcommittee on Economic Progress, *State and Local Public Facility Needs and Financing,* 89th Cong., 2nd sess., 1966. Federal agencies and commissions have asked that the manpower implications of these goals be estimated and the figures for increased labor

industry believed construction to be an expanding activity, well suited to sustain significant wage increases in the coming decade. Expectations of high levels of public expenditures obviated fears of any possible price elasticity in construction demand.

The Impact of Decentralized Collective Bargaining

Wage spirals in construction are facilitated by the decentralized collective bargaining structure of the industry. As the previous chapter showed, bargaining is fragmented among crafts, geographic areas, and branches of the industry. There are patterns of wage differentials and comparisons among localities and among the crafts in each locality. Deviations from traditional differentials in an area often set in motion a catching-up process. It matters less than it should (for economic efficiency) that local market conditions may require changes in historic craft and area wage differentials. Rather, a wage spiral begins in which some crafts and contractors attempt to widen differentials for economic reasons, while others attempt to keep pace or even close the gap.

The succession of contract termination dates for the various crafts in an area, together with traditional rivalries, creates a pattern of leapfrogging of settlements that is especially serious during full employment. Each craft seeks to better the settlements achieved by the other, and long and bitter disputes over wages may follow. During inflationary periods, this problem is exacerbated by the wage leadership exercised by very small bargaining units. Some crafts normally deal with an association of employers involving many small shops specialized in commercial and industrial work. The price inelasticity of this type of work, when it is coupled with ineffectiveness on the part of the contractors' associations at the bargaining table, exerts a significant upward pressure on wages generally. Other crafts are under strong pressure to achieve settlements large enough to maintain traditional earnings differentials with whichever crafts are obtaining the highest settlements. Resistance to change is increased by the common procedure of submitting proposed contracts to the union membership for ratification.[19] Finally, some employer

---

requirements be widely distributed. One study estimated that on-site labor requirements on new construction would rise 18.3 percent from 1965 to 1975 (assuming a 2 percent per year increase in real labor productivity). See John T. Dunlop and D. Q. Mills, "Manpower in Construction," in *Report of the President's Committee on Urban Housing: Technical Studies,* vol. 2 (Washington, D.C., 1968). Other studies have projected even greater manpower demands.

[19] Many members of building and construction trades local unions are very jealous of the privilege of approving or disapproving contracts negotiated by the leadership. Submission of contract disputes to resolution by national authorities or by neutrals

groups are in a position to negotiate conditions or wages that have little direct effect on their operations but that may have substantial adverse effects on rival or competitive contractor groups engaged in negotiations with the same trade.

Wage increases negotiated by one craft or by a group of crafts in one area may be transmitted to other crafts and areas in several ways.[20] Unfortunately, the dynamics of a wage spiral are difficult to trace in a comprehensive manner because of the number of crafts and areas involved[21] and because of ambiguities in settlement data.[22] But it is possible to determine in part the process by which, in the late 1960s, high wage increases spread from one region to another, and from one craft or branch of the industry to another within a limited geographic area. Thus, settlement packages that were high for the time were characteristic of the Pacific Coast region in 1962. In 1964 and again in 1968, negotiated settlements in the Midwest (especially in the Detroit-Toledo-Cleveland-Akron-Columbus area) were exceptionally high. In the summer of 1969, high increases were negotiated in New York City, Boston, and other cities of the Northeast, reflecting a pattern of increases tentatively agreed to in Buffalo early in the year. Within broad geographic regions with interconnected construction labor markets, a pattern of wage comparisons exists that tends to spread high settlements quickly among crafts and cities, and this often occurs even where economic conditions are far less favorable to the negotiated increases than in the crafts and cities that set the

---

may be vigorously opposed. For example, at the 1970 general convention of the United Brotherhood of Carpenters, a resolution was adopted that the Carpenters should declare "strong opposition to proposals. . .that would dilute or reduce the membership's right to approve or disapprove proposed agreements with contractors and builders." "Special Issue: 31st General Convention," *The Carpenter* 90 (October 1970): 4.

[20] Distinctly unfavorable economic or political circumstances might, of course, inhibit the spread of increases.

[21] More than 1000 collective bargaining contracts expire and are renegotiated each year in construction.

[22] For example, by 1968–1969 catch-up or piggy-back understandings were commonly included in the verbal or written agreements setting the wage and benefit provisions of a contract. These understandings provided that if a designated craft or crafts received a higher negotiated wage increase, the contract would be amended to provide the additional increase. As a consequence, terms of some agreements became directly dependent on other agreements, and the timing of announced settlements was no longer a reliable indicator of cause and effect. Similarly, in some cases contractor and union representatives reached agreement on a wage and benefit package that became the pattern for other settlements in the area but were unable to resolve work rules or other issues, so that the contract was not completed until several other contracts in the area were signed. Again, the timing of settlements would give no indication of the order of events in the determination of wages.

pattern. The rate of diffusion of pattern-setting increases is limited, of course, by the general practice of signing contracts for multiple-year (usually two- or three-year) terms. However, where rates in one area so clearly diverge from those in another that industrial relations on the job or the ability of contractors to recruit men is affected, agreements may be reopened by the consent of both parties in order to adjust the differential.

The complexity of this process of wage negotiation and diffusion can hardly be overstated; it is a direct result of the bargaining structure of the industry. Labor markets are interrelated and therefore wage comparisons are made among the various crafts and branches of the industry, while the geographic scope of negotiations of one craft or branch overlaps with other crafts or branches in a pattern that prevents simple or straightforward adjustments of differentials from being made at a single time. For example, a wage increase negotiated for operating engineers on highway work may become the standard for adjustment of the wages of engineers on building work in cities within or adjacent to the geographic jurisdiction of the highway agreement. Once adopted by the engineers for building work, the pattern may spread to other building trades employed with the engineers at sites. Because geographic jurisdictions of the engineers tend to be large, several local unions or district councils of the other trades may be affected, in turn affecting each of several adjacent locals of their own or closely related crafts. In any single negotiation, the full interplay of forces in the comparison of rates with other crafts and other geographic areas may be very great, leading to union members' taking the highest comparison as a target to be reached. Again, the point is not simply that this process of wage comparison occurs in construction, for it is true of virtually all collective bargaining,[23] but that it is probably most complex in construction owing to the decentralized bargaining structure.

In many cases, local unions have very small geographic jurisdictions, and negotiations cover only a small number of workers. In this situation, the special interests of a few local employers and workingmen often take precedence over wider interests in the negotiations. It is easier for the workers to remain on strike because they can work outside the local's jurisdiction. At the same time, the ability of contractors to sustain a strike or to be adamant in negotiations is increased, because they are likely to operate outside the affected area. It is common for the special circumstances of workers and em-

[23]See Arthur M. Ross, *Trade Union Wage Policy* (Berkeley: University of California Press, 1948), p. 6.

ployers in small areas to become major factors in the results of bargaining.

The Role of the Strike

In the high-employment economy, the use of the strike by the building and construction crafts assumed a separate and important role. The frequency of strikes at the termination of contracts in construction rose dramatically, and their effect on the size of settlements was pronounced. In 1969 and 1970, there were almost 1000 strikes during contract negotiations in construction, involving more than 36 percent of all contract renewals in the industry.[24] Strikes were often of several weeks' length, and the union was almost invariably successful in raising the size of the settlement. In the case of several very long strikes (lasting many months) in major cities, the final settlement package was above the union's demands at the beginning of the strike. In some instances, employers banded together for multicraft coalition bargaining and sustained long strikes, only to capitulate in the end. By 1971, a feeling of futility had become widespread among contractor groups, owing to their failure to gain concessions in so many strikes and to the damage the strikes had done to their businesses. As much as any other factor, the effectiveness of the strike contributed to the union's dominance of the bargaining process in the late 1960's.

It was the full-employment economy of the late 1960s that made effective strikes possible. Most important by far was the availability of work for strikers. Men from the striking jurisdiction were often able to find employment in other local unions' jurisdictions, at the jobs of nonassociation[25] employers who worked through the association contractors' lockout, as self-employed craftsmen, or even as maintenance workers in other industries. General shortages of skilled labor made it easier to find additional employment. Not all strikers were able to find other work, of course, but in many cases a remarkably large proportion (often more than half) was able to do so. Having strikers at work naturally reduces the pressure on a union to settle a contract. Although not as important, an additional factor was the impact that full-employment conditions had on the business position of contractors. Rapidly rising labor, material, and interest costs forced many contractors into cash-flow problems, which made long strikes very dangerous to the solvency of the

[24] Date from U.S. Department of Labor. Between 1960 and 1967, strikes over economic issues (generally occurring at the termination of a contract) averaged some 290 per year, or about 20 percent of contract renewals (author's estimate). See U.S. Bureau of Labor Statistics, *Compensation in the Construction Industry*, p. 28.

[25] That is, employers not bound to the collective bargaining position of the local contractors' association. These firms might be either independents or traveling contractors working on national agreements.

firm.[26] Industrial and office building owners, aware of the cost of construction delays and often needing the new facilities to reduce or hold down their own cost positions, were especially uncooperative toward the contractors.

To summarize: full-employment conditions exacerbated aspects of construction strikes that have long been familiar to students of the industry and greatly increased their effectiveness in the hands of the union.

A Statistical Model of Wage Determination

The following section presents a statistical model of wage determination in construction. It involves multiple-regression analysis of 605 wage settlements in contract construction occurring in the spring of 1968. These data were collected by the Federal Mediation and Conciliation Service, but they include 319 instances in which a mediator was *not* involved in the negotiations. The FMCS data included the total cents-per-hour increase negotiated (wages and fringes included) by craft and locality, the number of years of the contract term, whether a strike took place, and whether a mediator was involved. The cents-per-hour increase was converted to an average annual percentage increase over the term of the contract by applying base wage and fringes data obtained from the Bureau of Labor Statistics and the Davis-Bacon Division of the Office of the Solicitor of Labor. Additional data were prepared reflecting local labor market conditions in the areas from which settlement data were obtained.

Table 8 presents a cross-classification of the settlement data. The mean percentage increase, on *annual* average, in the 605 settlements was 12.005. In Region 4 (the Upper Midwest).[27] settlements averaged approximately 17 percent per year, well above the national average. Thus, there is considerable variation by region, craft, and the circumstances of the wage disputes.

A group of regression equations was estimated to show the relative importance of certain quantitative influences on the size of the wage settlement. The results of the regression analysis are presented in Table 9. Briefly, the study supports the view that the following factors influence settlement size in construction:

1.

Market conditions in construction, involving both the volume of demand for

---

[26] It was not uncommon for several members of a contractors' association to be forced into bankruptcy by prolonged strikes.
[27] Ohio, Indiana, Michigan, Wisconsin, Illinois, Kentucky, and Minnesota.

Table 8. Distribution of Settlements by Craft, Region, and Strike Incidence and Mean Size of Package Settlement Increases

	Percentage of All Settlements	Strike		No Strike	
		Percentage of All Settlements	Average Annual Percentage Increase in Wages and Fringes	Percentage of All Settlements	Average Annual Percentage Increase in Wages and Fringes
Basic trades[a]	47	17	13.09	30	11.40
Region 4[b]	10	6	16.52	3	14.94
Other regions	37	11	11.14	26	10.93
Mechanical specialty trades[c]	18	6	14.58	13	13.32
Region 4	4	2	17.88	3	17.75
Other regions	14	4	13.08	10	12.14
Other specialty trades[d]	34	11	13.40	23	10.23
Region 4	6	4	17.01	2	14.65
Other regions	28	7	11.47	21	9.73
Total	100	34		66	

[a]Includes carpenters, bricklayers, laborers, and others.
[b]Includes Ohio, Indiana, Michigan, Wisconsin, Illinois, Kentucky, and Minnesota.
[c]Includes plumbers, pipefitters, electricians, and sheet metal workers.
[d]Includes asbestos workers, lathers, painters, and others.

Table 9. Regression Results for Cross-Section Analysis of Settlement Size

Dependent Variable: Annual percentage change in wages and fringes as negotiated, 605 settlements, contract construction, spring 1968

Independent Variables	Estimated Coefficient	Significance Level (t test)
Strike: x_1 = 1 if a strike; x_1 = 0 if no strike	1.14730	0.05%
Percentage change in local contract construction employment, 1964–1967	−0.0368781	0.5
Region 4 (Upper Midwest): x_3 = 1 if Region 4; x_3 = 0 if not Region 4	4.94097	0.05
Number of employees covered by the agreement: x_4 = 1 if < 1000; x_4 = 0 if > 1000	−1.17401	0.5
Change in the local unemployment rate, all civilian workers, 1964–1967	−0.353307	5.0
Cities included in the BLS survey of union wages and hours in the building trades: x_6 = 1 if in survey; x_6 = 0 if not in survey	−0.971091	0.5
Basic trades: x_7 = 1 if a basic trade; x_7 = 0 if not a basic trade	0.741026	2.5
Mechanical specialty trades: x_8 = 1 if a mechanical trade; x_8 = 0 if not a mechanical trade	1.94440	0.05
Constant	10.3381	0.05

$F(8,596)$ = 32.9078, significant at 1%[a]

R^2 = 0.3323[a]

[a]Both the F and R^2 statistics are measures of the degree to which the equation provides estimates of the dependent variable closely approximating the actual values of the dependent variable.

labor and manpower supply conditions.[28] In 1968, settlements tended to be
marginally higher in cities that had experienced the greatest increases in contract construction employment from 1964 to 1967. Further, settlements
were higher where the local all-civilian worker unemployment rate had declined most between 1964 and 1967.

2.

The occurrence of a strike. Settlements were higher where a strike had occurred by approximately an additional percentage point of increase per year.

3.

The bargaining structure of the industry. Settlements tended to be much
higher in the Upper Midwest (Region 4) during the spring of 1968 than elsewhere in the country. A pattern of wage comparison and diffusion in that
region is indicated.

4.

The crafts involved. Crafts were grouped into three categories (as in Table 8):
the basic trades, the mechanical specialty trades, and the nonmechanical
specialty trades. Settlements were higher for the mechanical trades than for
other crafts and higher for the basic trades than for the nonmechanical specialty trades. I have noted previously the shift of construction demand into
sectors that draw heavily on the mechanical trades.[29] This change in the composition of construction demand contributed to the strong wage position of
the mechanical trades. By 1970, the situation had changed, and settlements
nationally were on the average larger in the basic trades than in the mechanical or other specialty trades.[30] Because there had been no major shifts in the

[28] Data were obtained on the percentage change in contract construction employment,
1964–1967, in the geographic areas for which wage settlements data were available.
These data were obtained from payroll reports of a sample of employers to the U.S.
Bureau of Labor Statistics (the bureau's establishment survey); see *Employment and
Earnings: States and Areas, 1939–67* (Washington, D.C., 1968). Also, the change in the
local unemployment rate for all civilian workers, 1964–1967, was obtained from unemployment reports for states and areas; see, for example, *Manpower Report of the
President* (Washington, D.C., 1970).
[29] For example, electricians, plumbers, and pipefitters provide, on a national average, 23
percent of total man-hours on hospital jobs, 18 percent on federal office buildings, and
16 percent on schools. On the other hand, they provide only 8 percent of total man-
hours on single-family homes and a negligible percentage on heavy and highway construction. (See Dunlop and Mills, "Manpower in Construction," p. 271.) These data are from
a series of reports entitled Labor and Material Requirements in Construction, prepared
by the Bureau of Labor Statistics and available from the Government Printing Office,
Washington, D.C.
[30] Report by the Construction Industry Collective Bargaining Commission, mimeo,
October 29, 1970.

pattern of manpower demand and supply in construction since 1968, it is likely that the increases achieved by the basic trades were in part owing to a catching-up process.

5.

Size of the bargaining unit. Regression results also indicated that the number of employees covered by the agreement was related to settlement size. In construction, bargaining units vary from very small units centered in a single locality to units as large as a metropolitan area or a state. Larger units often have broader geographic coverage and do proportionately more large-scale new construction than smaller groups. It is likely, therefore, that some elements of the bargaining structure are reflected in this variable. There has been a trend toward larger units, primarily by bargaining through district councils of locals, and apparently the larger units achieved higher settlements in 1968.[31]

The presence or lack of a mediator in each dispute was represented by a dummy variable that was statistically insignificant in the regression analysis. This finding lends quantitative support to the assertion of mediators and others that the mediation role is to facilitate agreement rather than to affect the terms of the bargain. However, to the extent that mediation and other mechanisms of dispute settlement reduce the occurrence of strikes, settlements will tend to be lower than otherwise.

Relative Importance of the Major Influences on the Size of Settlements
The relative impact of local conditions on the size of settlements can be measured by studying the behavior of the dependent variable in the regression equation under different assumptions regarding the independent variables. In this study, the independent variables represent conditions specific to each separate negotiation (for example, changes in local construction employment,

---

[31] The Bureau of Labor Statistics publishes an annual bulletin surveying union wages and hours in the building trades. A dummy variable representing the cities appearing in the BLS survey was included in the regression to check for any bias in the BLS reporting system (which is based on a much smaller sample than the data obtained for this study). In fact, wage increases in the 1968 period covered by the data collected for this study were somewhat lower in the cities included in the BLS survey.

Because the BLS survey is restricted to cities with population above 100,000 (though not all such cities are in the survey), the relation of city size to the size of the settlement was tested. A variable specifying population was insignificant in the regressions. In addition, a regression was estimated for the effect of the BLS cities on the other variables in the equation. The second variable (equal to 0 if the city was not included in the sample, actual value if the city was included) was not significant in a single case. Thus, there is no apparent reason for the tendency of the BLS sample cities to show lower settlement increases.

or the occurrence of a strike). More general influences, such as the changes over time in the state of the national economy, affect all areas in much the same way and cannot be reflected in the independent variables (that is, as differences between separate negotiations). It is, of course, possible that the average rate of increase in wages among all the settlements studied reflected national influences more than local factors.

A test may be made of the importance of national influences on the size of settlements in the spring of 1968 (the time of the survey) by specifying assumptions favorable to a *low* rate of wage increase and examining what the regression suggests would have been the resulting size of the settlement. In essence, if the constant term in the equation is large relative to the coefficients and values of the variables, then national influences are shown to be important. Therefore, assuming that locally (1) employment in construction had fallen by 5 percent from 1964 to 1967 (instead of rising, as it did, by an average of over 11 percent during the three years); (2) unemployment had risen 2 percentage points (rather than falling, as it did, by an average of a single point); (3) there was no strike; (4) the particular settlement was not in the Upper Midwest; and (5) the settlement was for a small local union (less than 1000 members) of a nonmechanical specialty trade, then the expected settlement size (by substitution in the equation and arithmetic calculation) would nevertheless have involved an increase of over 8 percent per year of the contract. The mean of the actual settlements was 12.005 percent per year increase. It would seem, therefore, that national economic and institutional influences, not reflected in the cross-section data used in this regression, dominated local conditions in determining the absolute level of the settlement increase.[32]

In order to isolate national influences on wage increases in construction, a statistical analysis of time-series data was made. Table 10 presents two regression equations, involving as dependent variables the annual percentage change in average hourly earnings in contract construction and the annual percentage change in the union hourly scale in selected cities (over 100,000 population) as prepared by the Bureau of Labor Statistics. The two time series on construction hourly earnings differ to some degree.[33] The average hourly earnings esti-

[32] It is possible that the relatively greater importance of national conditions is a characteristic only of the full-employment economy. It might be thought that in the fairly loose labor markets that characterized the early 1960s, with expectations regarding construction volume as uncertain as they were, local conditions would have carried relatively more weight than in 1968. Unfortunately, empirical evidence of a cross-section nature does not exist for other periods.

[33] The simple correlation coefficient of the two series is 0.79461.

Table 10.   Regression Results for a Time-Series Analysis of Wage Changes in Contract Construction

1. Dependent Variable: Annual percentage change in average hourly earnings in contract construction, 1950–1967

Independent Variables	Regression Coefficient	Significance Level (t test)
Average hourly earnings in nonagricultural industries, annual percentage change	0.7317	0.05%
Change in the construction unemployment rate, lagged one year	–0.1600	1.0
Constant	1.6208	1.0

$F(2, 16) = 33.4428$, significant at 5%
$R^2 = 0.8070$ Durbin-Watson = 1.5712

2. Dependent Variable: Annual percentage change in union hourly scale, Bureau of Labor Statistics index,[a] 1950–1967

Independent Variables	Regression Coefficient	Significance Level (t test)
Average hourly earnings in nonagricultural industries, annual percentage change	0.4515	0.05%
Consumer Price Index, annual percentage increase	0.2382	0.05
Change in construction unemployment rate, lagged one year	–0.0061	not significant
Constant	2.1945	0.05

$F(3, 15) = 38.0796$, significant at 1%[b]
$R^2 = 0.8839$[b]   Durbin-Watson = 2.2046

[a]U.S. Bureau of Labor Statistics, *Union Wages and Hours: Building Trades* (annual bulletin).
[b]See Table 9.

mates cover all workers in the industry, union and nonunion, and include all occupations except office and supervisory personnel. The union scale series involves only union rates and excludes fringe benefits (as do the average hourly earnings figures) and overtime (included in average hourly earnings estimates); it covers only a selected group of 68 major cities. The index is prepared by weighting the negotiated rates of the trades with estimates of union membership.

The regressions indicate the importance for construction earnings of the upward trend in labor earnings generally. Thus, annual percentage changes in average hourly earnings in all nonagricultural industry and in construction have a simple correlation coefficient of 0.84307, 1950-1968.[34] Increases in construction average hourly earnings are also well correlated (0.70560) with increases in the Consumer Price Index. A regression including both nonagricultural average hourly earnings and the CPI will, however, provide an insignificant regression coefficient for the CPI variable. Average hourly earnings also reflect changes in the construction employment rate, tending to fall as unemployment rises. The regression for changes in the union scale, on the other hand, reflects influences both from average hourly earnings generally and from the CPI, while unemployment conditions appear unimportant. In both equations, the elasticity of construction earnings of the period to changes in all-industry hourly earnings is less than unity. Thus, general increases in wages tend to be accompanied by less than proportional increases in construction earnings when other factors do not intervene.

Regression results indicate that the percentage rate of increase in construction average hourly earnings is positively related both to the percentage increase in average hourly earnings in nonagricultural industries and to the decrease in construction unemployment rates (the relationship is inverse, of course). Since the 1940s, however, rising wage levels in nonagricultural industries have made a larger contribution to rising construction wages than have changes in construction unemployment rates. This is because over the 1950–1968 period the mean annual change in construction unemployment rates was close to zero, while the mean increase in average hourly earnings in nonagricultural industries was some 4.3 percent per year. In consequence, generally rising wage levels have been the major contributor to the long-run increase in construction earnings. Had average hourly earnings in all industries risen at

---

[34] Employment in contract construction has averaged about 5.5 percent of nonagricultural employment in the postwar years, enough to influence only slightly the pattern of increases in nonagricultural average hourly earnings.

the 3.2 percent per year figure given by the Kennedy administration guidelines, construction earnings would have tended to rise at 3.9 percent per year, assuming that labor market conditions were unchanging. However, the unemployment rate for private wage and salary workers in construction fell at an average annual rate of 1.7 percent from 1961 to 1967, so that average hourly earnings in construction rose by an addition 0.27 percent per year in the 1960s.

Recently, labor market conditions in construction and the elements of the bargaining process that were described earlier, in Chapter 2, have combined to create widening wage differentials in favor of construction. There may be many reasons for these expanding differentials; they have not been successfully quantified. Nor is there clear evidence that the increased differentials can be maintained. Presumably, changes in institutional factors such as improved conditions of job security in other industries would aid in the maintenance of larger differentials.[35]

Finally, several economic time series were tested for their statistical relation to construction wage increases. In general, profit rates and productivity measures contribute nothing of statistical significance to explanatory regressions.

Limitations of the Analysis

1.

Bargaining structure in contract construction is more complex than the statistical analysis suggested. Labor bargaining units may be national unions, local unions, councils of local unions, multitrade councils, and regional or statewide units. Contractors' units may be single employers or trade associations or joint associations at a local, regional, state, or national level. The jurisdictions of the unions and the scope of the contractors' organizations create a patchwork quilt of overlapping bargaining units.[36] There is, in Cullen's words, "a maze of submarkets"[37] that are reflected in the wage structure. One result of this

[35] Increasing differentials in wage rates between construction and other industries reflect the provision of increased fringe benefits in nonconstruction industry. Provisions in collective bargaining agreements designed to protect or supplement the earnings of individual workers have become widespread in manufacturing (for example, seniority systems, supplemental unemployment benefits, paid holidays, vacation plans, severance pay) but remain very rare in construction. Construction work is also hazardous, seasonal, and often unpleasant, although probably no more so now than has been the case for many years. See U.S. Bureau of Labor Statistics, *Supplemental Unemployment Benefit Plans and Wage-Employment Guarantees,* Bulletin no. 1425-2 (Washington, D.C., 1965), and *Severance Pay and Layoff Benefit Plans,* Bulletin no. 1425-3 (Washington, D.C., 1965).
[36] See Chapter 2.
[37] Donald E. Cullen, "Union Wage Policy in Heavy Construction: The St. Lawrence Seaway," *American Economic Review* 49 (March 1959):68–84.

complex bargaining structure is to emphasize comparison of rates and attempts at whipsawing by both parties. The interplay of settlements, variations in differentials, and attempts to reassert or alter traditional differentials undoubtedly affects variations in settlements.

2.

The wage structure varies both by craft and by area. Thus, many trades normally negotiate a single journeyman scale; others agree to a range of rates. Some crafts have a range of rates in some geographic areas but not in others. In those crafts for which a range of rates is negotiated, the dependent variable in this study involved the increase in a major (in terms of employment) rate.[38] Variations not studied here occur in the structure of rates within the crafts that use multiple rates.

3.

As has been previously mentioned, the labor market data (excluding the information on wage settlements) used in this study were specific to area but not to craft or sector of the industry. Thus, much potentially significant variation in labor market conditions was not available as explanatory information.

4.

The study examined the determinants of the size of settlements in toto, both wages and fringes, by including a cost estimate of the fringes in the total settlement. The actual distribution of the package between wages and fringes, is, of course, important for many purposes. This study was unable to account separately for wage and fringe increases, but a few comments regarding fringe benefits in construction are appropriate.

Fringe benefits in construction normally include health and welfare plans, pension plans, vacation plans (in some areas), and, more rarely, supplemental unemployment benefit plans. Fringes began to develop in the 1940s but received a nationwide impetus only during the Korean War period. Local bargaining units normally negotiate a total economic package and then distribute the package between wages and fringes.[39] Fringe benefits are normally dispersed from jointly administered funds to which the employers (and in some cases the unions) pay agreed-upon amounts.

[38] For the operating engineers, who normally negotiate a different rate for each piece of equipment, the settlement data are changes in the rate for bulldozer operators; for teamsters, usually 1–1½-ton dump truck operators; for laborers, usually general building laborers.

[39] A significant departure from the local bargaining pattern is the National Electrical Benefit Fund (retirement) for the electrical contracting industry. The NEBF is a nationwide fund supported by the contractors' contributions (unit per hour) to the central fund.

The distribution of a settlement between wages and fringes depends on several considerations. First, there is pressure on the local unions from the national organizations to negotiate similar benefits in the same craft in different areas, in part to ease the problem of the portability of fringe benefits for the traveling members. Second, employers prefer certain fringes over others. Third, there are local labor market influences, from patterns set by other crafts in the same area. Fourth, the financial problems of the funds as currently established will be put before the negotiators by the trustees and consultants of the funds, and minimum adjustments agreed upon as necessary. Fifth, the benefits desirable to the membership of any craft will depend on the demographic characteristics of the local's membership. In many cases, the local itself can choose to divide a portion of the settlement between wages and a cents-per-hour contribution by the employer to fringes.

5.

The settlements data analyzed refer only to the average size of the yearly increase over the term of the agreement. In fact, increases are rarely proportioned evenly over time. Instead, agreements may have higher increases in later years ("back-loaded") or in earlier years ("front-loaded"). Several factors affect the timing of the increases. Contractors normally try to minimize increases in the first year of a contract, for these must be paid on ongoing work that was bid and awarded before the terms of the settlement were known. Increases falling later in a contract can be foreseen clearly and included in bids. Conversely, however, the catching-up process, by which a craft seeks to reestablish historic differentials with other crafts, may exert pressure for immediate large increases. Expectations of future demand conditions also affect the timing of increases. During the mid-1960s, expectations in construction were bullish, and agreements were generally back-loaded. By 1969–1970, expectations had shifted toward a future slowdown of work, and agreements became strongly front-loaded.

The timing of increases is important to stabilization policy. Strongly back-loaded agreements stimulate other crafts to a catching-up process in succeeding negotiations. Front-loaded contracts are less likely to accelerate a wage spiral.

Conclusions

This chapter has attempted to demonstrate that the increasing rate of wage settlements in construction in the high-employment economy of the late

1960s was due to a combination of economic and institutional factors. The most important economic factors were the rapid expansion of product demand in certain critical branches of the industry and the simultaneous shrinkage of the available labor supply because of the general expansion of the economy. The most important institutional factors were the decentralized structure of collective bargaining in construction and the increasing effectiveness of the unions' strike weapon. These factors are important elements of our economy and our collective bargaining system, and it will not be easy to achieve the reforms necessary to reconcile full employment with wage and price stability in the construction sector of the economy.

Perhaps it is the complexity of the problem of inflation or the difficulty of achieving fundamental reforms that causes many people to look for trivial explanations and simple solutions. It is not difficult to prepare a list of suggestions made by public authorities or private commentators as to what should be done to improve the economic and industrial relations performance of construction. The list is, for the most part, not a new list — it has been proposed often before in less difficult times than the late 1960s and has simply been dusted off to confront the problem of full employment. It includes recommendations such as abolishing the Davis-Bacon act, abolishing the hiring hall, establishing regional multicraft bargaining, expanding training, prohibiting the national contract, and organizing owners to support contractors.[40] Certainly some of these proposals require attention by industry and public officials,[41] not only for the contribution that reforms and improvements would make to the efficiency of the industry, but also because the abuses that have developed in some situations undermine the effectiveness of the particular institutions or legislation involved. However, such recommendations are at most an indirect and partial response to the problems of the industry and include both potentially useful and potentially damaging elements. Even if the recommendations were fully met, there would continue to be a difficult inflationary situation in construction in times of full employment.

Consider, for instance, the proposals to modify or repeal the Davis-Bacon

[40]See, for example, M. R. Lefkoe, *The Crisis in Construction: There Is an Answer* (Washington, D.C.: Bureau of National Affairs Books, 1970); John C. Garvin, "A Plan for Regional Bargaining in Construction," address to the Builders Exchange of Greater Lansing, Michigan, printed in *Daily Labor Report* (Bureau of National Affairs), no. 189 (September 9, 1970), pp. D-1 ff.; and "Bribing the Building Trades," *Wall Street Journal* editorial, December 14, 1970.

[41]Apprenticeship training, manpower utilization, and planning are discussed in later chapters.

Act as a response to rising labor costs. The act requires that the prevailing wages in an area for a given type of work are the minimum wages that must be paid on the federal or federally assisted projects covered by the act.[42] The Department of Labor administers the act, and the Secretary of Labor generally issues a determination of wages to be paid in advance of the job.[43] The argument has been that the act and its administration, by spreading union scales to federal work, raise the cost of federal projects and protect the high wages of workers under union contracts against nonunion competition. Yet the potential net impact of Davis-Bacon on construction labor costs is very difficult to estimate. It does tend to increase costs by certifying higher wages and fringe rates in some areas and for some types of work than the government would have to pay under open competition.[44] But repeal of the act could result in greater total costs on government projects by increasing industrial strife, by facilitating awards to incompetent contractors competitive only by virtue of low wages, and by making it difficult to obtain men for work in distant areas.

It should not be imagined that the Davis-Bacon Act is as effective a barrier as it may appear to be against lower-than-union rates on federal jobs. First, the administration of the act is based on the prevailing, rather than on the union, rate. Often on federal jobs, especially housing jobs, rates different from union rates prevail in the area. Second, enforcement of the act (as opposed to its administration, that is, the issuing of determinations as to the prevailing rates) is often weak. There are many ways to cheat on its requirements, and it is often quite difficult to produce evidence of violations.[45] In general, re-

---

[42] Federal funds provided some 10 percent of all construction expenditures in 1966, the most recent year for which data are available. Public (all levels of government) new construction was 32 percent of new construction expenditures in 1966 and 31 percent in 1969. Several states have prevailing wage laws similar to Davis-Bacon. See *Construction Review* (U.S. Department of Commerce, Business and Defense Services Administration), *passim.*

[43] See Joseph Stone and J. R. Brunozzi, *The Construction Worker under Federal Wage Laws,* (Washington, D.C.: Livingston Press, 1959).

[44] The impact of Davis-Bacon is most pronounced in highway construction, where federal funds are a major proportion of total construction dollars. Davis-Bacon has made union organization easier in this branch of the industry and has probably contributed to a rising level of wages. Its impact on other branches is far less significant. For a description of Davis-Bacon as an organizing weapon in highway construction, see Garth Mangum, *The Operating Engineers: The Economic History of a Trade Union* (Cambridge: Harvard University Press, 1964), pp. 257 ff.

[45] For example, labor costs as a whole may be minimized under a Davis-Bacon determination by the employer's assigning work to employees in lower wage classifications than is common practice in the industry. Prevention of such action by a nonunion contractor is very difficult.

peal or modification of the Davis-Bacon Act could be expected to have only
a small impact on federal and federally assisted construction costs, and even
less on privately financed work.[46]

Brief criticisms may be directed at the other elements of the list of recommendations. First, the hiring hall serves a useful and important role in the
allocation of labor in construction which no other mechanism is now equipped
to fulfill. In most cases, elimination of hiring halls would add to, rather than
reduce, inefficiencies in the industry, although reforms may be necessary in
particular instances. Second, multicraft regional bargaining cannot be expected
to work in the absence of a greater degree of unity of interest among contractors and their associations than is now apparent. Rather, reform of collective bargaining must follow the pattern of the business interests of contractors
in different branches and geographic areas. Third, the nation has no widespread
mechanism for the training of skilled construction workers except apprenticeship. Most federal nonapprenticeship training programs are provided for persons
in the laborer classification or for aspects of carpentry. The time lag involved
in training men for many of the trades (especially the mechanical trades, which
are in shortest supply) is such that government programs sensitive to immediate
needs are unthinkable. Apprenticeship programs, however, require different
measures of reform in different crafts and areas. What is most needed in apprenticeship generally is improvement in the process of planning by which training
is adjusted to actual manpower needs. Fourth, the national contract facilitates
the operation of large national contractors whose specialization is an efficient
response to the needs of large-scale construction. Reforms in the relationship of
the national contractor to the bargaining position of local firms must be carefully considered in order not to sacrifice the competitive interests of the former
to the latter, lest the economies of specialization be lost. Fifth, the organization
of owners to support contractors in collective bargaining is likely to produce
results in only a limited number of situations and for only brief periods. The
interests of owners are too divergent, and their involvement in construction too
variable, to be a reliable basis for fundamental changes in the industry.

The long-run adjustment of construction to the full-employment economy
must involve changes other than the ones discussed. There must be avoidance,
through aggregate economic policy or specific measures, of demand conditions likely to generate unreasonable short-run pressure on labor markets. Re-

---

[46]The President's suspension of the Davis-Bacon Act in the spring of 1971 was too brief
to provide any significant empirical evidence of what its impact might be. During the
suspension of the federal statute, most of the 28 state laws of a similar nature remained
in force.

form of government and large-industry procedures for the planning and scheduling of construction projects could be extremely helpful in this area. Improvements in the adjustment of manpower allocation and utilization to labor demand are vital, and within reach both of the industry and of public authorities.[47] If the fragmentation of the collective bargaining structure in construction were reduced, the long-run needs of the industry could be reflected more fully in the results of bargaining. Fragmentation can be reduced in several ways, including the merger of international unions and their local affiliates, enlargement of the geographic scope of bargaining in many trades, and multicraft bargaining where appropriate. The reform of bargaining structure should also provide a greater role for national union and contractor authorities in local collective bargaining. The creation of larger bargaining areas would require the establishment in a single contract of differentials in wages and conditions of work among branches of the industry.[48] Currently, the different product market characteristics of the various branches (for example, home building and road building) can be accommodated informally in small areas in ways that would not be possible in larger areas. Therefore, it is likely that specific adjustments in wages and conditions for different branches will be necessary in large-area agreements. It is possible that separate rates and conditions by branch will render different wages and conditions by locality less important than they now would appear to be.

As has already been shown, the geographic scope of negotiations partly depends on the territory of the union and contractor organizations involved. Thus any changes in scope must be sensitive to the internal structure and leadership of the union and contractor organizations. The task of developing a consortium among contractor associations or melding a number of associations into a new one is complicated and characteristically takes a long time. Similarly, on the union side, the formulation of a district council or the merger of local unions, or the intervention of the national union as spokesman for local union organizations, is fraught with complex questions of leadership, rivalries, and special local interests. The history of such mergers on both

---

[47]See Chapters 4 and 5.
[48]See, for example, the agreement between the Laborers International Union, State of Indiana District Council, and the Employers Negotiating Committee (April 1, 1970), which replaced 16 agreements between laborers local unions and various contractors' associations in Indiana. The agreement excludes heavy and highway work and gas distribution; it covers primarily building construction. Eight categories of work and four geographic areas of the state are classified separately for wage rates and fringe benefits.

sides suggests that persuasion and active leadership on the part of national groups has been vastly more effective than force, compulsion, or formula.

Finally, development or extension of procedures for the settlement of disputes over the terms of new contracts will minimize the disruptive effect of the strike and are widely needed in the industry. Many union officials and employers recognize that short-run wage concessions have often been gained by the unions at too great a cost to the industry, by disrupting the work of other trades, lessening demand in the product market, and encouraging non-union competition. More stable industrial relations in many sectors of construction that now lack dispute settlement machinery will contribute to the general good of the industry.

II

The Labor Market in Construction

4

Manpower Planning

The Impact of Tight Labor Markets

The need for manpower planning[1] in construction has never been more obvious than in the decade just past. During the 1960s, labor market conditions in the American economy tightened considerably, and a prolonged period of labor shortages and near shortages developed in much of construction. The industry has long been adapted to shortage conditions in all production factors in the peak season, but shortages in crafts and materials in the off-season have been unusual. Building recessions have historically followed close upon the heels of booms, but they did not materialize in the 1960s. Localized downturns occurred, but they were short-lived and followed by strong expansions. Unemployment rates fell to fifteen-year lows in the industry and remained until 1970 at levels never before experienced in the absence of wartime central economic controls.

This description of tight labor markets in construction should be qualified to account for the fact that unemployment rates in the industry have remained high in relation to other sectors of the economy. To a large degree, construction unemployment rates reflect the casual employment conditions in the industry. But the gap between construction and other unemployment rates has narrowed. Between 1948 and 1964, the construction unemployment rate (on annual average) never failed to be double or more than double the national rate. Yet in 1964 the construction rate fell to less than double the national rate and remained at the new level for several years.

Unemployment rates in most construction crafts fell dramatically during the 1960s. From 1962 to 1969, unemployment rates among carpenters fell 4.5 points, among bricklayers 5.5 points, among electricians 3.3 points, and among cement finishers 7.1 points (see Table 11). Only among plasterers did the national rates of unemployment rise, reflecting unfavorable changes in construction technology and materials usage. By 1969, unemployment rates in many crafts had reached historically low levels: electricians, 1.6 percent unemployed, plumbers and pipefitters, 2.0 percent unemployed; bricklayers, 3.2 percent unemployed.[2]

---

[1] Planning is used here to mean a process by which expected demand for labor is related to the available supply, and adjustments made in either demand or supply to reduce the pressure of surpluses or shortages. Planning may, of course, involve many types of adjustments, including a better allocation of the work force, changes in the timing of projects, increased training, and so on.

[2] These data include persons working at the occupation cited in all industries, not only construction. See Table 11 for an estimate of the proportion of each craft working in construction.

Table 11. Unemployment Rates for Construction Occupations

Occupation	Number in Labor Force (000)				Unemployment Rate (%)				Change in Unemployment Rate (%)		Approximate Percentage of Total Number in the Occupational Category Employed in Construction[a]	
	1962	1967	1969	1970	1962	1967	1969	1970	1962–1967	1967–1970	1966	1970
Craftsmen and Foremen												
Bricklayers, stone masons, tilesetters	206	209	219	205	8.7	4.8	3.2	8.8	−3.9	+4.0	74	93
Carpenters	896	876	925	906	8.9	5.0	4.4	8.4	−3.9	+3.4	77	84
Cement and concrete finishers	54	61	69	73	12.9	10.3	5.8	9.6	−2.6	−0.7	95	97
Electricians	407	454	431	448	4.9	1.5	1.6	2.7	−3.4	+1.2	45	48
Excavating, grading, and road-building machine operators	248	290	342	347	11.7	5.5	5.6	7.5	−6.2	+2.0	78	81
Painters and paper-hangers	389	403	414	407	12.6	6.3	4.1	7.4	−6.3	+1.1	67	83
Plasterers	36	28	33	30	7.7	12.5	9.1	6.7	+4.8	−5.8	95	100
Plumbers and pipefitters	279	344	354	378	6.7	3.6	2.0	4.0	−3.1	+0.4	64	70
Roofers and slaters	62	59	67	72	10.1	3.3	4.5	6.9	−6.8	+3.6	98	95
Structural metalworkers	57	76			10.9	6.2	3.2	7.2	−6.8	+1.0	56	69
Tinsmiths, coppersmiths, and sheet metalworkers	138	154			5.5	2.5			−3.0		35	

Source: Data from the Bureau of Labor Statistics.

[a]Includes employees of contractors, government construction agencies, the self-employed, and unpaid family workers. Excludes the construction and maintenance personnel of private nonconstruction firms.

The labor shortages that developed were confined largely to certain crafts and areas, but they were undoubtedly more widespread than at any time since the Korean War. Shortages were most significant among the mechanical trades and in areas of considerable industrial and commercial construction.[3] In the mid-1960s, contractor groups began to conduct continuing surveys among their membership of labor shortages. In 1966, *Engineering News-Record* began to publish a survey of shortages and found some contractors anxious to report shortages even in winter months.[4] During that year, international union officials also admitted increasing shortages and called upon local unions to increase apprenticeship training, to accept permitmen as members (where necessary), and to make other adjustments to a rising volume of manpower demand.[5]

The existence and the extent of shortages were disputed in the industry. Union members normally view current jobs only as one element of their employment opportunities; they are concerned about future unemployment as well. In the casual labor markets of construction, employment insecurity is endemic among workers and creates a desire to spread the work over a longer period of time, by shortages and delays if necessary. To a considerable degree, a real divergence of interests separates contractors and owners from unions and workmen on this issue.[6] However, regardless of their exact extent, shortages increased considerably in the 1960s and by the latter years of the decade were generally recognized as a problem in the industry.

The press of demand against the available labor supply was reinforced by other aspects of the industry's labor market. The seasonal pattern of constrution had diminished but continued to involve a severe underutilization of

[3] In many cases, complaints of an inadequate labor supply in construction are directed at the availability of skilled men, or the better-trained mechanics, not at the total volume of manpower. See Samuel M. Burt, *Industry and Vocational-Technical Education* (New York: McGraw-Hill, 1967), p. 92.

[4] These surveys, including that in *Engineering News-Record,* are not scientifically chosen samples and cannot be cited as an accurate measure of labor market tightness or job availability.

[5] Carpenters' President Maurice A. Hutcheson discussed the developing situation at his union's convention in 1966 and suggested, by implication, an approach to the problem: "Generally speaking, manpower shortages are most acute in those areas which pay the lowest wages and maintain the poorest working conditions. Men are not very likely to move from one area to another if it means taking a substantial cut in pay." "General President's Report," in United Brotherhood of Carpenters and Joiners of America, *Proceedings of the Thirtieth General Convention* (1966), p. 110.

[6] For a fuller discussion of shortages, see John T. Dunlop and D. Q. Mills, "Manpower in Construction," in *Report of the President's Committee on Urban Housing: Technical Studies,* vol. 2 (Washington, D.C., 1968), pp. 253–254.

the industry's labor force.[7] Localized recessions in building construction continued to occur and, because of the inefficient mechanisms of manpower allocation, generated pockets of large-scale unemployment in the industry. Finally, past experience with building cycles caused the industry to be conservative regarding the expansion of the labor force in the absence of reliable extimates of future requirements.

The impact of tight labor markets was to make the need for comprehensive planning to meet manpower requirements more evident than before. Planning in construction remains very decentralized and largely limited to the operation of apprenticeship programs. Improved planning awaits advances in the quality of information on which decisions can be based and in the mechanisms by which the labor market situation is evaluated. In the absence of reliable information, it has proved most politic to allow local authorities to handle manpower planning in their own largely expedient manner. In addition, the slack labor markets that reappeared in the early 1970s were no less a problem than the period of shortages, for unemployment remained a hardship for the worker, led to a waste of national resources, and contained the seeds of future shortages (by imbuing the work force with concern for the scarcity or potential scarcity of jobs). This chapter describes advances in manpower planning mechanisms of the industry.

Manpower Forecasting and Planning at the National Level

The Current State of Forecasting

Advances in projecting manpower demand   Despite the need for more effective utilization of the construction industry's labor force, methods of manpower forecasting and planning developed only slowly in the 1960s. Although manpower forecasting for construction is more advanced on the national level than on the local level, its current stage of development is nevertheless quite primitive. The availability of manpower forecasts is limited, and methods of preparation have been inadequate in many cases. Projections of total employment in the industry and of the growth or decline of major occupations are published,[8] but, until recently, breakdowns for the construction industry of forecasted employment by craft were not available.[9] Estimates of future

---

[7]See Chapter 5.

[8]See U.S. Bureau of Labor Statistics, *Occupational Outlook Handbook* (bulletin series).

[9]See U.S. Bureau of Labor Statistics, *Tomorrow's Manpower Needs* (Washington, D.C., 1969); Alan F. Salt, "Estimated Need for Skilled Workers, 1965–75," *Monthly Labor Review* 89 (April 1966): 365–371; and U.S. Bureau of Labor Statistics, *Projections 1970,* Bulletin no. 1536 (Washington, D.C., 1966). The record of these projections has on the whole been one of considerable overestimates. For example, in 1966 Dan Hol-

employment by craft in the different major branches of construction (such as highway construction) have been available only on a spotty basis.[10]

Beginning in the late 1960s, projections of manpower demand specific to craft and construction sectors were prepared. It became possible to obtain direct estimates of the magnitude and craft distribution of manpower demand for the residential construction industry under various assumptions about future private residential construction and public housing assistance.[11] Similarly, the impact on manpower demand of expected activity in other sectors of the industry was estimated. These improved projections allowed considerably more range for the development of manpower policy, by placing forecasts on a basis consistent with the institutional and economic structure of the industry. For example, it became possible to analyze future requirements for manpower in industrial and commercial building construction. Until this time, this important sector of construction was either lumped together with all other private construction or scattered in exclusively occupational forecasts that included industries other than construction.[12]

---

land, relying on projections published by the Bureau of Labor Statistics, in *Manpower Report of the President* (Washington, D.C. 1963), p. 95 and by the National Bureau of Economic Research, predicted annual average employment in contract construction would reach 4 million in 1970. The 1970 annual average was some 3.4 million. See D. M. Holland, *Private Pension Funds: Projected Growth*, National Bureau of Economic Research, Occasional Paper no. 97 (New York, 1966), pp. 26–28. Similarly, in 1955, Stucke and Gordon projected annual average on-site construction employment in highway construction of 500,000 for 1960. The actual figure was less than 300,000. See A.L. Stucke and E.M. Gordon "Manpower Impact of the Proposed $101 Billion Highway Program," *Construction Review* 1 (February 1965): 5–8. The overestimates of these projections were due to a variety of causes, including the failure of anticipated spending volume to materialize.

[10] See, for example, "Estimating Future Occupational Labor Requirements for Private Construction," *Monthly Labor Review* 65 (July 1947): 73–75. See also U.S. Congress, Joint Economic Committee, Subcommittee on Economic Progress, "Labor Requirements for State and Local Public Works, 1946–1975," in *State and Local Public Facility Needs and Financing,* vol. 1, 89th Cong., 2nd sess., 1966, pp. 75–94; Stucke and Gordon, "$101 Billion Highway Program"; and U.S. President, *Second Annual Report on National Housing Goals* (Washington, D.C., 1970), pp. 140–146.

[11] See Dunlop and Mills, "Manpower in Construction."

[12] The most recently developed techniques of manpower forecasting derive from a group of studies of labor and materials requirements in different types of construction begun by the Bureau of Labor Statistics in 1959. Projected expenditures by type of construction are applied to the estimated labor requirements by craft per dollar expenditure to obtain manpower demand forecasts. See *ibid.,* pp. 240 ff. The continuance and improvement of these manpower projections depends on the updating and extension of the studies on which they are based. Previous projections began from estimates of total expenditures on all construction activity and obtained an aggregate employment estimate from the expenditure figures. An industry occupational distribution was then applied to the aggregate figure to obtain employment by occupation. Separate sectors of construction could not be directly distinguished. (This is the essence of the previous Bureau of Labor Statistics methodology. See Salt, "Estimated Need for Skilled Workers," p. 367.)

Forecasting manpower supply Techniques of forecasting manpower supply have been less well developed than those for projecting demand. Analysis of the availability and development of manpower in construction has generally treated those currently employed in the industry as a stock of labor which is reduced only through death or retirement and which is increased only through apprenticeship.[13] Because the relative importance of apprenticeship as a source of manpower differs among crafts, sectors of the industry, and geographic regions, and because apprenticeship is rarely the major source of increase in the construction labor force, this procedure leaves a great deal to be desired. In fact, the construction labor force is considerably more flexible than is commonly supposed. Indeed, the flexibility of the labor force is an outstanding characteristic of the industry.

The ratio of the total number of persons employed at some time during the year to the number of annual full-time jobs is high in construction.[14] In 1968, for example, some 6.4 million workers were employed in contract construction to fill an average of 3.3 million full-time jobs — a ratio of 1.8 workers to each job. In manufacturing the ratio was about 1.3. Certain building trades skills (including elements of carpentry and masonry, for example) are widely distributed throughout the economy, and when necessary the construction industry has often been able to increase its work force at a fairly rapid rate by recruitment from other industries.[15]

The mobility of the construction labor force has four basic dimensions.[16]

[13] See, for example, Building Research Advisory Board, National Academy of Sciences – National Research Council, "Historical Evaluation of Industrialized Housing and Building Systems," in *Report of the President's Committee on Urban Housing: Technical Studies,* vol. 2 (Washington, D.C., 1968), pp. 177–190.

[14] David A. Farber, "Apprenticeship in the United States: Labor Market Forces and Social Policy," *Journal of Human Resources* 2 (Winter 1969): 88.

[15] The seasonal expansion of employment is one reason for the flexibility of the labor force. For example, for construction craftsmen other than carpenters, expansion in the construction labor force averaged some 76.5 percent of the net increase in employment in the spring months of 1961–1966 (a reduction in the numbers of the unemployed accounted for the remaining 23.5 percent of the increase). For carpenters, the figure is identical (76.5); for laborers it is 88.5 percent (these figures refer to wage and salary workers employed by contractors and government construction agencies).

[16] The industrial distribution of earnings among contract construction workers indicates considerable mobility. In 1957, only 72.3 percent of the approximately 5 million male wage and salary workers employed in contract construction earned most of their year's income from contract construction employment. With the exception of the service industries, this was the lowest reported percentage. See U.S. Social Security Administration, *Handbook of Old-Age Survivors, Disability Insurance Statistics: Employment, Earnings, and Insurance Status of Workers in Covered Employment, 1957* (Washington, D.C., 1965), pp. 34, 41. (These are the most recent data available.)

For example, the work force of carpenters on residential jobs might be increased by drawing from: (1) employment on other construction in the same locality; (2) the maintenance crews of local manufacturers; (3) residential construction in other geographic areas; or (4) other related occupations. There appear to be many people in other jobs but with some construction experience who gravitate to construction at certain times. Informal entry is most important for the basic trades and occurs primarily during the seasonal upswing or when an area undergoes a sudden large increase in work volume.

The flexibility of the industry's work force requires that manpower forecasting at the national level consider the magnitude, direction, and determinants of manpower flows to and from the industry. The availability of manpower to construction over the short run depends on the interaction of relative wages, general unemployment, and the volume of demand in construction itself. The volume of construction employment and training in previous years determines the rate of adjustment to high levels of activity in the industry. When general unemployment is growing, manpower is likely to be more easily available to the industry than when tight labor markets prevail.

Technical note: A manpower planning model The preceding discussion has shown that analysis of manpower requirements in construction is further advanced than understanding of manpower flows to the industry. Nevertheless, both are sufficiently developed to allow an exploratory forecasting model to be prepared. (Unfortunately, there remain some very significant interrelationships between manpower demand and supply that cannot yet be modeled.) This section presents a description of a manpower planning model for construction.

Simplifying assumptions regarding economic conditions are necessary to the development of a model. Thus, the model cannot be used to predict with accuracy what changes in economic conditions (such as labor costs) will occur as the result of any imbalances that are forecast. Instead, the model is a recursive method of indicating levels of anticipated activity and of identifying potential problem areas. It is not a general model of the labor market in construction and cannot, in its present stage of development, be utilized to simulate the operation of the market in response to any of the conditions it predicts.

The model proceeds from estimates of construction expenditure by category or type of structure. These estimates are normally generated by econometric or input-output models of the national economy and rest upon assumptions about behavior in the areas of consumer expenditures, business investment, government expenditures, and real rates of growth in the economy. Construction expenditures are the sum of projected private capital investment, public capital investment, and expenditures on residential construction (based largely on population growth, changes in the housing stock, geographic mobility, and so on).[17]

Estimates of construction expenditure by type may be converted into estimates of manpower demand by use of a matrix of coefficients expressing the man-hour requirements by craft for each $1000 (or whatever standard unit is desired) of construction cost. For each type of structure, there is a vector of coefficients representing requirements in each of the several crafts. Multiplication of the vector of expenditures (by type of structure) by the matrix of man-hour coefficients (by type of structure and craft) generates a vector of total man-hours required by craft for all types of construction. This vector of total man-hour requirements is reduced by the factor representing the number of man-hours in a full workyear in order to estimate annual average employment in the craft.[18]

The use of a matrix of coefficients to estimate manpower requirements by craft involves some basic assumptions. The most important one is that substitution is not allowed between labor and other factors of production or among the different crafts. In effect, relative factor prices are assumed to be unchanging (or, for an equivalent result, factor demand is assumed to be inelastic to changing relative factor prices). These assumptions are necessary because of our current inability to estimate production functions that allow factor substitution for the various types of construction activity.[19]

The relationship between manpower demand and the supply conditions of the labor market can be analyzed by relating estimated annual average employment to wage and unemployment conditions. The capacity of the industry to meet labor requirements without undue costs and delays depends on the manpower available to it at existing relative wage rates and on the extent of nonconstruction employment opportunities. The relationships be-

[17]See, for example, U.S. Bureau of Labor Statistics, *Patterns of U.S. Economic Growth,* Bulletin no. 1672 (Washington, D.C., 1970).

[18]This method of manpower projection is more fully presented in Dunlop and Mills, "Manpower in Construction," pp. 263–273. A later section of the present chapter discusses an adaptation of the demand forecasting aspects of the model to the local labor market.

[19]Peter J. Cassimates, *Economics of the Construction Industry,* National Industrial Conference Board Studies in Business Economics no. 111 (New York, 1969), has estimated a Cobb-Douglas aggregate production function involving total man-hours and capital input for all construction (pp. 69–75). This function is far too aggregative to be of any use in manpower forecasting. Data and other limitations prevent disaggregation.

tween the manpower pool available to construction and other variables have already been described. Parameters estimated from time-series data allow the degree of tightness in the labor market to be predicted at projected levels of demand.

Unfortunately, it is not possible to perform an analysis of this nature on an occupational basis. A measure of the total manpower pool available to the industry can be obtained from the Social Security Administration, but it cannot be disaggregated on a craft basis.[20] Thus it is possible to make only a rough evaluation of the ease or tightness of the entire manpower pool, and all problems arising from occupational imbalances must be ignored. Similarly, the data do not allow disaggregation by state or locality, so that all potential geographic imbalances are also unknown.

The model may be expressed symbolically as follows:

$$AAE = \sum_i v_i,$$

$$v = a^{-1}BA,$$

$$E = f(AAE, w, UE, u, \dots),$$

where

AAE = annual average employment in contract construction,

  A = matrix of coefficients of man-hours per $1000 construction cost by type of structure,

  B = vector of estimated total expenditures by type of structure,

  a = number of man-hours per workyear,

  v = vector of man-years of work by craft,

  w = relative wage, construction and other industries,

 UE = annual average all-industry unemployment rate,

  E = total number of persons reporting employment in contract construction,

  u = an index of labor utilization which affects the average ratio of all employees (E) to full-time jobs (AAE), and

  i = indicates a particular craft.

B, w, u, and UE must be forecast exogenously.

A number of different specifications, each with varying properties, may be made of the functional relationship in the third equation. The specification depends on how the estimates are to be used, as well as on statistical properties. In any case, the equation provides an estimate of the total number of

[20]The Social Security Administration collects no occupational information.

persons needed for work in the industry under various conditions, such as the level of manpower demand (for yearlong workers), relative wages, and unemployment. When the estimate of total persons required is compared to availability, the degree of potential labor market stress is demonstrated; in this way, expectations regarding subsequent changes in other economic variables (for example, wages) may be developed or corrective policy measures initiated.

Models of this nature are in use, though it should be noted that some important relationships and interrelationships are subsumed under them. Thus the volume of construction demand B is presumably not independent of the aggregate level of employment UE. Similarly, the matrix of labor input coefficients is not actually invariant with changes in the relative wages of the several crafts, which are subsumed under the overall relative wage variable w. However, for the kinds of predictions for which the model is intended, these relationships are of secondary importance.

Balance Sheet Manpower Planning

Forecasting has now progressed sufficiently so that aggregate manpower planning for construction may soon become a reality. The basic purpose of such planning is to achieve, as efficiently as possible, a balance between manpower demand and supply. Through planning it will be possible to tap various sources in order to reach a desired volume of manpower and to determine the costs and implications of each source for the future progress of the industry. Industry or public officials might choose among alternative sources with several objectives in mind. For instance, it might be public or private policy to attempt to increase real labor productivity in construction rather than to expand entry into the industry, because when labor market conditions are generally tight, expanded manpower demand can cause undesirable wage increases or raise recruitment and training costs. It might be less expensive to increase real labor productivity; however, no matter which policy is selected, there are costs, both direct and indirect, associated with expansion of the effective labor supply through any given means. Manpower policy must be based on knowledge of the volume and incidence of these costs, as well as on the need for additional labor.

At present, labor market mechanisms operating in a traditional manner either induce entry or increase labor utilization as a response to increasing demand. The purpose of forecasting and planning by private or public bodies is to anticipate the operation of decentralized market forces and intervene to affect their results. Often, market processes generate short-run adjustments, such as undesirable wage and cost increases and unanticipated delays, that undermine the long-term objectives of public or private policy. Forecasting, even in its current state, may help to avoid these conflicts.

It is useful to prepare numerical projections of the volume of manpower entry into construction by various routes and of the increases in the effective manpower supply obtainable through better utilization of labor. Past experience may provide insights into the reasonableness of expectations about each means of increasing manpower supply, but even where numerical estimates are subject to considerable inaccuracy and differing interpretations, they may identify potential problem areas. Table 12 presents a balance sheet of manpower demand and supply on an aggregate level for construction and quantifies the sources of manpower available in 1978 to meet expected requirements. The balance sheet is a planning device, intended to reveal potential problems and alternative policy choices. It is not so much a prediction of the future (although it is largely based on manpower forecasts) as a device for developing a comprehensive and consistent manpower plan. The complexity of the balance sheet and the large variety of alternative policies open to decision makers are an accurate reflection of the complexity of real-world processes.

Table 12 is a manpower balance sheet in the sense that net manpower demand (derived from estimated construction expenditures) is made to balance with manpower supply. The item by which the table is made to balance is informal entry, so that increases in, for instance, apprenticeship are offset by assumed reductions in informal entry. The volume of informal entry is assumed to be dependent on the gap between the formal entrants and the net demand requirement, but a high volume of informal entry will be difficult to achieve in tight labor markets without increases in compensation. Higher levels of federal training assistance may help to bring this about.

The following is a brief commentary on the elements of the balance sheet:
1.
Formal training

(a) Apprenticeship: in 1968, some 132,000 apprentices were registered in the construction trades; by Bureau of Apprenticeship Training estimates, a similar number were nonregistered. This was an increase of some 30 percent in registered programs since 1960 (and of 9 percent from 1967 to 1968). If a 50 percent increase in the annual rate of training was achieved between 1968 and 1978, more than 100,000 additional apprentices (registered and nonregistered) would be employed in 1978. Furthermore, an additional

Table 12.   A Construction Manpower Plan

	Number of Persons[a] (millions)	1800-Hour Man-Years (millions)
Requirements 1978[b]		
Total net increases	1.85	1.10
Residential	0.85	0.50
Nonresidential	1.00	0.60
Gross losses (deaths and retirements)[c]	0.40	0.24
Total requirements	2.25	1.34
Availability 1978		
Without special efforts from		
Apprenticeship[d]	0.70	0.60
Nonapprenticeship formal training[d]	0.05	0.04
Improving safety	0.04	0.03
Total	0.79	0.67
Required informal entry[e]	1.46	0.67
Total	2.25	1.34
With special efforts from		
Nonapprenticeship formal training[f]	0.15	0.13
Better utilization[g]	0.51	0.30
Additional productivity increase[h]	0.09	0.05
Total	0.75	0.48
Total with and without special efforts	1.54	1.15
Required informal entry[e]	0.71	0.19
Total	2.25	1.34

Note: This table considers only gross flows of manpower. Implementation of manpower policy must consider the distribution of entry and training among trades, since appropriate distribution is essential to success.
[a]Estimated at 1.7 persons per yearlong job, or 1100 hours per year.
[b]Author's estimates. See for example, U.S. President, *Second Annual Report on National Housing Goals,* p. 35, and Dunlop and Mills, "Manpower in Construction," pp. 265–269.
[c]Bureau of Labor Statistics estimates adjusted to reflect the fact that only two-thirds of all construction craftsmen are in the (new) construction industry, as defined for manpower needs projections (others are in maintenance and other nonnew construction work).
[d]Assuming relatively high rates of annual hours worked for mechanics with apprenticeship and other formal training.
[e]These estimates are not to be taken as implying a manpower "gap" of this size. Informal entry has and will continue to be a major source of manpower to construction. Further, not all entrants require extensive training, especially in unskilled categories of work.
[f]Assuming a tenfold increase of federally financed construction outreach and training by 1978.
[g]Dependent upon project scheduling and deseasonalization.
[h]Dependent upon special efforts to improve the rate of labor productivity increase in construction.

350,000 persons who have completed apprenticeship or spent one to three years in programs will be working in the industry (a large portion of those who do not complete apprenticeship nevertheless become construction crafts-men). These figures, adding up to some 700,000 workers, may be considered estimates of the total volume of apprenticeship contribution to the man-power supply by 1978, although a pattern of increasing manpower demand at the jobsite will be necessary to achieve these incremental increases.

Because of the intermittency of construction employment, the reason for low annual average hours worked in the industry, these 700,000 workers rep-resent only 600,000 yearlong jobs (1800 hours). I have assumed a higher annual average hours figure for apprentices and apprenticeship-trained per-sonnel than for others (1530 hours per year for apprentices and apprenticeship-trained personnel; 1100 hours per year for all mechanics in construction). This assumption reflects the widely held belief that apprenticeship-trained mechanics, because of their greater range of skills, often obtain more employment in the course of a year than others.

(b) Nonapprenticeship formal training: federal MDTA and JOBS training in construction now approach 11,000 training slots per year, or about 7000 to 8000 trainees. Many of these trainees go into apprenticeship programs. If this volume were increased to 110,000 slots per year (estimated federal cost $180 million authorized), some 150,000 persons might be trained or work-ing in 1978, excluding apprentices. It might be anticipated that, at 1500 hours per year in construction work, some 125,000 yearlong jobs would be filled by these persons in 1978.

2.

Informal entry: estimating informal entry is the most difficult problem, and its magnitude is best treated as the necessary residual after the size of other programs has been projected. Informal entry has been quite large in the past but is clearly a function of economic conditions. Generally, informal entry to construction will be hampered in the future by several factors, including a decreasing number of new labor force entrants and a high volume of em-ployment in other sectors of the economy. Inflows will tend to increase some-what over past levels as a result of additional opportunities for entry into the industry offered members of minority groups. On balance, in the future informal training will be less attractive, lower in volume, and more costly.

3.

Better utilization: increased manpower planning, better scheduling of work, and deseasonalization would increase manpower by some 300,000 yearlong jobs, or 510,000 men. These increases are not to be anticipated in the absence of special public and private efforts to achieve them.

4.

Productivity increases: real output per man-hour (labor productivity) increases of 1 percent per year in residential construction and 2 percent per year in nonresidential construction were assumed in order to obtain projected manpower demand.[21] Should federal and other efforts toward technological innovation double the rate of productivity increase in residential work, 50,000 fewer yearlong jobs will be provided in 1978, a reduction in demand of some 90,000 workers.

5.

Improving safety: a halving of the accident rate in construction would reduce the number of men required to fill the expected jobs by 45,000.

6.

Mobility: The impact of improved mobility has been considered in the section beginning on p. 104, "Manpower Forecasting and Planning in a Local Labor Market Area."

The value to policy makers of this scheme is that it quantifies, to a degree not previously possible, the various means of increasing available manpower, along with their cumulative effects — thereby locating the need for discretionary action. For example, if there were to be no better utilization of the industry's labor force (item no. 3), the impact on manpower needs would be very great (510,000 additional men), with all that this implies in the way of shortages, delays, cost increases, and industrial relations turmoil.

Development of Planning Mechanisms

Manpower forecasts can do more to facilitate necessary adjustments in the manpower process in construction if they are accompanied by improved mechanisms for preparation and implementation. Forecasts of manpower requirements in construction are now used by several institutions nationally, but there is little long-term planning on a coordinated basis. The Bureau of Labor Statistics prepares estimates of the employment outlook for construction and other occupations and publishes these estimates for the use of high school guidance counselors and others concerned with suggesting career opportunities for youths and returning veterans. Similarly, industry bodies,

[21] The rate of productivity increase in residential construction is subject to considerable confusion. In the conventional (as opposed to prefabricated) industry, it has apparently been relatively slow compared to the rates of increase in other branches of construction. For this reason, the text assumes a 1 percent increase, but the effect of higher rates of increase are also specified.

especially national joint apprenticeship and other training committees, study manpower trends in construction and suggest action to local affiliates. There is, however, very little interaction between the government agencies responsible for projections and the industry personnel who operate training programs, except when the availability of manpower assumes political implications.[22]

It is appropriate that joint private-public bodies meet regularly to assess the manpower situation in construction and make recommendations for private and public action as needed. The Construction Industry Joint Conference and more recently the Construction Industry Collective Bargaining Commission have served as mechanisms for occasional discussions among national industry and government officials regarding manpower development. However, meetings of joint bodies are best organized by branch of the industry,[23] for while in some cases public agencies play an important role in the activities of a particular sector, in others they play little or no role.[24] Conferences among industry and public officials may be technical and advisory only. It is appropriate that the industry retain its training responsibilities, both administrative and financial. However, conferences could perform useful functions regardless of their authority to take action as a group. First, the special conditions of each branch of construction could be confronted directly and evaluations made in the specific context of the branch. Public officials need to understand more clearly the operation of the branches of the industry with which they deal. Second, it is important that both public and private parties interpret correctly the intentions and commitments of the other. Labor organizations and contractors have sometimes prepared training programs and special work agreements to facilitate federal work that they thought was imminent, only to find that it is never begun. Conversely, the industry has at times discounted the intention of public authorities to put

[22] BLS manpower projections have sometimes been used to suggest that the construction unions are limiting entry of workers to the industry or are restricting the supply of manpower to areas of public concern, such as housing.

[23] The interdependence of construction manpower in the several branches of the industry means that a general framework of manpower forecasts must be developed against which more detailed sectoral studies can be measured. General forecasts might be prepared by the BLS in association with the industry through the CIJC, the CICBC, or an equivalent body.

[24] For example, manpower planning for housing should directly involve representatives of several employers' associations, the affected international unions, the Department of Housing and Urban Development, and the Department of Labor. Highway planning should involve four or five international unions, several employers' associations, the Department of Transportation, and the Department of Labor.

through large-scale construction programs, only to find difficulty manning the jobs when they began. Third, joint conferences could provide a mechanism by which public officials may judge more accurately the capacity of the industry to meet the requirements of their planning. The use of outside experts by federal agencies and commissions to evalute the manpower potential of the building trades has been far less useful to the government than a direct and continuing dialogue with the industry would be.

Manpower Forecasting and Planning in a Local Labor Market Area

Short-Run versus Long-Run Planning
Labor market planning at the national level has been described in the previous section as a process in which anticipated future requirements are set against anticipated future supplies of manpower and an adjustment between the two is made. In a local labor market area, the short-run planning problems are those of allocating manpower among projects and expanding the local labor supply to meet temporary conditions. Manpower planning for the long run is considerably different, for it involves recruitment, training, and considerable time lags from inception to completion.

Both short- and long-run manpower planning in the local labor market would be more effective if better projections of manpower demand were available. The short-run process of allocating men among projects would be usefully supplemented by an information system designed to provide current job data. Such a system, perhaps involving computerization, would allow employers and unions to improve the operation of referral processes. Electronic processing of manpower data has been introduced in longshoring[25] and in some areas in construction; it could without too much difficulty be adapted to construction generally. A more elaborate use of an information system to facilitate manpower allocation would involve anticipating major changes in the volume of work in an area. When potential labor shortages were identified, prejob conferences between contractors, owners, and labor representatives could be held to arrange means by which a labor force could be assembled for the project. Such conferences have been held for many years in conjunction with large-scale or isolated projects.

It might also be possible to develop a long-run forecasting system for local

[25] Verne H. Jensen, "Decasualizing a Labor Market: The Longshore Experience," in Abraham J. Siegel, ed., *The Impact of Computers on Collective Bargaining* (Cambridge: M.I.T. Press, 1969), pp. 226–242.

areas. The system could be used as a basis for manpower planning over a period of several years, involving adjustments in the volume of manpower development and training activities. Forecasting is a considerably more sophisticated task than the development of an information system to supplement the short-run allocation process. A short-run information system, since it would be designed to estimate manpower demand a few months in advance, could be based on a sample survey of current and planned activity in the area.[26] A forecasting system, however, cannot depend strongly on reports of individual projects because they are too unreliable and their coverage too limited when the projection target dates are years in advance. It is necessary to have recourse to economic models, if only to predict the future status of current construction plans. The introduction of very large jobs into an area is a problem in itself; the project may become public knowledge only at a late date, and because of its decisive effect on local conditions, it may be beyond the capacity of a forecasting model to make predictions without information about the project's specific nature. Finally, economic models of local areas and the relationship of construction activity to other economic variables are far less fully developed than national economic models. For these reasons, forecasting conditions on a local basis in construction is a far more difficult and treacherous task than forecasting at the national level.

Nonetheless, while manpower information and forecasting in construction at the local level can be improved significantly, the process of adjusting manpower supply to demand cannot be made mechanical. Individual judgment remains a basic input to the determination of actual needs; decision makers will continue to differ in their expectations. Expectations, the response to them, and the effect of responses on the existing labor force and on employers will therefore remain appropriate subjects for labor-management resolution.

Current Mechanisms of Local Area Planning by Contractors and Unions

It should not be inferred from this discussion of possible improvements in the forecasting process that no planning is done by unions, contractors, or joint committees. Nevertheless it is frequently haphazard and is based in all cases upon only partially informed expectations of the future demand for manpower and its supply. While the interaction between the two sides of the labor market

[26] The Center for Architectural Research at Rensselaer Polytechnic Institute, Troy, New York, has developed and begun to operate on a limited basis a construction information system much like that described in the text. See "A Construction Information and Analysis System for the State of New York," Reports no. 1 (June 1969) and no. 2 (September 1969), Status Report 1 (May 15, 1970), and a brief description, "BIDS" [Building Industry Data System] (1971).

limits the value of simple techniques for making separate projections of manpower supply and demand, planning can nonetheless be accomplished with
either supply- or demand-side information alone. In fact, planning is commonly
done with analysis of one side of the market considerably more advanced than
the other. For example, a local apprenticeship committee may base its actions
regarding the numbers to be trained on virtually complete information about
formal training in the area while knowing little or nothing about changes in
future demand for workers or about the current level of informal entry.

It is important to distinguish planning from the process of manpower development itself, for training and recruitment may occur without formal
planning. Not all organizations that perform a part of the manpower development function do so as part of a comprehensive program in a local area. In
most cases, comprehensive planning occurs only where a joint apprenticeship
committee exists. However, where there is not a joint apprenticeship committee, individual employers may plan formally in order to meet their individual companies' manpower needs. In many crafts and areas, especially in
smaller towns and rural areas, there is neither planning nor formal training, although informal training and recruitment do take place.

Joint planning by unions and contractors normally occurs through joint
apprenticeship committees for each trade, which determine the absolute numbers to be trained and establish requirements for apprentices, subject to federal
and state law and national standards. Decisions about the volume of new
training are made in the light of expected future manpower needs in the
carfts. Apprenticeship programs and the planning associated with them are
most relevant to larger urban areas. Where nonunion apprenticeship programs
exist, they are normally run by single employers and operate differently from
joint apprenticeship programs.[27]

Some manpower planning in construction is associated with the negotiation and approval of federally funded training programs. The federal government has sometimes been reluctant to approve projects for individual employers in construction, preferring that an association conduct training in order
to insure more continuity of employment to trainees than an individual employer could offer. In applying for a program, association representatives are
normally asked by the government to specify the volume of training they
propose and to provide a rationale for it. In some cases, federal personnel offer
employers technical services for manpower planning, supplying concepts and

[27]See Chapter 8 for a more detailed discussion of the activities of joint apprenticeship
committees.

methods. The impact of federally assisted training on the total volume of construction manpower planning and development has of course not been large.

There is very little that need be said about the procedures and tools of the planning process as it is exercised by contractors and unions. For the most part, planning is very primitive and does not make much use of formal estimates of future manpower availability and requirements. At most, the informed expectations of the individual contractor and union representative (or the individual nonunion employer) are the basis for planning. Often these expectations are very short-range and depend almost entirely on extrapolations from the experience of the recent past. In the case of joint apprenticeship committees, the differing expectations of members are compromised by a bargaining process in which unions normally (but not always) argue for fewer and the employers for greater numbers to be trained.

Because the technology of the planning process is quite primitive, improvements in the formation of expectations about future needs could be important. Furthermore, there do not appear to be any serious impediments to the introduction of better techniques of forecasting and planning, once they are developed and become generally available for use by local decision makers. The new procedures will, of course, be required to demonstrate their reliability, but once they have done so, their adoption should in most cases face no major restraints. Planning mechanisms already exist; what must be done in the coming decades is to improve their functioning. One of the best ways of accomplishing this is to develop the technology of forecasting that they employ.

Improving the Techniques of Manpower Forecasting

Problems involving the scope of forecasts To be useful in the planning process, estimates of manpower demand in contract construction must be made by craft and geographic area. The concept of craft is relatively straightforward, since it corresponds to the work jurisdictions of different labor organizations. In some cases, however, work jurisdiction is quite broad, and it is necessary to make separate projections of demand for specialties within certain crafts. Where labor organizations do not exist, it is necessary to project demand in the occupations into which the work force is normally specialized. (There is an occupational structure in the construction industry even in the absence of labor organizations. The exact nature and boundaries of each occupation in a nonunion situation depend on the branch of the industry and the employer involved. Carpentry, brickmasonry, electrical work, and plumbing, for example, remain separate specialities into which the work force is organized.) It is inadequate for manpower projections to estimate only total manpower demand, because ability to perform the work is critically dependent upon the skills possessed by the work force. If better techniques of estimating manpower demand are to be used as a mechanism for adjusting labor shortages or surpluses, estimates (both of supply and of demand) must reflect the craft structure of the labor force.

Projecting manpower demand for the appropriate geographic area is a more difficult problem. Usually, the appropriate geographic area for projections would be a local labor market area. The local labor market is defined as an area from which projects tend to draw their labor force. There is generally a greater degree of mobility within areas than between them. In the past, labor market areas were distinguished primarily by distance from the center of one geographic area to another, because distance effectively insulated markets from each other. The development of transportation, particularly automobiles, has considerably enlarged the geographic area in which workers travel to jobs, so that local labor markets may now be quite large. However, there are other impediments to mobility than distance alone. The geographic jurisdictions of local unions may create an additional series of boundaries. In the case of many labor organizations, members from one local working in another local's jurisdiction must obtain permit cards from the local in whose jurisdiction they are working. In practice, if not explicitly, preference is often given to local employees. Thus, the territorial jurisdiction of local unions or district councils helps to define the local labor market. The volume of work available to a craft is the final and perhaps the most important factor in determining the labor market area. In some trades, work is sufficiently specialized and jobs sufficiently scarce that the jurisdiction of a local union may cover large areas. In other crafts, especially carpentry, the geographic scope of markets is much smaller. Manpower forecasts that cover too broad a geographic area may be worthless because there are no suitable means of disaggregating the estimates for use by planning bodies, which normally function on the local union or district council level. Thus, if projections are to be really useful, they must coincide, or be capable of being made to coincide, with the appropriate planning area.

It is for these reasons, and because of problems with the more technical aspects of projections, that the technology of forecasting in construction has developed so slowly. Recently, however, important advances have been made in projecting manpower demand in construction, and considerable thought and preliminary work have been applied to anticipating changes in manpower supply.

Techniques of manpower forecasting: Demand Projections of manpower demand in local areas require a methodology similar to the one described for national projections. The process begins with estimates of the anticipated volume of construction work over the period for which projections are to be made. Estimates of product expenditures may be obtained from several sources (for example, public agencies or private researchers), or they may be prepared by the analyst himself. These estimates must then be translated into estimates of manpower demand. To perform this operation, the analyst must know the composition by type of projected construction activity in order to consider the manpower requirements involved of the various types of construction.

Derivation of estimates of construction product demand in an area depends on several sets of assumptions or forecasts about the state and progress of the local economy. First, levels of construction activity in the target period must be estimated. Normally, the immediate future would be the simplest period for which to make projections, while the most difficult would be a period of several months or years. In addition, it is relatively simpler to project the average volume of work over some future period than to project the exact time path of expenditures. The volume of information that would be necessary to make specific projections of the time patterns of the flow of construction work is quite extensive.

Second, the composition of construction in the target period must be estimated. Confirming estimates of total construction activity by means of estimates of its composition provides most of the basis for manpower projections.[28]

Third, the rate of increase of real output per man-hour must be estimated. Unfortunately, there are little or no data to allow estimates of productivity changes by craft or area in construction. It is likely that productivity changes vary, and will continue to vary, by craft, geographic region, and type of con-

---

[28] "The construction industry has many indicators which enable us to gauge its short-run future. Construction contracts are let in advance of construction operations. Small contracts and building permits may indicate work to be done in the first and second months following the signing of the contract or the authorization of work. Larger contracts may require months before maximum employment is given. During World War II, very accurate projections were made of construction activity and reliable estimates were made of how much additional work could be initiated at any given time without straining the capacity of the industry." Robinson Newcomb and Miles L. Colean, *Stabilizing Construction* (New York: McGraw-Hill, 1952), p. 300.

struction. It may therefore be necessary to provide a range of rates of productivity increase which judgment suggests to be reasonable but which further analysis and investigation may modify.

Fourth, large-scale changes in technology need to be anticipated. Analysis of labor productivity rarely anticipates dramatic and extremely rapid changes in the nature of technology. Labor productivity is ordinarily conceived as an evolutionary or discontinuous but finite set of changes in the technology of an industry. Were there to be a considerable shift in the physical character of a product, then projections would have to be adjusted to take it into account. One method of dealing with such a shift would be to make separate models of the technologies of the two types of construction (single-family versus high-rise systems). The change in the composition of the volume of work that would result from a shift in expenditures from the first type to the second would alter manpower requirements. In general, when new technologies are likely to have a serious impact on future manpower requirements, it becomes necessary to include a detailed description of them as part of the process of translating expenditures into manpower demand.

The transition from product estimates to estimates of manpower requirements utilizes a mechanism that converts dollar demand by type of construction[29] into labor requirements by craft (in the terminology of economics, a production function). For a variety of reasons, including availability of data and simplicity of analysis, the most suitable current mechanism for translating product demand into manpower requirements is a matrix of coefficients reflecting fixed relationships among the crafts. Summations can be made of manpower demand by type of construction in order to obtain a set of total man-hour requirements by craft for all construction in the target year.

In general, the methodology of preparing manpower demand estimates involves estimating future construction expenditures by type of structure, adjusting for evolutionary productivity changes and possibly discontinuous major shifts in technology, and applying expenditure estimates to unit manpower requirements by craft on different types of projects. This methodology

[29] The number of different types of construction must be kept to a manageable size but must adequately reflect the diversity of projects. One limitation of current data on labor requirements by craft is that the building categories too often represent final-use characteristics rather than structural types. Often the structural and mechanical systems of projects with different final uses may be similar, while projects with similar final uses may have quite different structural characteristics. The most suitable way to categorize labor requirements information is, of course, by similarity of structural and mechanical systems. Future labor requirements studies should emphasize structural and mechanical characteristics rather than the end use of the project.

has already been fully applied on a national and regional (multistate) basis but has yet to be utilized for local areas.[30]

There are special problems in making labor projections for a local area rather than on a national level. Initially, a mechanism for obtaining expenditure estimates must be devised. It is tempting to base these estimates on surveys of the plans and ongoing work of owners in the area. An organization preparing projections might contact several sources in order to obtain information relevant to anticipated local construction demand. There are many sources of information, including architects, engineers, trade publications, labor unions, contractors' associations, individual contractors, and state, local, and federal government agencies. The problem is less the availability of data than the cost of obtaining it. Surveys of all possible projects would have to be very extensive, yet many projects intended for a local area are never started. The process of planning and designing a construction project and finally putting it out for bid or negotiation is a long one, often involving months and perhaps even years. At any stage in the process, the project may be dropped, substantially altered, or moved to another area. Therefore, in order to obtain reliable estimates, a large volume of anticipated and planned projects would have to be monitored, but at the same time the cost of such coverage would have to be limited. The issue is the volume of information needed to do an adequate job of projecting. Mainly because of the complexity and cost of collecting information and updating it, hardly anywhere in the country have formal efforts been made to provide projections of anticipated market demand and supply, except in certain sectors of the industry (especially residential construction).

Feasibility studies indicate that it is possible and financially practical to collect a volume of information adequate to represent accurately the future status of construction activity in a local area.[31] The basic unit of expenditure data would be the project description. Project descriptions must indicate location, character, and scheduling. The character of the project includes its type (for example, an apartment building), nature (for example, prestressed concrete), and budget. Scheduling information includes the date of bidding, start of contracting, duration, and completion date.

[30]See Dunlop and Mills, "Manpower in Construction."
[31]The following paragraphs draw heavily from a document prepared by the Center for Architectural Research of Rensselaer Polytechnic Institute for the State University Construction Fund [New York], "A Construction Information and Analysis System for the State of New York: A Feasibility Study" (Troy, N.Y., 1969).

Given a description of a project, it is necessary to allocate the project expenditures over time. To provide an estimate of total demand in any region over a period of time, the work on each project must be allocated over the project's duration and a sum taken of all projects in each time span. Unfortunately, jobs of different types rarely possess the same scheduling pattern, so that it is necessary to develop a model by type which will distribute the total volume of a job over its duration. Manpower estimates are derived by multiplying the dollar volume of different types of projects in separate time periods by the manpower requirement coefficients on the projects Thus, the labor requirements on different types of projects are estimated directly and then summed.

Unfortunately, detailed information regarding projects is always much more accurate very close to the particular time when they will begin, or when they are already under way, than at any previous time. For projects whose anticipated starting date is still in the future, accuracy and coverage of information are reduced dramatically. As a result, demand estimates tend to be most accurate for the immediate future. The immediate future is important, but considerable information about more distant periods of time is also needed. For longer-term projections, plans become extremely difficult to obtain on an accurate basis. However, sampling techniques should allow preparation of reliable demand estimates several months in advance. Information on more distant projects must be supplemented by estimates of economic and other conditions in obtaining probabilities of the volume of work to be expected. Expenditure estimates made several years in advance must be almost entirely economic in nature rather than based on samples of project plans.

A further major difficulty in local area forecasting involves means of validating the statistical models. There are virtually no data available on a local area basis (or nationally, either) for employment by occupation in each type or sector of construction. Thus projections made of craft employment in the different types of construction are not comparable to any available statistics on employment in recent years. As a result, it is very difficult to analyze the degree to which projections are reasonable. It will not be possible to check the accuracy of projections against actual experience except by further special efforts.

The most potentially valuable sources of local area manpower information are the records of health, welfare, and pension funds. Fund data will reveal the volume of employment in past periods. These data, if available, might be used to check the accuracy of the manpower demand estimates derived from expenditure plans. Fund records could provide bench marks from which sample estimates of employment could be made.[32]

Techniques of manpower forecasting: Supply   Rudimentary and confusing as they may appear, the techniques for projecting manpower demand are far better developed than those dealing with supply. To a large degree, this situation reflects the primacy of demand. The labor supply responds to demand conditions; it rarely has a constraining effect on the volume of demand. In the long run, manpower supply conditions affect manpower demand through costs and relative prices, but in the short run, compensation is relatively fixed, and demand conditions are the result of factors largely extraneous to the construction industry. As a consequence, the number of men working at a trade measures effective demand better than it measures potential supply. Unemployed mechanics are a part of the potential labor supply, but their numbers may be deceptive. Many mechanics may be working outside the jurisdiction of a local union yet be available for work in the area if it develops. Similarly, if construction is slack in nearby areas, a much larger work force may be available to draw on than is indicated by local conditions alone. Hence current labor shortages do not necessarily imply that additional jobs could not be manned. Local unions and their membership may be seeking to stretch out current work, fearing joblessness in the near future because of seasonal or other factors. The work force might increase rapidly if future conditions were expected to be more favorable.

In general, the geographic and industrial mobility of construction mechanics creates a great deal of interdependence among labor markets. Furthermore, in some cases unions and contractors' associations exercise considerable influence over the number of men working at the trade, normally in response to demand conditions. Thus it is very difficult to make a successful model of the supply side of a local labor market. At the least, conditions in closely related markets would have to be explicitly considered, and there may be many related markets. Achieving balance between quantity supplied and demanded is therefore best left to the unions and contractors, rather than being made a function of some central forecasting and planning system. But a forecasting system could indicate where an adjustment was needed and, in some instances, even the magnitude of the adjustment.

[32] This is essentially the process followed by the BLS in its survey of monthly employment by establishment, although the data used to set up bench marks for the estimates do not come from private health, welfare, and pension funds but from the records of the Unemployment Insurance System.

The membership of local unions, the number of men working in the jurisdiction of a local, and the number who have recently worked in its jurisdiction are all potentially available to researchers. The local union or contractors'
association would be the best source for the local's membership, men on permit, and apprentices. Pension or health and welfare trust funds would be the
appropriate source for estimates of the total number of men employed at the
trade in the past year or so. Normally, trust fund records will indicate a considerably larger number of men employed in the course of a year or more at
the trade than the records of the local indicate (this degree of divergence is a
measure of the fluidity of the labor market and varies by craft and area).
Thus, a variety of measures of past or present manpower supply are available
for analysis.

The best procedure would be to project manpower demand for a group of
key trades and compare the forecast to several measures of supply. These
comparisons should be made available to users of the forecasts. It would not
be appropriate, however, for the forecasts to try to predict the response of
the labor market to apparent shortages or surpluses. The complexities of the
supply adjustment process are so great that attempts to model the process
explicitly will surely be expensive and misleading.

Two further complications on the supply side give support to this conclusion. First, if a construction job is awarded to *local* contractors, the labor
force will normally be drawn entirely from the area. If, however, the award is
to out-of-town contractors, in whole or in part, a significant proportion of the
work force, especially the most skilled men and supervisors, will be brought
into the area. Thus, the effective supply of labor will depend partly on which
contractors get which jobs. Second, where a significant volume of work is
done nonunion, it will be difficult to obtain any kind of comprehensive
supply-side estimates. As a consequence, forecasting systems for local areas
must concentrate on achieving reliability in manpower demand estimates and
resign themselves, under the current structure of the industry, to far less
knowledge and certainty on the supply side.

Initiating Local Area Manpower Planning

Techniques are now adequate to establish construction forecasting systems on
a local area basis. The projections they provide may be compared to various
measures of manpower supply and made available to appropriate groups for
whatever action they desire. Yet there is some question as to who ought to
prepare these projections, and to whom they should be made available. Furthermore, operation of the forecasting system would require fairly substantial

financing. Either public or private bodies might provide the service, but it would be unlikely to be self-sustaining. Public funds might be used to provide support.[33] Alternatively, the industry itself might wish to fund and operate a forecasting mechanism through jointly administered funds.

Questions of financing and control are related to the more significant issue of access to forecasting results. Industry sources fear that the system may be used in some cases to relocate projects planned for an area on the grounds that the local labor market is inadequate to receive them. Conversely, projects might be delayed or redesigned because of indicated manpower shortages. Whether such changes are warranted or not, they pose a threat to work opportunities for some crafts and contractors. If the system is used in this way, it is unlikely to receive industry support, and without support the system may be impractical.[34]

The flexibility of owners in relation to the scheduling of projects should not be underestimated. Owners often have a considerable degree of discretion in the location, timing, and design of particular projects. Normally this discretion is exercised with the assistance of architects, engineers, and construction managers. In some cases, cost consultants advise owners on such aspects of a project as its design, scale, and the appropriate time at which to offer the job for bid and construction. The actual amount of flexibility in design and timing varies among projects and tends to lessen as each stage of the planning and development process on a project is passed. Yet the design of a project may remain more flexible, even late in the planning process, than the owner and his representatives realize. In the tight construction markets of recent years, many owners have discovered that jobs must be redesigned to reduce their costs after unexpectedly high bid prices have been received.

It should be possible through a construction forecasting system to improve the information on which the scheduling of projects is based. When construction volume is relatively high, many owners are willing to delay putting projects out to bid if a more favorable period can be identified in the near future. The relative demand for manpower in an area may be an important element of the decision about when the owner should schedule the start of a project. Decisions about scheduling are made continually, and the provision of better market data to owners and contractors might improve the scheduling process.

[33] The Rensselaer Study (see fn. 26) is supported by public funds.
[34] Union support is necessary to obtain supply-side estimates. Contractors must provide reports on project starts, progress, and completion and must provide the craft and time profiles for the separate types of projects.

Were the owners to use a manpower forecasting system in a local area simply to reschedule the timing of projects in order to extend the work over a longer period of time — thereby helping to reduce the variability of demand in the industry — it is unlikely that there would be opposition to forecasting from contractors or unions. But there are factors that suggest this might not occur. First, the current construction project planning process is very decentralized among owners, architects, and contractors.[35] Initially, most projects are scheduled entirely independently, although perhaps with a rough notion of volume of work other owners have or are expected to have under way. However, were decision makers in the decentralized process provided with forecasts of future construction activity, they might react similarly and in large numbers to projected peaks and troughs in construction volume. The resultant changes in scheduling might be quite destabilizing to the flow of work — that is, the result of improved forecasting might be perverse.

Second, there is reason to believe that owners might respond to projected long-range manpower shortages by having projects redesigned to reduce the contribution of the crafts that are expected to be in shortages. Architects might also shift designs in response to expected future shortages. Because the manpower supply situation several years in advance is always extremely uncertain in construction, the trades affected unfavorably by redesign could be expected to oppose using the system in that way. However, a forecasting mechanism that identified potential peak load periods and facilitated the solution of such problems by increasing capacity rather than reducing demand might be welcomed by the industry.

In summary, manpower planning in local labor market areas must involve the use of forecasts differently for different functions. Estimates of manpower demand in the immediate future may facilitate adjustments in the labor allocation process by each local union and contractor. Forecasts of demand over a period of a few months or a year are an appropriate basis for scheduling projects and might be submitted to local committees of owners,

[35] Ideally, there might be a centralized mechanism to utilize product and labor market information in the scheduling of construction projects. Such mechanisms do not now exist at any level in this country and have been strongly resisted in peacetime because of the necessity of imposing priorities in allowing work to proceed. It is perhaps possible that one owner, for example, a public owner, might agree to schedule construction in a stabilizing manner. In "Seasonal Unemployment in the Construction Industry: Report and Recommendations of the Secretary of Labor and the Secretary of Commerce to the President and to Congress," mimeo (Washington, D.C., December 1969), it is suggested that federal projects be scheduled to introduce an element of stability into the progress of work in local markets.

contractors, and unions for discussion and action, if desired.[36] Long-run forecasts, if available, are the proper concern of each local union and its employers and should be used to determine the volume of manpower training appropriate to the area.

Conclusions

Tight labor markets have demonstrated the need for improved manpower planning to meet future construction demand, especially in periods of full employment. Among Western industrialized nations, the United States has been conspicuous for the absence of major efforts to improve the quality of forecasting and planning in construction.[37] The time is long overdue for cooperation by public and industry authorities in improving the capability of construction to meet both short- and long-term fluctuations in demand. In the United States, improved planning will depend critically on advances in the quality and coverage of information made available to industry and public authorities. Advanced techniques for forecasting manpower demand are now in operation at the federal level; means for analyzing the supply of labor to the industry have been suggested in this chapter. Unfortunately, mechanisms for manpower planning and for utilizing forecasts are poorly developed in all branches of the industry.

Local area manpower forecasting systems are in an embryonic stage of development. The techniques of forecasting require considerable elaboration but at present are adequate for experimental implementation. The functions of a local area manpower forecasting system would be as follows:

1.
Survey or sample local area construction demand and forecast demand over appropriate periods with continual updating and revision of projections.
2.
Apply job progress patterns and craft profiles for each type of job in order to obtain a time profile of manpower demand by craft.

---

[36] For preliminary work regarding construction scheduling, see Eugene C. Holshouser, *Construction Budgeting in State Highway Departments* (Lexington: University of Kentucky Bureau of Business Research, 1962). The essence of the problem of scheduling is to allot priorities to different projects.

[37] See E. Jay Howenstine, *Action against Seasonal Unemployment in the Construction Industry* (Washington, D.C.: Department of Housing and Urban Development, International Affairs Division, 1971), Chapter 4, "Construction Scheduling and Active Manpower Policy."

3.

Circulate demand projections by expenditure, volume, area, and type of work among owners, architects, contractors, and unions.

4.

Compare manpower demand projections with each of several measures of labor supply in each craft and circulate the forecasts to appropriate labor and management groups to be judged and acted upon.

Both national and local area forecasting and planning require attention and financial support by public and private groups if the construction industry is to develop manpower planning responsive to tight labor markets and rapid variations in the volume of work.

Improving the Utilization
of Labor

Underutilization of Labor in Construction

The expansion in construction activity that occurred during the years of high
employment demanded a larger work force, but many traditional channels of
manpower supply were depleted. The industry sought to utilize traditional
methods of adapting to these conditions, including the lengthening of building
seasons, training of new workers, and labor-saving innovations in the production
process. But in many cases the necessary adjustments did not occur quickly or
completely enough to prevent rapid cost increases. In addition, many of the
most basic characteristics of the industry were not altered by the inflationary
conditions, and persons in the industry preferred to retain the institutional
arrangments that corresponded to these characteristics.

Employment in construction has always been extremely variable in response to changes in market demand. During the 1960s, market demand
was strong in construction but remained as uncertain as ever. A number of
communities experienced great volumes of construction, while certain other
markets were depressed. Booms hit an area and passed within a few years. The
individual firm continued to insist on flexibility in its manpower planning as a
necessary element of its operation. Job security remained essentially nonexistent, though the journeymen could follow the work. In consequence,
employment was intermittent, with time lost due to weather conditions, to the
ebb and flow of demand in local markets, and to work stoppages, scheduling
errors, and other interruptions of on-site work.

Underemployment (that is, less than full-time employment of the work
force) remained relatively high in construction at all times. Not only did
workers experience considerable unemployment by the standards of other
industries, but many construction workers were forced to find work outside
the industry at intervals throughout the year. In consequence, the underutilization of the industry's work force in construction itself was larger than
unemployment statistics alone suggest. A special Bureau of Labor Statistics
study made in 1966 found that of 13 crafts surveyed in 4 major metropolitan
areas, in no case did average annual hours worked in construction exceed
1300 hours.[1] As a result of the low average utilization of labor, construction
employs during the course of the year almost two persons for every year-

---

[1] See U.S. Bureau of Labor Statistics, *Seasonality and Manpower in Construction*,
Bulletin no. 1642 (Washington, D.C., 1970), pp. 68–72.

long job, the highest ratio among nonagricultural industries in the United States.[2]

Seasonality continues to be a major problem. During most of the winter a considerable volume of construction activity is either shut down or slowed, and unemployment rates among the basic trades rise dramatically. During years of labor shortage and high construction activity, seasonality lessens, but the process is inefficient and costly, and considerable underutilization remains.

Some intermittency of employment in construction is inevitable because of the nonrepetitive nature of projects and the continual shifting of the work site. In construction, the labor force bears a very large part of the cost of uncertainty and fluctuations in demand. Discharge of employees by contractors serves as a mechanism to cushion the effect of imperfectly forecast changes in demand and the movement of contractors among jobs and areas, just as in manufacturing inventories and order backlogs reduce the effects of changes in demand.

Labor is able to soften the impact of instability somewhat through high hourly wage rates and, in some cases, by spreading work by means of temporary shortages and by geographic and industrial mobility. However, high wage rates and delays only shift the burden through increased costs to the consumer and do not lessen the public interest in eliminating the need for costly standby capacity in the labor force and in contractors' organizations generally. Measures to stabilize construction employment are justified when the cost of stabilization is less than the benefits gained from reducing the number of men who are idled when demand is at a low point.[3]

The additional volume of man-hours of work potentially available from reduced intermittency is very large. An increase of 200 hours per year in the average workyear of the present labor force would provide an additional two-thirds of a million man-years of labor. To provide this volume of additional manpower to the industry without reducing intermittency would require the addition of more than one and one-third million persons to the industry's labor force. In periods of relatively tight labor markets, better utilization of the industry's labor force may be the most efficient means of increasing the manpower available to the industry.

[2] *Ibid.*, pp. 62–67.
[3] This discussion closely follows that in "Seasonal Unemployment in the Construction Industry: Report and Recommendations of the Secretary of Labor and the Secretary of Commerce to the President and to the Congress," mimeo (Washington, D.C., 1969), pp. 6–7.

Reduced intermittency of employment has also been viewed as an important means by which several of the industrial relations problems of construction might be resolved.[4] Hourly wage scales that would reflect yearlong employment might be lower than those currently existing without affecting the annual earnings of construction workers. Lower hourly wage scales could result in lower unit labor costs and savings to the consumer. Greater employment security might also create a less conservative attitude on the part of the current labor force regarding expansion of the supply of well-trained men and less concern for strict observance of craft jurisdictional boundaries. Thus labor relations in construction, many aspects of which are connected to the issue of work opportunities, might benefit from improved job security. The problems of achieving increased job security for the individual worker are explored in the following sections.

Reducing Seasonality

The Scope of the Seasonality Problem
Seasonality in construction is only one of several causes of intermittency in employment, but it is a major cause.[5] In 1969, for example, the number of employees in contract construction rose 674,000 from February to August, or more than 23 percent. This represents a volume of manpower larger than the total annual average employment in the basic steel industry or in mining. Were it possible to maintain employment at its peak monthly level during the entire course of the year, a quarter of a million additional man-years of labor would be available to the industry.

The seasonal pattern varies among types of construction, contractor specialities, building trades, and geographic areas. Normally, seasonality is greatest in the northern tier of states and in heavy, highway, and homebuilding con-

---

[4]See, for example, William Haber, *Industrial Relations in the Building Industry* (Cambridge: Harvard University Press, 1930); and Robinson Newcomb and Miles L. Colean, *Stabilizing Construction: The Record and the Potential* (New York: McGraw–Hill, 1952).
[5]Considerable attention was devoted to seasonality in the late 1960s. See "Seasonal Unemployment in the Construction Industry"; Robert J. Myers and Sol Swerdloff, "Seasonality and Construction," *Monthly Labor Review* 90 (September 1967): 1–8; U.S. Congress, House, Committee on Education and Labor, Select Subcommittee on Labor, *Seasonal Unemployment in the Construction Industry: Hearings on H.R. 15990*, 90th Cong., 2nd sess., July 1968; U.S. Building Research Advisory Board, National Academy of Sciences – National Research Council, *Proceedings of the Year-Round/All-Weather Construction Conference* (Washington, D.C., 1968); and *Proceeding of the AGC Conference on Seasonality in Construction* (Washington, D.C.: Associated General Contractors of America, 1968).

struction. Seasonality is more pronounced for smaller general contractors and for laborers, carpenters, bricklayers, and other outdoor trades. Construction work does not stop in winter. Even highway construction continues to some extent, and building construction sites are rarely closed down entirely during cold weather. Instead, there are winter layoffs, reductions in the sizes of crews, fewer starts, and slowdowns and delays — all of which add up to a significant pattern of seasonal work reduction. In general, not all trades, areas, and contractors experience seasonality in the same manner or to the same degree; not all journeymen in a trade are affected by seasonality — the better mechanics do well, for the most part, all year round; and there are persons in construction who have adapted to a seasonal pattern of work, so that winter slowdowns are welcomed in some areas.

Before and during World War II there was a considerable reduction in the seasonality of construction employment. The improvement was associated with better techniques and materials for winter building, with larger-scale jobs, and with the year-round rush of construction activity at the beginning of the war. Since 1947, there has been less change in seasonal patterns. As measured by seasonal adjustment factors[6] (which net out the variations due to business cycle trend and irregular influences) for monthly estimates of employment in contract construction, the pattern and amplitude of employment seasonality in the postwar years has been virtually stable.

A similar seasonal pattern of employment in construction extends to all regions of the United States, although its severity varies. While in some southern and western states the winters are not particularly harsh, they are characterized by rain, which also tends to hamper construction operations. In these states construction employment reaches its lowest point in midwinter, just as in colder northern states, although seasonal fluctuations tend to be greater in the more northerly states.[7]

Seasonality means not only fewer jobs during the winter months but also a reduced level of operations. Like employment, average weekly hours worked in the industry follow a seasonal pattern. Overtime work is of considerable significance in summer, especially in highway work, and adds to the cost of construction.

[6] See U.S. Bureau of Labor Statistics, *The BLS Seasonal Factor Method* (Washington, D.C., 1966).
[7] Thus employment in Arizona in August exceeds that in February by an average of 10 percent. In Minnesota, employment rises 65 percent from February to August.

Adjustments to Tight Labor Markets and High Construction Demand

During periods of high aggregate employment and intense construction activity, seasonality declines. Thus, in the period 1968–1970, the increase in employment in contract construction from February to August was the smallest percentage increase since 1953.[8]

Statistical analysis of monthly employment data indicates the factors that determine the magnitude of seasonal variation. Of major importance among these factors are employment and unemployment conditions in other sectors of the economy. It may be inferred that high rates of building activity do not normally result in lessened seasonality unless economic conditions generally are tight. There has been some misunderstanding of the dynamics of this situation. Haber and Levinson[9] suggest that fluctuations in the degree of seasonality in construction employment nationally are primarily a function of the level of building activity. Thus, in a year of particularly vigorous construction activity, the level of winter employment would be expected to be higher with respect to the preceding summer's employment than in a less expansive year. High levels of construction activity tend to generate shortages, but the interaction of the rate of construction activity and conditions in the economy generally must be stressed. High levels of activity in construction will yield markedly different short-run seasonal patterns, depending on the economic environment in which they occur.[10] The regression analysis on which these conclusions are based is presented in the following technical note.

[8] Circumstances specific to the months involved are partly responsible for year-to-year changes in the seasonality measure. For example, analysis of trough-to-peak changes on a quarterly rather than on a monthly basis indicates lessened variation in recent years, but not so dramatically as the February to August figures.

[9] William Haber and Harold Levinson, *Labor Relations and Productivity in the Building Trades* (Ann Arbor: University of Michigan Bureau of Industrial Relations, 1956), pp. 57–58.

[10] The question of the impact of high levels of construction activity on short-run seasonality is not academic. The Haber and Levinson position is naive in suggesting that by keeping the general level of building activity high, the nation may be able to minimize the waste associated with seasonal letdowns. On the contrary, in the absence of generally vigorous economic conditions outside construction, the seasonal pattern of construction, in terms of both amplitude and phasing, will tend to remain unchanged. See Howard G. Foster, "Labor Supply in the Construction Industry: A Case Study of Upstate New York" (Ph.D. thesis, Cornel University, 1968), p. 98. At the risk of oversimplification, it can be said that this is because a capacity constraint in summer (which leads to a spillover of activity into winter months) occurs only when economic conditions generally are tight, since elasticity of construction supply to quantity demanded is high when there are underutilized resources elsewhere in the economy.

Technical note: Determinants of seasonality in employment Short-term changes in the severity of employment seasonality in contract construction are the result of several influences, including labor market conditions in the economy generally. A group of regressions was estimated to explain statistically annual trough-to-peak variation in contract construction employment. Two dependent variables were examined: trough-to-peak (February to August) variation in each calendar year from 1947 to 1967, and peak-to-trough variation within a "construction" year (i.e., August to the following February).

The first equation in Table 13 presents the analysis of February to August percentage change in national contract construction employment. Note, first, that the composition of construction activity during the year is strongly related to the seasonal measure. Some branches of construction are more subject to seasonality than others. When the composition of total con-

Table 13.   Short-Run Variation in the Seasonality of Contract Construction Employment

1. Dependent Variable: February to August percentage change in contract construction employment

Independent Variables	Regression Coefficients (*t* values)	Partial Correlation Coefficients
Nonhighway, nonresidential value put-in-place as a percentage of total value put-in-place (annual)	−1.155 (−3.5001)[a]	−0.6705
February to August, percentage change in employment in noncontract construction industries	1.478[b] (2.8285)	0.5898
August, nonconstruction unemployment rate	1.199 (1.4091)[d]	0.3589
Linear time trend, annual	0.639 (2.6689)[b]	0.5674
Intercept	71.3960 (4.1743)[a]	

R^2 = 0.8197 R^2 (corrected for degrees of freedom, 15) = 0.7596

Durbin-Watson = 2.1915[e]

2. Dependent Variable: August to February percentage change in contract construction employment

Independent Variables	Regression Coefficients (t values)	Partial Correlation Coefficients
August to February, percentage change in employment in noncontract construction industries	1.188 (3.7607)[a]	0.6850
August, private wage and salary worker unemployment rate in construction	−0.479 (−1.9294)[c]	−0.4344
Linear time trend, annual	−0.342 (−3.6069)[a]	−0.6697
Intercept	−14.1173 (−6.8312)[a]	

$R^2 = 0.6216$ R^2 (corrected for degrees of freedom, 16) = 0.5270

Durbin-Watson = 1.7823[e]

Source: *Construction Review* (monthly issued by Department of Commerce, Business and Defense Services Administration); *Monthly Labor Review:* and data from the Bureau of Labor Statistics.
Note: The second and third independent variables in Equation 1 and the first independent variable in Equation 2 were constructed by removing construction employment and/or unemployment data from the aggregate data. The employment variables are based on the Bureau of Labor Statistics' establishment Survey. The unemployment variables are derived from the Current Population Survey. The private wage and salary worker unemployment rate for construction (the second independent variable in Equation 2) is identical, in industry concept, to employment figures for contract construction (the dependent variable).
[a]Significant at 0.5 percent.
[b]Significant at 1.0 percent.
[c]Significant at 5.0 percent.
[d]Significant at 10.0 percent.
[e]There is no significant (at 5 percent) indication of serial correlation.

struction activity shifts toward the more seasonal branches, measured seasonality in the industry as a whole tends to increase. The compositional variable is the percentage of calendar-year value put-in-place that is in nonhighway, nonresidential construction (normally the less seasonal work) and is negatively correlated with seasonality. Second, a nonconstruction employment variable is used to represent short-run changes in business cycle influences. Third, seasonality tends to be greater in years when nonconstruction unemployment is high during the peak of the building season. Statistically, the nonconstruction unemployment rate in August is positively related to the seasonality of contract construction employment.[11] Presumably, lesser manpower availability in August constricts the volume of work in that month. Unfortunately, data limitations prohibit specifications of shortages of equipment, managerial manpower, financing, and materials, which along with (or in place of) labor may contribute to reducing peak season activity. As a consequence the impact of unemployment conditions on other industries probably reflects these other influences as well, especially the availability of materials.

The fourth point regarding the first equation in the table is that there appears to have been a trend toward greater seasonality in the postwar years. A linear time trend, 1947 to 1967, assumes considerable importance in the multiple correlation framework. The simple correlation coefficient between the time trend and the February to August percentage change in contract construction employment is 0.1739 (which is not significant at 10 percent). However, in the multiple correlation framework, the partial correlation of trend and seasonality climbs to 0.5674, and the regression coefficient is 0.6387, significant at the 1 percent level. The trend toward greater seasonality, other things being equal, is consistent with the evidence of seasonal adjustment factors regarding the long–term, underlying stability (or slow worsening) of construction seasonality. Had employment and other conditions generally not favored lessened seasonality in recent years, the seasonality of construction employment apparently would have increased.[12]

The second equation in Table 13 presents an analysis of the percentage decline in contract construction employment from August to February of the next calendar year, utilizing the concept of a construction year, which explicitly involves hypothesized spillovers of work from August to the following February. February is conceived as the end of a construction year that began the preceding spring. The regression explaining the August to February variation in employment is somewhat less successful than the February to August study. However, the significant variables are consistent in the two analyses.

---

[11] For comparative purposes, the correlation between August to February percentage change in contract construction employment and change in the construction unemployment rate between those two months is –0.7633; the correlation between February to August changes in the two variables is –0.8097. It is assumed that these simple correlations reflect the interdependence of the two variables, with changes in employment affecting unemployment, and labor availability affecting seasonality. The use of nonconstruction employment and unemployment in the regression largely avoids this interdependence, for there is little causal connection between construction employment changes and aggregate conditions.

[12] Analysis of the residuals of the equation indicates that it is most *in*accurate in explaining the dependent variable during the late forties and mid-fifties. The percentage error is quite low in more recent years. (The average absolute error is approximately 4 percent, 1961-1967.)

The percentage change in noncontract construction employment is positively related to the August to February change in contract construction. The August to February change in construction employment is, of course, always negative. An increase in employment in other sectors between the two months tends to lessen the construction decline, and vice versa. This independent variable appears to act as surrogate for general business conditions. The construction unemployment rate in August is negatively related to the seasonality measure.[13] Thus, a high August rate implies a larger decline in employment from August to February than a low rate. This result is consistent with the hypothesis that a spillover of employment occurs from the peak month to the trough when there are shortages in the peak season. Finally, the time trend in the seasonality measure is negative, implying a worsening situation. As in the previous equation, the partial correlation of time and seasonality is stronger than the simple correlation.

Seasonality in Unemployment

The rate of unemployment in construction also shows a distinct seasonal pattern. Unemployment rates are highest in the winter months and lowest in summer. But winter unemployment rates are responsive to the availability of jobs for construction workers in other industries. When unemployment rates in the economy generally are declining, the construction unemployment rate declines more than proportionally (except during the summer months). Construction unemployment rates fall to a very low level in the summer and are only slightly responsive either to changes in construction unemployment or to the all-industry unemployment rates. It may be inferred that summer unemployment rates in construction are practically irreducible, since they are associated with job changes and localized slumps in demand. The following technical note describes the statistical analysis on which the preceding conclusions are based.

Technical note: Determinants of seasonality in unemployment   A group of explanatory regressions was fitted to monthly changes in the private wage and salary worker unemployment rate in construction, 1958 to 1968 (see Table 14). Changes in employment in contract construction were used as a measure of construction demand conditions. Changes in the all-civilian worker unemployment rate represented job opportunities in nonconstruction industries.

---

[13] The construction unemployment rate was used as an independent variable in this regression rather than the nonconstruction unemployment rate (as in the first equation) in order to represent directly unemployment conditions in construction, as is consistent with this study of the impact of possible shortages in construction on the flow of work in the industry.

Table 14   Unemployment Absorption Equations

Dependent Variable: Monthly change in private wage and salary worker unemployment rate in construction, 1948–1968[a] (248 observations)

	Total (d. o. f. 242)	(N-D-J-F) 1st Quarter (d. o. f. 58)	(F-M-A-M) 2nd Quarter (d. o. f. 60)	(M-J-J-A) 3rd Quarter (d. o. f. 60)	(A-S-O-N) 4th Quarter (d. o. f. 58)
R^2 (corrected)	0.8223	0.7190	0.4681	0.0584	0.6084
Regression coefficients and t values					
Percentage change in employment in contract construction	-0.39761[b] (-12.9191)	-0.40947[b] (-7.4235)	-0.28590[b] (-4.0799)	-0.20425[b] (-2.4859)	-0.38857[b] (-3.6295)
Change in all-civilian worker unemployment rate	1.37306[b] (8.8028)	1.54003[b] (4.4583)	3.14877[b] (4.6176)	0.52188[c] (2.2384)	1.6568[b] (4.3003)
Seasonal dummy N-D-J-F	0.44769[c] (1.8371)				
Seasonal dummy F-M-A-M	-0.13254 (-0.4327)				
Seasonal dummy M-J-J-A	0.89019[b] (3.3119)				
Intercept	-0.1720 (-1.0568)	0.1380 (0.4557)	-0.2474 (-0.6023)	0.0181 (0.581)	-0.1457 (-0.5800)
Durbin-Watson	2.3621	1.8423	2.2134	2.4598	2.4065

[a]Through September 1968.
[b]Significant at 1 percent.
[c]Significant at 5 percent.

Finally, seasonal dummies were employed to allow for other influences specific to the periods involved. Regressions were run for the entire period and for the four quarters separately. The pooled (all quarters) data regression explained some 82 percent of variation in the dependent variable. Changes in construction employment conditions and in employment opportunities elsewhere are significant in this explanation; a seasonal dummy variable for the summer quarter is also an important contributor.

The influence of these variables on changes in the construction unemployment rate varies in the different quarters. During all quarters except the third (summer), the two variables representing employment and unemployment conditions contribute significantly to the explanation of variation in the dependent variable. The combined importance of these variables (as expressed by the multiple correlation coefficient) varies with the season, as does the relative importance of each. The crucial importance of other industries' unemployment conditions in the spring (second) quarter is evident. During the second quarter a change in the all-worker unemployment rate of one percentage point will induce a threefold change in the construction unemployment rate (contract construction employment conditions unchanged). On the other hand, during the winter quarter, changes in employment conditions in the industry itself are of major importance. The summer quarter is unusual. Neither employment conditions in construction nor unemployment conditions in other industries are major determinants of changes in the construction unemployment rate during this period. Most likely, variations in the composition of construction activity and its geographic location dominate summer changes in the unemployment rate.

Mechanisms for Reducing Seasonality

Earlier it was shown that seasonality in employment tends to diminish when construction demand is high and labor markets in the economy are generally tight. Yet the process is largely an unintended one, resulting from peak season shortages and delays, and it entails considerable unanticipated costs to both contractors and owners.[14] These costs can be minimized if formal programs are developed in the industry to reduce seasonality.

Development of mechanisms for increasing winter construction beyond

---

[14]The additional costs of winter construction depend greatly on whether planning and preparation for winter work are undertaken in advance. Where adequate precautions are taken, additional costs of winter work rarely exceed 1 to 2 percent of project cost and may actually be nonexistent—there may even be a saving. See the testimony of Mr. A.T. Bone in *Hearings on H.R. 15990*, p. 121; also, a survey by the Structural Clay Products Institute, "Cold Weather Construction Techniques" (Washington, D.C., 1967).

current industry levels have proved quite difficult. In part, the problem has been the complexity of the construction process, which involves owners, architects, contractors, and labor organizations. Arrangements by any of these parties with regard to winter construction must not violate the requirements of the others. For example, the collective bargaining contract must not conflict either with architects' specifications or with the multiple prime contract laws of some states in the field of public construction. Similarly, willingness by contractors to perform winter work should not conflict with the desire of architects and labor organizations to maintain quality of construction. Increasing winter work must therefore involve due regard for the requirements of each element of the construction process.[15]

Some effective mechanism for enforcement of the obligation to perform winter work is also necessary. In the American construction industry, enforcement of employment- and wage-related standards is traditionally performed by the labor organization rather than by government or joint labor-management committees.[16] An effective winter work program will probably also involve enforcement by labor organizations. Furthermore, public agencies and private owners as well are not normally able to enforce a contractor's obligation to work in winter unless he would otherwise fail to complete a project on time. Completion dates are sometimes so tight that the contractor encloses the job and works through the winter. In the more usual case, there is considerable latitude for scheduling, and winter-weather construction can be minimized. Because many jobs enter the market late or are altered in the course of construction, completion dates become elastic. Among public authorities in the major northeastern states, there have been few instances of the enforcement of liquid damages (that is, monetary damage payments) against a contractor for late completion. Thus, although owners and architects are in a position to specify winter construction, in fact they are rarely in a position to enforce the requirement.

A solution to the problem of increasing wintertime construction beyond current levels would appear to require the following elements:
1.
Collective bargaining agreements must specify the contractors' obligation to carry out winter work through enclosure and temporary heating as required.

[15] See *Hearings on H.R. 15990*, p. 74, for a brief review of the activities of the All-Weather Masonry Committee of the masonry industry and the Committee on Seasonality of the AGC.
[16] This is true even with respect to enforcement of the Davis-Bacon requirements, where complaints are often initiated by labor organizations.

Further, the labor organizations involved must be prepared to work out jurisdictional and manning agreements for temporary heat and lighting such as to
facilitate winter work through economy of operation. Currently, the laborers,
electricians, operating engineers, and pipefitters each assert some jurisdiction
over temporary heat and light on a winterized job, jurisdiction that sometimes
involves nonproductive or standby personnel. It is very important that jurisdictional and/manning requirements be developed that are both economical
and consistent with the requirements of health and safety on the job.
2.
The willingness of owners and of architects to allow and if possible require
winter construction must be made explicit. Public owners (federal, state, and
municipal) should develop statutes that indicate the desire of the owner and
his representative to have work proceed through the winter months. Further,
legislation should require that public agencies design and award jobs for a four-
season workyear. The current bunching of contract awards and starting dates
in spring and summer occurs in part because public owners intend a three-
season schedule. Statutory requirements for wintertime construction should
of course include provisions for exceptional cases in which the nature of the
job is such that all-weather work becomes prohibitive.[17]

Further, public owners must adopt, as many already have, detailed specifications for winter work, including specifications for temporary heating, lighting, and enclosure, as required. These specifications are especially important
where there are laws requiring multiple prime contracts on a single project.
The responsibility of each contractor must be clearly indicated, and collective bargaining agreements should not conflict with these specifications.

Private owners must similarly avail themselves of requirements and specifications for winter work. Temporary heat, light, and enclosure should not be
extras on a job or subject to negotiation but should be specified in the bid
documents, consistent with collective bargaining agreement obligations, and
included in the bid price.

Both public and private owners might consider a specific allowance for
temporary heat, light, and enclosure in the contractual arrangements. Presumably, if such an allowance existed, the obligation of the contractor would

[17]See *Hearings on H.R. 15990*, pp. 59–71, and for a summary, pp. 3–5, regarding
methods for federal assistance in stabilizing employment in construction through more
effective use of science and technology and through winter scheduling of federal construction projects. The report refers for further study a suggested counterseasonal
unemployment insurance tax for construction.

not extend beyond this sum, except for what might be required by a labor agreement.

Subsidies versus Specifications

The procedures just outlined envisage that requirements for winter work would apply uniformly to contractors,[18] so that the costs of winter work would appear as elements of the bid document (or as an allowance uniformly applied). Fair competition in the industry demands that contractors be placed on an equal footing regarding winter construction requirements. Competition among bidders would then mainly center on achieving relatively low unit costs. Other things being equal, the bidding mechanism would tend to insure that the additional cost of winter work was competitively established and therefore minimal.

Considerable interest has existed abroad in government subsidies to encourage winter work.[19] Subsidies in the form of a lump sum or a percentage of the job cost, available on a performance basis (not negotiated, or cost-reimbursement), would act much in the manner of specification to achieve winter work at minimum cost. Thus, if contractors differ in their costs for winter work, a subsidy would always tend to improve the competitive position of the most efficient winter builder (so long as the amount of the subsidy exceeds his marginal winter cost). Nevertheless, there are several possible disadvantages to a subsidy program. First, the subsidy might not achieve winter work, for it may be set too low to be attractive to any builder, or it may fall below the marginal winter cost of the successful builder and be unclaimed. Second, a public enforcement mechanism, involving the monitoring of jobs, would be necessary and might be cumbersome to administer and expensive. Third, subsidies of whatever nature encourage cost pass-throughs, tending to raise the cost of all employers toward the subsidy level. Labor particularly is in a position to see that the full amount of the subsidy is expended on temporary facilities, so that the more efficient winter builders might find their costs increased. In general, subsidies and cost-plus arrangements are best avoided in construction.

[18]For contractors not subject to collective bargaining agreements, statutes requiring winter work on public facilities might specify that the standards of the area be met.
[19]See Jan Wittrock, *Reducing Seasonal Unemployment in the Construction Industry* (Paris: Organization for Economic Cooperation and Development, 1967), and U.S. Department of Housing and Urban Development, *Action against Seasonal Unemployment in the Construction Industry: Lessons from Foreign Experience* (Washington, D.C., 1971).

Intermittency of Employment

Nonseasonal Sources of Employment Intermittency

Employment variations associated with nationwide fluctuations in the amount of construction activity have been relatively unimportant in the post-World War II period. The 9 percent decline in annual average employment between 1956 and 1958 has been the largest since the war. Changes of this magnitude are dwarfed by seasonal fluctuations in the industry and by localized (but nonseasonal) variations in employment.

There have been significant shifts in the composition of construction, however. Residential construction expanded from 1950 to a peak in 1954 and declined precipitously until 1957; it expanded again, peaking in 1959, fell off until 1961, and then rose, peaking again in 1963 and declining steadily thereafter until 1967. These fluctuations in residential construction were offset considerably by steady growth in the nonresidential construction market. For example, the impact of the residential building trough of 1959 was considerably offset by a nonresidential boom. Again, in the 1960s, the residential downturn of 1963-1966 was more than compensated for by a nonresidential boom. Figure 1 shows these movements in private construction activity since 1946. Public construction has given a steady expansionary impetus to the industry.

Thus the stability of total construction activity and of employment may be explained by compensating alterations in the composition of output. The four severe declines that residential building has suffered since 1947, have largely been associated with tight federal monetary policy. In three cases, expansion in the level of capital expenditure by business buoyed the industry against a general decline.

The compositional changes that have characterized construction stability over the postwar period have been connected with important shifts in the locality and craft requirements of building. Declines in the residential construction sector produce large reductions in employment opportunities for carpenters, bricklayers, and painters, who are likely to be released from work in greater numbers than the increasing activity in nonresidential construction is able to absorb. The geographic distribution of work has also altered, with centers of building activity shifting from suburban areas to central city locations — or again, from large areas of residential building like Southern California, Florida, and Arizona toward industrial centers in the Middle West, the

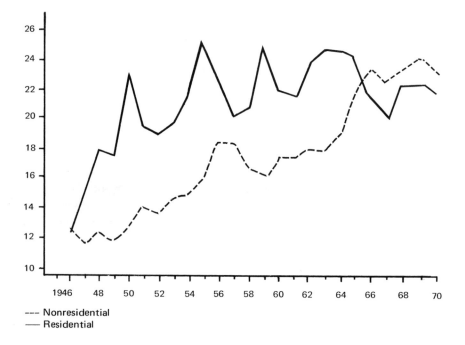

--- Nonresidential
—— Residential

Figure 1. Gross Private Domestic Investment, Nonresidential and Residential Structures, 1958 Dollars (Billions), 1946–1970.
Source: *Construction Review* (monthly issued by Department of Commerce, Business and Defense Services Administration).
Note: It is necessary in these estimates to obtain constant dollar estimates through the use of price deflators, which are known to overstate the rate of inflation and thereby to depress unduly constant dollar output in recent years. These deflators are used because of the lack of better ones on a current basis. See Robert J. Gordon, "$45 Billion of U.S. Private Investment Has Been Mislaid," *American Economic Review* 59 (June 1969): 221-238; and George Jaszi, "Reply," *American Economic Review* 60 (December 1970): 934-939.

Gulf Coast, and the East. Conversely, the expansion of nonresidential building requires operating engineers, plumbers and steamfitters, electricians, sheet-metal workers, boilermakers, and ironworkers in greater numbers than declines in residential building are likely to release.

One consequence of this pattern of changing construction demand has been the intensification of the problem of the coincidence, both geographic and occupational, of pockets of unemployment and areas of shortage. Since neither contractors nor workers are perfectly mobile, and since neither skills nor equipment are perfectly transferable from one sort of activity to another, there have been inherent and persistent adjustment difficulties. When construction activity has declined or altered in composition, workers have experienced periods of unemployment, journeymen have been reluctant to expand apprenticeship opportunities, pension and welfare funds have been plagued with difficulties of coverage, and policies designed locally to reduce the seasonality of employment in the industry have been the victims of local depressions in construction activity. Conversely, rapid expansions in building activity have left contractors unable to fill work crews and have caused union officials to charge that the mobility of their members has declined. Furthermore, the continual procession from boom to bust has burdened management with the costs of repeatedly establishing and dismantling organizations.

Variation in employment experience extends to differences in experience among crafts, among locals of the same craft, and among members of the same local. Each variation in employment experience has its influence on the institutional structure of the industry — and, within that structure, upon wages, work rules, and collective bargaining relationships. The influence of divergent employment conditions on manpower phenomena in the industry is so tangled in its complexity that it is not possible here to examine it in detail.[20] I will limit myself to describing the most important aspects of divergence and their significance.

Common to all crafts are wide annual variations in the amount of work available locally. Data on employment fluctuations by craft and area are rare, but some data with wide coverage are available from payments by contractors to the National Benefit Fund, established by the IBEW and the National Electrical Contractors Association (NECA). These data indicate considerable variation in the amount of work done in particular cities over periods of only a few years. For example, in Boston, hours worked in the electrical contracting industry rose 60 percent in 1964–1965 and fell 10 percent in 1965–1966; in Detroit, hours worked rose 40 percent in 1964–1965 and 4 percent from 1965 to 1966; in Los Angeles, hours worked fell 17 percent in 1964–1965 and rose 5 percent in 1965–1966.[21]

There is a great divergence in the number of hours worked by craftsmen within most locals of building trades unions. For example, according to reports made to the pension fund on behalf of operating engineers in New Jersey in 1964, 14.2 percent of those reporting at least 1 hour worked less than 700

[20]This task is best undertaken with regard to the individual crafts. See, for example, Garth Mangum, *The Operating Engineers: The Economic History of a Trade Union* (Cambridge: Harvard University Press, 1964).
[21]Compiled by the author.

hours during the year; a total of 34.2 percent worked less than 1300 hours. On the other hand, 27.1 percent reported over 1999 hours worked.[22] Among electricians in Los Angeles, 10.23 percent of those reported to the fund worked under 250 hours between August 1964 and June 1965. A total of 28.72 percent reported over 2000 hours, and 46.49 percent reported between 1500 and 2000 hours.[23]

The work experience accumulated by members of a local seems to vary with the craft, the degree of seasonality to which workmen are subject, and the degree of organization of the labor market. First, lower-skilled workmen are subject to considerably more competition from entrants to the industry when jobs are scarce elsewhere in the economy. Second, where operations are commonly discontinued in large measure in winter months, some workers nevertheless remain employed at their crafts, and the gap in hours worked between the seasonally out of work and those at work is widened.[24] Finally, locals that operate referral systems often give preference to workers from the locality or with long service and in this way try to provide steady employment for some of the men in the local.[25]

In summary, employment variability in construction is a result of several causes other than seasonality, including changes in the composition of demand, fluctuations in the volume of work available in local labor markets, and an uneven distribution of available work among craftsmen in a trade in a par-

[22]These data were obtained by the Department of Labor in conjunction with the Secretary of Labor's determination of the dispute between Local 825, International Union of Operating Engineers, and the Associated General Contractors of New Jersey. It is clear that some persons who reported very many hours worked in 1964 did not actually work as many hours as claimed. Apparently, employers filing late reports failed to attribute them to the pay period worked and in this way distorted the estimates of hours worked.

[23]See the special study of hours worked in U.S. Bureau of Labor Statistics, *Seasonality and Manpower in Construction.*

[24]It might be useful to distinguish two construction labor forces. One consists of journeymen fairly regularly employed by a contractor or homebuilder — his key men. The contractor is quite reluctant to allow these employees to go elsewhere and may even be willing to undertake jobs simply to keep them on his staff during slack periods in the building market. The other labor force consists of craftsmen who fall into the traditional pattern of the journeyman, following the work and going from employer to employer (and, perhaps, industry to industry). See A. H. Belitsky, "Hiring Problems in the Building Trades, with Special Reference to the Boston Area" (Ph.D. thesis, Harvard University, 1960); also, Maurice Parodi, "Wage Drift and Wage Bargaining: A Case Study of the Building Industry in Marseilles, *"British Journal of Industrial Relations* 1 (June 1963): 213–227.

[25]Because referral systems, where operative, determine to a degree a man's employment opportunities, exclusive referral systems often provide for binding arbitration of disputes arising from the operation of the hiring hall.

ticular area. The result of these factors and the seasonality of work is to provide a relatively low average number of hours worked in construction for those persons employed at some time in the industry. The intermittency of construction employment is reflected in part in the relatively high rate of unemployment that the industry continually reports.

The Limitations of Mobility

The contribution of localized building slumps to intermittency and unemployment in construction depends largely on "imperfections" in the labor market. If all workers in construction were fully mobile, an increasing level of aggregate demand for construction labor would be likely to reduce intermittency in the industry (assuming that employment conditions in other industries are unchanging). For example, the existence of areas of unemployment and areas of labor shortages may seem to demand mobility as its solution.

However, the mobility solution is only partially effective for several reasons. The mobility envisaged for construction workers would have to be both geographic and occupational. Geographic mobility would be required because downturns in employment may occur in local areas at the same time as jobs are available elsewhere. The institutional barriers to significantly greater geographic mobility should not be underestimated. Home ownership, community investment, family ties, credit standing, and so on, impede it.[26]

Some of these impediments are social goals, whose reduction would be inappropriate. In addition, the lack of appropriate vesting and reciprocity arrangements for benefits arising from health, welfare, and pension funds for construction workers may cause a man to be reluctant to move to another area or another craft for fear of losing service credits. And yet the level of benefits and their adequacy are partly a function of the breadth of coverage and the expense of reciprocity arrangements.[27] Occupational mobility would be necessary because a downturn might be centered in a particular sector of construction activity employing a particular mix of skills. Yet specialization, work experience, and development of skill itself limit occupational mobility. The design of jobs in such a way that all craftsmen can perform them easily, or of training so general that the individual has a bit of

[26] Geographic mobility also threatens the work opportunities of craftsmen in areas to which there is heavy migration. See "Unions Fighting for Alaska Jobs," *Engineering News-Record,* January 30, 1969, p. 42; also, *ibid,* June 6, 1968, p. 13.
[27] In some trades, national health, welfare, and pension reciprocity are now in existence, and others are moving toward this goal. For a comprehensive discussion of the problems associated with reciprocity or national coverage, see "U.A. 29th Convention Proceedings," *United Association Journal* 78 (November 1966): 208-211.

knowledge in all areas, is neither technologically nor economically desirable. Thus perfect mobility would exact a heavy price in social well-being, personal security, and economic efficiency. A balance between these objectives and that of mobility must be struck, and that balance is certain to contain obstacles to perfect mobility.

Viewing localized unemployment in construction as a mobility problem is an error resulting partly from loose terminology. "Construction" workers are given a verbal homogeneity by the term and therefore are expected to obtain jobs in construction. Construction workers are in many cases already very mobile, not only within but outside the industry. More than one-quarter of construction workers (carpenters, other construction craftsmen, and construction laborers) are employed in nonconstruction industries at any given moment. Consequently, mobility for construction workers must be interpreted widely (if the statement refers at all to normal patterns), to include intermittent employment in nonconstruction industry. The problem of unemployment in a local construction labor market often includes the workers' inability to find jobs elsewhere in the economy and thus extends beyond construction.

There have been remarkably few data available regarding the geographic mobility of construction workers. Some crafts are commonly believed to be more mobile geographically than others, and the circumstances of their employment support such inferences. For example, the construction crews on highways, pipelines, transmission lines, and heavy construction projects are mobile because of the location of projects and their nature. Structural ironworkers and boilermakers follow a relatively small volume of work around large areas, though worker mobility in some branches of the ironworkers' trade has probably decreased in recent years. In any case, the absence of mobility data is such as to prevent a quantitative analysis of the volume of geographic mobility and the impact of inducements to increased mobility.[28] It is unlikely, however, that considerable increases in construction mobility will be achieved in the context of generally tight labor markets, in part because jobs in other industries are readily available on a temporary or permanent basis.

Determinants of Unemployment Rates in Construction

Unemployment rates for construction are usually higher than for any other

[28]The Bureau of Labor Statistics has prepared a study of the geographic and industrial mobility of construction workers based on Social Security data. The lack of occupational information limits the usefulness of the survey for analytic purposes. See *Hearings on H.R. 15990*, pp. 62–68.

nonagricultural sector of the economy and are normally double the national unemployment rate.[29] There are several sources of unemployment in the industry, including movement among jobs, localized building recessions, the seasonal downturn in employment, and the inflow of workers from other industries when aggregate employment in the economy declines.[30] Because unemployment due to job mobility, local conditions, and seasonality is fairly stable over time, most variation in annual average unemployment rates in construction is due to the influence of other industries.

Variations in the annual average unemployment rate of private wage and salary workers in construction are very highly correlated with those in the all-civilian worker unemployment rate. For the period 1948 through 1966, the simple correlation coefficient between the two series is 0.9739. In essence, statistical explanation or prediction of changes in the annual construction unemployment rate can rest solely on the all-worker rate. The very close relationship between the all-worker and construction (private wage and salary worker) unemployment rates is an effect of the availability or non-availability) of job opportunities in other industries. Because construction is an industry that is relatively easy to enter, many persons obtain short-term jobs in construction and then, if they are unable to find other work later, are reported as unemployed construction workers.

Specifically, changes in nonconstruction employment opportunities have accounted for about 70 percent of the variance in the annual average unemployment rate in construction since 1948.[31] A time series was constructed to reflect changes in job opportunities outside construction by measuring percentage changes in annual average employment in nonagricultural, nonconstruction employment, as estimated by the Current Population Survey. This series exhibits a correlation coefficient of –0.8543 with changes in the construction unemployment rate. Therefore, it is reasonable to conclude that aggregate demand measures directed at the general economy may have a considerable impact on construction unemployment. A decrease of one percentage point in the all-industry unemployment rate will tend to reduce

[29] Ibid., pp. 38–43.
[30] See D. Q. Mills, "Factors Affecting Patterns of Employment and Unemployment in Construction" (Ph.D. thesis, Harvard University, 1967), pp. 94–108, for a discussion of the relative significance of the different sources of unemployment in construction.
[31] "Construction may represent a special case [among American industries], since its cyclical sensitivity is due not so much to its own declines in employment as to the inflow of disemployed labor from other sectors." Edward D. Kalachek, "The Composition of Unemployment and Public Policy," in R. A. Gordon and M. S. Gordon, eds., Prosperity and Unemployment (New York: John Wiley & Sons, 1966), p. 234.

the construction unemployment rate (both rates on annual average) by over two percentage points.

Achieving Job Security in Construction

The Role of Contractors and Unions
This chapter has emphasized stabilization of the volume of construction demand as the major means by which an improved utilization of manpower may be achieved. More intensive utilization of labor may be translated into job security for the individual worker, which may be expected to have a desirable effect on attitudes toward change and innovation. Although increased job security is not likely to be realized within the individual firm, it may be possible to achieve it within the industry generally. In either case, it is sought as a means to affect the economic and industrial relations behavior of the industry.

The reason that the individual firm is not able to provide job security for most of its construction employees is that for the most part its jobs are short-term, vary as to location, and demand somewhat different compositions of the work force. Often the firm works in the jurisdictions of different locals or district councils of a craft union and is required to hire a number of local people. Furthermore, the firm experiences fluctuating levels of demand for manpower, involving the phasing of separate jobs. Economical operation requires that a large portion of the firm's work force be available at its discretion from central pools of manpower.

More often, job security is attempted through the division of jobs among a limited group of mechanics. Traditionally, building and construction tradesmen seek to allocate work opportunities among themselves through participation in a trade union. In many trades, labor organizations operate hiring halls, exclusive or nonexclusive,[32] to which the discharged worker goes to seek employment. Continuing referral from a pool of workers is the only mechanism by which job security is attainable for many journeymen. For most craftsmen, however, the hiring hall mechanism is imperfect, particularly in periods of labor surplus, although it is then most important to them. Considerable intermittency continues to exist in employment, especially over periods of several years.

Suggestions have been made for work stabilization on a local basis by

[32] An exclusive hall involves a commitment by contractors to try to hire first through the hall.

exercising tighter control over the allocation of jobs than is currently practical. For example, a guarantee might be made by employers as a group to provide an annual rate of hours of work to an eligible group of journeymen. Presumably, these men would then have first claim on job opportunities until the guarantee is reached. Such plans are not impossible to envisage in construction. They exist in longshoring, another industry of "casual" employment. But there are considerable differences between the construction and longshoring situations which complicate the introduction of work guarantee plans to construction. First, construction is less a single industry than a complex and shifting conglomeration of many different specialties — each with its own employment and industrial relations policies. Second, employers and specialties are much more numerous in construction. Third, the separate specialties are intimately related in the production process, so that work guarantees in one trade might be quite expensive were other trades to continue to have considerable freedom for layoffs and delays. To a degree, job security much be achieved simultaneously in many separate and somewhat distinct specialties, and the problem is therefore more complex and difficult than in longshoring. Fourth, unlike longshoring, in construction there is continual shifting of the workplace from one site or area to another, so that centralized mechanisms for job referral and reporting are difficult to operate effectively. Yet despite the differences in the two industries, efficient utilization of manpower resources in construction may well require an approach to intermittency of employment that includes some form of work guarantee.

The Role of Owners
Stabilization of employment in construction depends critically on stabilization of the work flow. This cannot be done by contractors or unions but only by owners and their representatives. Thus far, owners have indicated little or no concern for problems of manpower utilization, other than public complaints about manpower shortages and enforced delays or cancellation of some projects due to high costs or lack of bidders. Public owners, such as states and the federal government, have resisted establishing central coordinating mechanisms for their construction activities for many years. Local market coordination of projects occurs only when the complete inability of the industry to cope with an intended volume of work is evident.

Each year's collective bargaining negotiations bring protests from owners, public and private, regarding spiraling construction costs and proclamations of an intent to rationalize scheduling in the industry (among other things). Each year nothing is accomplished. Until owners develop more responsible attitudes regarding priorities for work and scheduling mechanisms, job security in construction is likely to be unobtainable. The pattern of local boom and bust, with its associated inefficiences, will continue.

At present, as in the past, work stabilization in construction awaits two major developments: first, a willingness by owners, particularly public owners (who are potentially the more centralized), to schedule work with due regard for local labor market conditions; second, the initiation of serious discussions among contractors' associations and unions with a view toward developing feasible job guarantees. Ultimately, only these parties can determine what will be accepted.

6

Quantitative Measures of Racial Integration in the Building Trades

Few disputes in recent years have been so persistent, so bitter, and have led to so much misunderstanding as the disputes over the racial composition of the construction industry's work force. Racial discrimination has been and remains a problem, especially in some crafts and areas, yet the record of the industry as a whole in terms of minority group participation is better than that of most industries. Considerable racial imbalance exists in several of the skilled trades; unfortunately, the situation in the skilled occupations in other industries is no different. Recent years have seen the development of special approaches to increasing the integration of the building trades. In order to put these efforts in perspective, the following pages examine the statistical evidence regarding minority participation in construction, the causes of racial imbalance, and methods of improving the integration of the industry's work force.

The Racial Composition of Construction

Employment in contract construction and the building trades may be measured in many ways, as is to be expected in an industry of casual employment. Each different measure will provide a slightly different estimate of the racial composition of the industry's work force. About the only valid generalizations that the data allow are that (1) a larger proportion of nonwhites is employed in contract construction than in American industry as a whole,[1] that (2) these persons are represented in relatively larger numbers than whites in the laborers' trade, and that (3) nonwhites are a very small proportion of certain crafts.

The Social Security Administration reported that in 1964 (the most recent year for which data are available) 13.5 percent of persons who reported any income from contract construction employment were black.[2] However, while 14.3 percent of those with *most* of their earnings in contract construction were black, only 11.4 percent of those with *all* of their reported earnings from contract construction were black. Similarly, average annual earnings from all sources for whites employed in the industry were almost double the annual earnings of blacks.[3]

---

[1] In the economy as a whole, nonwhites constitute approximately 11 percent of annual average employment of persons 16 years of age and older. *Employment and Earnings* (monthly issued by the U.S. Bureau of Labor Statistics).
[2] Spanish-speaking persons are generally classified as whites in these data.
[3] These data are from a special Bureau of Labor Statistics study of Social Security data prepared by Mr. Joe Russell.

Table 15.   Racial Composition of Wage and Salary Workers in Contract Construction, 1964

	Minority Workers as a Percentage of Workers Who Received Most of Their Total Earnings from Contract Construction	
	All Workers (%)	Workers Employed in Contract Construction in All Four Quarters of 1964 (%)
General contractors	13.7	11.5
Heavy contractors	14.2	12.1
Highway and street contractors	14.4	12.6
Other heavy contractors	14.0	11.8
Special trade contractors	10.4	7.8
Plumbing, heating, and air-conditioning	5.9	4.1
Electrical	3.2	1.9
Masonry, plastering, stone, and tile work	24.3	19.3
Roofing and sheet metal work	11.2	9.0

Source: Social Security Administration, 1% sample, special tabulations made by the Bureau of Labor Statistics.

Black participation in employment has been much more extensive in some sectors of the construction industry than others. In 1964, black employment among workers most of whose earnings came from a particular sector of the industry varied from 24.3 percent for masonry contracting (including large numbers of laborers and bricklayers) to 3.2 percent for electrical contracting (primarily electricians). In each of these sectors, the proportion of blacks among workers employed in construction in all four quarters of the year was somewhat lower (see Table 15). Unfortunately, there are no data available on the racial composition of the branches of the industry (for example, residential and heavy and highway).

The Social Security Administration collects no occupational data. While occupational data are available from other sources, they do not allow disaggregation to the construction industry alone. Table 16 presents estimates of the racial composition of employment in the building trades covering almost eighty years. However, these data (except for the laborers) refer to

Table 16. Percentage of Blacks Employed in Selected Building Trades, All Industries, Selected Years, 1890-1970

	1970	1967	1950	1940	1930	1910	1890	Approximate Percentage of Total Number in Occupational Category Employed in Construction	
								1966	1970
Bricklayers	15.5	13.5	10.9	6.0	6.9	7.5	6.1	74	93
Carpenters	6.6	6.1	3.9	3.9	3.5	4.3	3.6	77	84
Cement finishers	30.3	37.7	26.2	15.2	15.8	13.0	10.3	95	97
Electricians	3.4	3.6	1.0	0.7	0.7	0.6	n.a.	45	48
Painters	9.8	9.9	5.2	3.8	3.6	2.9	2.0	67	83
Plumbers and pipefitters	3.9	3.2	3.3	2.2	2.0	1.7	1.1	64	70
Excavating, grading, and road machinery operators	5.0	6.9						78	81
Roofers	10.5	15.3						98	95
Structural metal workers	6.7	3.9						56	69
Tinsmiths, coppersmiths, and sheet metal workers		1.9						35	
Laborers in construction		26.9						100	100

Source: 1890–1950: F. Ray Marshall, *The Negro and Organized Labor* (New York: John Wiley & Sons, 1965), p. 157; 1967, 1970: Current Population Survey data; the last column contains author's estimates based on unpublished CPS data.

all persons employed in the building trades, many of whom are not employed in construction.[4] By the late 1960s, many crafts had a significant proportion of black membership. The bricklayers, cement finishers, roofers, and laborers each had a larger proportion of blacks than the national all-industry labor force as a whole. The electricians, plumbers and pipefitters, structural metal workers (ironworkers), and sheet metal workers were predominantly white.[5] Further, the proportion of blacks in all trades for which data are given has increased over the period surveyed, especially since the 1940s.

By 1968, of some 410,000 nonwhites employed on an annual average in the building and construction trades (including laborers), more than half were in the skilled trades.[6] Nonwhites are concentrated to some degree in lower-paying construction occupations, but the evidence is mixed. In 1968, the average union wage rate plus employer hourly contribution to fringe benefits was $5.68 for all trades. The average laborers' scale was $4.47, but the brick-layer earned an average of $6.31 per hour, among the highest rates. By 1968, the plumber ($6.65 per hour) and the pipefitter ($6.47 per hour) were on the average the highest-paid tradesmen. Roofers earned $5.45 per hour, and cement masons $5.60.[7] Although these data are for union wages, and al-though comparable estimates for nonunion scales are not available, there is little evidence that blacks are disproportionately represented in the nonunion sector of the industry.[8]

[4] Employment in the "construction" industry is composed of the employees of contractors (contract construction) and of government construction agencies (for example, public highway departments), comprising perhaps 15 percent of all construction employment.

[5] It is interesting to note the positive correlation between the 1967 percentage of black craftsmen and the proportion of the craft employed in construction. Those crafts with the largest construction membership also have the largest proportion of blacks. It is unlikely that any simple causal factor is operating here.

[6] *Employment and Earnings* 16 (December 1969): 36. This estimate includes some black construction foremen among the skilled. Because the estimates of minority participation in the skilled trades include those employed not only in construction but in all industries, it is possible that in construction itself the number of minority laborers exceeds that of craftsmen. The 1967 Survey of Economic Opportunity (a CPS sample survey taken in February 1967 for data to cover the year 1966) reported that 64 percent of nonwhites in construction were laborers.

[7] U.S. Bureau of Labor Statistics, *Union Wages and Hours: Building Trades, July 1, 1968,* Bulletin no. 1621 (Washington, D.C., 1969), p. 10.

[8] The 1967 Survey of Economic Opportunity indicated that only 27 percent of nonwhite craftsmen and 35 percent of nonwhite laborers in construction reported union membership. These data, however interesting, are suspect. First, not all skilled crafts were included in the estimates of nonwhite craftsmen (sheet metal workers, teamsters, glaziers, operating engineers, asbestos workers, and apprentices were omitted due to classification differences). Second, the statistical basis for the estimates is very small, and the estimates may be much in error.

The Equal Employment Opportunity Commission has released some results of its surveys of the racial composition of building trades local unions that operate referral systems.[9] The data are based on returns from only 3700 of 5000 locals operating hiring halls and cover less than one-third of the industry's work force (coverage is high in the mechanical trades and low in the basic trades). The data are generally in accord with the patterns revealed by the Current Population Survey, but the nonwhite percentages are generally lower for the mechanical trades than those reported by the CPS.

Finally, surveys made in specific cities have indicated that there may be crafts with few minority members even where the industry as a whole is well integrated. For example, the Office of Federal Contract Compliance found that in the five-county Philadelphia area in the summer of 1969 "the overall construction industry. . .has a current minority representation of employees of 30 percent. . . .Despite that fact, there are few minorities in. . .six trades."[10] In the Washington, D.C. area, the Office of Federal Contract Compliance found "approximately 26 percent of the total work force in the Washington, D.C., SMSA is minority workers. The over-all minority representation. . .in the Washington SMSA construction industry is approximately 50 percent. . . .[But] minority representation averages 3.3 percent among [5 crafts]."[11]

The most dramatic improvements in racial balance within the building trades have been achieved in apprenticeship programs. It has been reported that, as recently as 1966, blacks constituted only 2.3 percent of all of the registered apprentices in the United States (the construction industry accounts for approximately two-thirds of all registered apprentices). By January 1, 1969, nonwhites were 6.5 percent of all registered apprentices; 4 percent were blacks. Most of this expansion has come in the building trades, in large part as a result of federally financed outreach programs (first estab-

---

Whatever the data, it would not be surprising if a larger proportion of nonwhites were in the nonunion sector, since this sector is concentrated in the South and in residential construction (which generally requires men with lesser skills). Still, it is likely that the allover distribution of nonwhites between the union and nonunion sectors of construction is approximately equal. Although nonunion work in some crafts in the South is largely black, this factor is somewhat or entirely offset by the lesser proportion of blacks in homebuilding in the North and West — largely because residential construction is found on the fringes of metropolitan areas, well away from the black work force concentrated in the inner city.

[9] See *Engineering News-Record,* October 16, 1969, p. 29.

[10] Order of Assistant Secretary of Labor Arthur Fletcher, "Setting Goals for the Philadelphia Plan," September 23, 1969.

[11] Order of Secretary of Labor George P. Shultz, "The Washington Plan," June 2, 1970.

lished in 1964 in New York City), which recruit and prepare minority youth for apprenticeship. By mid-1970, over 7500 minority apprentices had become registered through the outreach programs, and over 11 percent of new apprentices were nonwhite. Nonwhites were recruited through outreach for all trades, but the majority were placed with the carpenters, electricians, plumbers, painters, and sheet metal workers. In the spring of 1968, James J. Reynolds (then Undersecretary of Labor) predicted that as a result of the extensive affirmative action program adopted by the building trades for apprenticeship, a realistic numerical participation by blacks in apprenticeship would be reached within three years.[12] By the spring of 1971, that prediction had been fairly well fulfilled.

Minority Participation in Construction Compared with Other Industries
To the extent that there is a nationwide problem of racial imbalance in construction employment, it is centered in a few of the skilled trades.[13] This problem is certainly not unique to construction. On the contrary, there is a serious problem of racial imbalance in the skilled blue-collar occupations in all industries, and in professional and managerial occupations as well. The racial imbalance in the building trades is neither greater nor less than in most other skilled crafts, and it is considerably less serious than in higher-status white-collar occupations.

In 1967, the proportion of nonwhite workers employed in occupations classified as "construction craftsmen other than carpenters" (and excluding laborers) was 8.2 percent — higher than the average for all craftsmen and foremen (6.2 percent), for metal craftsmen excluding mechanics (5.5 percent), for all sales workers (3.0 percent), and for all clerical and kindred workers (7.3 percent). The only "higher status occupation" group (that is, excluding operatives, laborers, service, and farm workers) in which the percentage of nonwhites was higher than for construction craftsmen was noncollege teachers (9.4 percent). For carpenters, the nonwhite percentage was 6.2, slightly above the median percentage for the "higher status occupations" (17 in number) listed in a recent BLS study.[14]

[12] Manpower Administration News Release, USDL-8716 (May 16, 1968); the data on apprenticeship programs are from news releases dated October 7, 1968, August 15, 1969, and November 4, 1969. See also Robert W. Fisher, "Labor and the Economy in 1969," *Monthly Labor Review* 93 (January 1970): 35.
[13] There are, of course, local imbalances in other crafts, including, in some cases, the laborers.
[14] C. C. Hodge, "The Negro Job Situation: Has It Improved?" *Monthly Labor Review* 92 (January 1969): 20–28. These data are BLS estimates of annual average employment by occupation. The data include all persons described as working at the occupation listed, regardless of the industry of employment.

In the past two decades, the proportion of nonwhites in construction trades has increased at about the same pace as among other skilled blue-collar occupation groups; it has increased by some 2.6 points (from 4.9 percent non-white in 1950 to 7.5 percent nonwhite in 1968) in eighteen years (see Table 17). By 1968, there was remarkably little variation in the nonwhite proportion among the skilled trade groups, despite considerable differences in the occupations involved (for example, mechanics and repairmen versus construction craftsmen) and the industries in which the different occupation groups are characteristically employed. Only foremen, in all occupations, show a distinctly lower minority group participation, and no skilled craft group is dramatically ahead of the others. The situation in the numerically much larger white-collar categories is far less favorable to nonwhites than in the skilled blue-collar trades. By 1968, less than 5 percent of all white-collar employees were nonwhite, and among managers and officials the proportion was 2.5 percent.

Skilled blue-collar occupations in most manufacturing industries are not more fully integrated than in construction. For example, in 1966, nonwhite em-

Table 17. Nonwhites as a Percentage of Total Annual Average Employment for Selected Occupations, 1950–1968, and Change in Percentages

	1950	1960	1968	1950–1968	1960–1968
Blue-collar	3.9	4.5	6.5	+2.6	+2.0
Foremen	1.3	1.6	3.4	+2.1	+1.8
Mechanics and repairmen	4.5	5.8	7.9	+3.4	+2.1
Metal craftsmen	2.8	3.4	5.4	+1.6	+2.0
Construction craftsmen	4.9	5.7	7.5	+2.6	+1.8
Other craftsmen	3.3	3.7	6.4	+3.1	+2.7
White-collar		3.5	5.7		+1.2
Professional and technical		3.4	4.8		+1.4
Managers and officials		2.1	2.5		+0 4

Source: *Employment and Earnings* (monthly issued by the Bureau of Labor Statistics).

ployment in the big three automobile companies as a proportion of total employment was as follows:[15]

Craftsmen   3.0%
Operatives   20.2
Laborers   27.6

Among 32 plants organized by the Aluminum Workers, it has been reported that 10.5 percent of laborers are black and that 0.6 percent of craftsmen and foremen are black. Ratios for Spanish-Americans were reported to be substantially the same.[16] Apparently, the industrial unions in these and other industries have had little more success in integrating the skilled crafts than some of the construction trades.

The prevalence of racial imbalance among skilled craftsmen and the even poorer performance of the professional and managerial occupation groups suggest that the problem in construction is not unique but is to a large degree an element of a larger pattern in American industry. Presumably, the same factors that generate racial imbalance elsewhere in the economy also affect construction, including racial discrimination, social and educational barriers to blacks, certain patterns of labor market operation, and so on. A detailed analysis of the causes of racial imbalance in construction will show that in addition to these general factors there are some that are unique to the building trades.

The Relative Importance of the Racial Imbalance Problem in Construction
An increasingly publicized goal of public policy is to achieve a distribution of nonwhites among higher-skilled and higher-paying jobs that is similar to the white distribution. For this to happen in the building trades, many nonwhites must enter certain of the skilled crafts. Such a redistribution would also require a movement of nonwhites from the occupations in which they are now disproportionately represented. Yet the total magnitude of the inflow of nonwhites to skilled construction is only a very small proportion of the total occupational redistribution of nonwhites that must be accomplished to achieve racial balance in the entire economy.

In 1968, 205,000 nonwhite males were employed in the building trades

[15] Herbert R. Northrup, *The Negro in the Automobile Industry* (Philadelphia: Wharton School of Finance Industrial Research Unit, 1968), p. 36. For a sympathetic discussion of the auto companies' attempts to improve this racial imbalance, see pp. 37–41.
[16] Statement by William H. Brown III, Chairman of the EEOC, to the Aluminum Workers Annual Convention, June 25, 1969, in *Daily Labor Report* (Bureau of National Affairs), no. 122 (June 25, 1969), p. A-3 .

Table 18.   Black Employment in Selected Occupations, Males, 1968

Occupation	Black Employment (000)	Black Employment after Redistribution (000)	Deficit (000)
White-collar	896	1975	1079
Professional and technical	310	663	353
Managers and officials	170	691	521
Blue-collar	2808	2168	-640
Craftsmen	629	983	354
Construction craftsmen	205	277	72

Source: *Statistical Abstract of the U.S., 1969* (Washington, D.C., 1970), p. 223, and computations by author.

crafts, exclusive of laborers and helpers.[17] Were the black employment distribution similar to that of white males, an additional 72,000 blacks would be employed in the skilled trades in construction.[18] This is less than 2 percent of total black male employment in 1968 (see Table 18). The relative deficit (present distribution compared to figures after redistribution) of nonwhites in the skilled building trades is not large compared to other occupations. In 1968, the percentage deficit (the deficit divided by the current level of employment) among the building trades was 35 percent. Among all craftsmen, the deficit was over 50 percent; among professional and technical employees (males only), more than 110 percent; among managers and officials (males only), more than 300 percent.

More significantly, the absolute number of job opportunities that would be available to nonwhites if racial balance were achieved is higher in certain other sectors of the economy than in construction alone. Over 1 million new jobs for nonwhite males would be necessary to equalize the white male–nonwhite male employment distribution in white-collar jobs.[19] Among white-

[17]Also excluded from the construction craftsman category are boilermakers and sheet metal workers (classified as metal craftsmen), glaziers and operating engineers (classified as other craftsmen), and asbestos workers, apprentices, and construction teamsters (classified as operatives). Statistically, these omissions have a substantial effect on the measure of the total number of construction craftsmen. Probably the figures given in the text for black employment should be raised by one-quarter, and the increase necessary to achieve racial balance raised by about the same amount.

[18]Author's estimates.

[19]Excluding service and farm workers, but including professionals. managers, and sales and clerical workers.

collar and skilled blue-collar jobs, some 1.4 million new jobs for nonwhite males would be necessary to equalize the employment distribution. Jobs in the skilled building trades would constitute some 3 percent of these.[20]

At some point, nonwhites may come to constitute a greater proportion of workers in skilled crafts in construction than in the economy as a whole. There are reasons to expect this development within a decade or so. Many construction industry leaders more or less share the view that nonwhites are a major potential source of manpower in an industry that has had some difficulty in recruiting young men in recent years and that for several years has experienced considerable manpower shortages in certain crafts and areas. In consequence, the job opportunities available to nonwhites in the skilled trades may rise to a higher level than that needed to achieve racial balance.

The construction industry has received perhaps disproportionate attention from civil rights groups. There appear to be many reasons for this. Some observers stress the symbolic importance of construction jobs to blacks because they are masculine jobs and pay well. Others stress that blue-collar jobs seem to require less education and other qualifications than white-collar occupations. Furthermore, many blacks are familiar with construction and with a large number of trades. Finally, much construction is publicly financed, providing civil rights organizations with a means of exerting pressure for nonwhite hiring.[21] Nevertheless, more American males earn their livelihood as professionals, managers, and technicians than as skilled craftsmen, and the trend is toward increasing the relative importance of the former occupational groups.[22] It is inappropriate for public policy to stress nonwhite entry into the slowly growing blue-collar occupations at the expense of the occupational groups that in the future will outweigh them in importance.[23]

[20] There are those who anticipate a large increase in the number of jobs in construction as a result of massive federal expenditures on urban redevelopment. Should these expectations come to fruition, many more jobs will be available for blacks in the building trades than previously. This would of course be a welcome addition to nonwhite employment opportunities. Unfortunately, those who put faith in the promises of the federal government regarding housing and urban development are likely to be disappointed if past experience, especially recent experience, is any guide.

[21] George Strauss and Sidney Ingerman, "Public Policy and Discrimination in Apprenticeship," in L. A. Ferman et al., *Negroes and Jobs* (Ann Arbor: University of Michigan Press, 1968), pp. 314–315.

[22] For example, between 1950 and 1970, males employed as professionals, managers, and technicians increased from 20 to 28 percent of all male workers; craftsmen (in all industries) increased from 17 to 19 percent of all male workers. During the 1960s, construction craftsmen declined as a portion of all employed males, while professionals, managers, and technicians rose steadily. *Statistical Abstract of the U.S., 1970* (Washington, D.C., 1971).

[23] There is not necessarily any connection whatsoever between success in integrating the building trades and progress in integrating white-collar or other blue-collar occupations.

Causes of Racial Imbalance in Construction

The racial imbalance that exists in some sectors of the construction industry is a result of a complex and interacting group of factors. For the most part, racial imbalance is not a result of any single cause, whether it be overt racial discrimination by whites or the supposed failure of will or performance of blacks. In general, problems of equal employment opportunity are derived from the heritage of past imbalances, from the failures of school systems, and from employment practices in the industry, including in some cases overt racial discrimination.[24]

Racial Discrimination: The Employers

Overt racial discrimination may occur at the behest of the employer, the union, or both. In construction, employers are subject to a set of attitudes regarding minority group workers that have been widespread in our society. Often social attitudes are buttressed by unfavorable stereotypes of blacks as employees. White employees may be preferred because of their supposedly greater reliability, skill, honesty, and so on. However, employers are largely covered by the provisions of federal, state, and local laws regarding nondiscrimination in employment, so that efforts are generally made to conceal any discrimination.

It is impossible to know the extent of overt discrimination by employers in construction. Many thousands of contractors employ workers, some in a more steady relationship than others. It may well be that racial discrimination is most likely to occur in the small firm and in the presence of relatively stable employment relationships. Such employers are numerous in certain sectors of construction, especially the subtrades in residential, commercial, and public building construction. Larger contractors are more common in industrial, heavy, and road construction and, given the impersonality of many employment relationships, are probably less likely to practice racial discrimination in employment.

In recent years, circumstances have combined to make employment discrimination a risky and potentially expensive exercise for a large employer. Many owners, both public and private, are insisting on extensive efforts by contractors to hire and train (if necessary) minority workmen. Failure to do so to the satisfaction of his client subjects the contractor to penalties varying from harassment to litigation or even blacklisting. While penalties as extreme as blacklisting are rarely employed, the threat is not an idle one, and the pub-

[24]See especially Vernon M. Briggs, Jr., and F. Ray Marshall, *The Negro and Apprenticeship* (Baltimore: Johns Hopkins Press, 1967).

lic notice that generally accompanies charges of racial discrimination can be very damaging to a firm. In addition, conditions in the labor market have increased the contractor's incentive to hire men wherever he can. Manpower shortages occasioned by high levels of construction activity and low aggregate unemployment rates have made minority workers appear a potential source of new mechanics to many contractors. In many areas, there are no more insistent and (in some cases) effective advocates of increased minority participation in the building trades than the employers. Where qualified black mechanics are available, employers' needs for manpower are generally enough to increase hiring. Where training is necessary, the building trades unions have become direct parties to the process.[25]

Racial Discrimination: The Unions

There can be no doubt that elements of the building trades unions have for many years followed overtly discriminatory policies in membership, referral, and training and in some cases continue to do so. Several local unions have been found by courts to have engaged in overt racial discrimination on the basis of evidence so explicit as to require no inference whatever as to the purpose of their behavior.[26] Scholars have condemned the building trades both generally and individually for racial discrimination. Thus, Ray Marshall comments:

The pattern of exclusion in the building trades has been second only to the railroad industry in its rigidity. The craft locals of the . . . IBEW and the . . . UA have had an almost consistent pattern of discrimination throughout the United States.[27]

This situation is not universal, however, nor is it unchanging. In many areas, local unions of both the UA and the IBEW have made efforts to alter

[25]The following statement was made to the 1961 convention of the United Association (plumbers and pipefitters) by G. Allen Briggs, President, National Association of Plumbing Contractors:

"It is these few localized instances which worry us. NAPC is concerned with this matter because it is the contractor — not the union — who will be the first to 'take it on the chin' if and when a case of discrimination is found. If discrimination by a union whose members are used by the contractor on government work is established, then the contractor's government work will be cancelled under the new regulations. We don't relish the idea of being 'knocked off' our jobs, nor do we want to see any of you 'knocked off' because of any discrimination."

"U.A. 28th Convention Proceedings," *United Association Journal* 76 (November 1961): 79.

[26]See, for example, Dobbins v. Electrical Workers (IBEW), Local 212, 58 LC No. 9158 (S.D. Ohio, 1968), amended 61 LC No. 9527 (1969).

[27]F. Ray Marshall, *The Negro and Organized Labor* (New York: John Wiley & Sons, 1965), p. 168.

past practices, often with some degree of success. Other trades have not had
so dismal a record. Thus, Marshall continues:

The Unions in the so-called trowel trades [bricklayers, plasterers, cement
masons] and the Roofers have many Negro members in integrated or virtually
all-Negro locals in the South, but there have been charges of segregation in
the South and other forms of discrimination in many places in the non-South.
Other organizations like the IUOE [operating engineers] and the Teamsters
have had reputations for barring Negroes in some places and accepting them in
others.[28]

The patterns of discrimination and integration vary. In the South, some internationals have maintained segregated locals, often with separate work jurisdictions. The painters, carpenters, and bricklayers, who have had segregated
locals in the South, have recently sought to merge them. In some cases black
locals have balked at merger out of fear of discrimination, loss of identity, or
(in some cases) loss of favorable work arrangements. For the most part, the
bricklayers have had a century-long policy of racial integration and have had
few segregated locals. Carpenters' locals in the South, however, have been
generally segregated until recently.[29]

It has not been a practice of the building trades to include racially exclusive clauses in their international constitutions. Since 1930 more than 22
international unions have at one time formally barred blacks from equal membership. However, most of the unions were railway and maritime brother-
hoods. Only one building trades union (the boilermakers) had such a bar.[30]
Rather, the international unions have often sought to extend equal employment opportunity within the jurisdiction of the union. There have been long
and persistent struggles in most trades between the internationals and recalci-
trant local unions involving issues of racial discrimination.[31] The international
officers have usually been more sensitive than local officers to public opinion
regarding racial discrimination and less sensitive to the desires of the mem-

---

[28]*Ibid.,* p. 169. Marshall's general conclusions are of interest:
"There is ample evidence of discrimination against Negroes by unions, but it would be
false to allege either that there has not been a significant lowering of racial barriers in
unions in the past thirty years, or that the union movement has not made significant
contributions to the Negro's welfare" (p. 183).
[29]See *ibid.,* pp. 170 ff., for a discussion of these questions.
[30]See F. Ray Marshall, "Union Racial Practices," hearings before the U.S. Senate Committee on Labor and the Public Welfare, Subcommittee on Employment and Manpower,
September 10, 1963, reprinted in Herbert R. Northrup and R.L. Rowan, eds., *The Negro
and Employment Opportunity* (Ann Arbor: University of Michigan Press, 1964), pp. 167–
185
[31]See Marshall, *The Negro and Organized Labor,* pp. 111, 169, for a discussion of such
matters involving the Bricklayers, the UA, and the Carpenters.

bership of certain locals. In consequence, the internationals have exercised a constructive influence on the locals for several decades regarding racial policies. However, they normally lack either the authority or the power to dictate membership policies to the local unions. The limited influence of an international president must be used for many purposes, and racial discrimination is only one of a host of problems he may confront. For these reasons, local policies of racial exclusion may persist in the face of strong international policy in the other direction and in spite of efforts by the national leadership to eliminate them.[32]

Racial discrimination in the building trades arises out of the sentiments of union membership, not, in most cases, from the desires and practices of its leadership.[33] The local unions are among the most democratic in the labor movement and among the most cohesive.[34] The root causes of exclusionary practices lie in the attitudes and behavior of the union membership and must be examined in that light.

It is possible to speculate on the sources of racial discrimination among the construction work force where such attitudes exist. Presumably, they originate outside the industry and are then reflected in its practices. In this sense, the problem has its origins in the wider context of the society. But characteristics somewhat peculiar to the industry are also relevant. The entrance of blacks (or other workers, for that matter) to the work force may threaten the job opportunities of current journeymen. In construction, this threat is more prominent than in industries characterized by more stable employment relationships. While the fear of expanding the work force extends in some degree to all potential applicants regardless of race, it is also clear that this fear reinforces racial prejudices and creates a set of attitudes peculiarly difficult to modify. Union leadership often spends considerable efforts attempting to dispel such fears by indicating that the magnitude of the inflow of minority workers is likely to be small, that job opportunities are plentiful

[32]See Gus Tyler, "Contemporary Labor's Attitude toward the Negro," in Julius Jacobson, *The Negro and the American Labor Movement* (New York: Doubleday, 1968), pp. 363–364:
"The policy of the AFL-CIO is to create a consensus on civil rights policy by (1) avoiding expulsion of national unions where discrimination exists; (2) passing legislation for fair employment to include union practices; (3) putting pressure on affiliates through the civil rights committee of the Federation; (4) setting an example through the statements and acts of national . . . labor bodies; and (5) involving local unions in action for civil rights."
[33]See Derek C. Bok and John T. Dunlop, *Labor and the American Community* (New York: Simon & Schuster, 1970), pp. 134–136.
[34]See George A. Strauss, "Controls by the Membership in Building Trades Unions," *American Journal of Sociology* 61 (May 1956): 527–535.

(if they are), and so on. Attempts by the leadership to play down the importance of integration are largely motivated by a desire to defuse a dangerous
situation. Thus, President Schoemann of the UA said in 1966 to the international convention that "members of minority groups will come into our
local unions in gradually increasing numbers; there will be no great flap about
it; life will go on as it has in the past."[35]

Ironically, the threats that minority groups pose to the job opportunities
of members of some trades are best answered not by exclusion but by organization. Where large numbers of skilled or semiskilled nonunion craftsmen exist, they pose a potential threat to the business of the union contractor
and to the conditions of the union mechanic. The response of local unions to
such threats may be of several sorts, some favorable to racial integration,
others not. The union may attempt to organize a nonunion contractor
and offer to accept whatever number of his employees he desires to retain on
his payroll in lieu of current union men. Often this is a small number, and
nonunion men are organized out of a job, so to speak. Conversely, the union
may organize the nonunion men and attempt to control the labor supply, not
the jobs. Such a strategy is sometimes favorable to minority mechanics, especially in the South. The attempts by painters, carpenters, and bricklayers,
especially, to organize homebuilding mechanics, if pursued effectively, will
tend to increase the number of minority mechanics in these unions in areas
in which large numbers of minority workers are employed.[36]

The difficulty that the union as an institution (including both national and
local leadership) has in dealing with problems of racial discrimination must
not be overlooked or minimized. Union leadership is elected leadership and
may be dismissed. Where the social prejudices and economic fears of union
membership interact, a very difficult, almost intractable problem is created
for union leadership. Only sustained education of the members and progress
at a largely nonthreatening rate can be effective in this context, regardless of
the pressures brought to bear from inside or outside the union. In the extreme case, only extensive litigation and the compulsion of federal court

[35] "U.A. 29th Convention Proceedings," *United Association Journal* 78 (November 1966):
62.
[36] There is very little competition in the mechanical trades from nonunion minority
workers for commercial and industrial construction work, the heart of the mechanical
sector of the industry. In the trowel trades, in painting, roofing, and in other trades, the
opposite is true. There are historical and technological reasons for this situation, but its
impact is to make the exclusionary response to threats from nonunion mechanics more
successful in the mechanical trades than in other crafts.

orders may finally break a really racalcitrant local. Fortunately, few locals have adopted so unbending a position.

Assertions have been made that craft unions by their nature are more racially discriminatory than industrial unions.[37] Normally, these arguments rest on the craft unions' supposed control of the labor supply in the occupation involved.[38] Industrial unions, conversely, are said to have welcomed blacks as members and to have fought for racial equality. Yet some authors have begun to recognize that there has been racial discrimination by industrial unions also, though it has expressed itself differently than in the craft unions.[39] Further, it is increasingly clear that racial discrimination is less a function of the character of the union than of the occupation and area involved. Craft unions of the unskilled (for example, the laborers) and of some of the skilled trades (for example, bricklayers, roofers, and cement masons) have large minority memberships. Other craft unions have few minority members. Most industrial unions have very few minority members in the skilled trades.

Nevertheless, construction unions differ in important ways from other unions, more because of the casual nature of employment in the industry than because of their craft structure. Discrimination tends to occur, therefore, in the hiring and training aspects of the employment relationship rather than in transfers, promotions, and layoffs, which are affected by industrial seniority systems. It is perhaps poor comfort to those discriminated against, but comfort nonetheless, that employment in construction offers new entrants far fewer barriers to advancement to supervisory positions and to continued employment in the face of declining business than do the seniority systems of industrial employment.

Social and Educational Patterns

It has not proved a simple task to recruit or retain minority group workers for training or journeyman's work in construction. There have been large numbers of applicants or potential applicants who have been screened out by

[37]". . . the craft unions generally have supported the practices of racial discrimination. . . . Quite different from the policy of craft unions . . . has been that of industrial unions." Sumner H. Slichter, J. J. Healy, and E. R. Livernash, *The Impact of Collective Bargaining on Management* (Washington: Brookings Institution, 1960), pp. 37–38.
[38]See Marshall, *The Negro and Organized Labor,* p. 173: "Craft unions influence job opportunities for Negroes by controlling entry into the labor market through closed-union, closed-shop conditions, job referral systems, apprenticeship programs, and pressure on employers to have or not to have Negroes."
[39]"Industrial unions affect job opportunities through control of hiring, transfer, promotion and layoffs." *Ibid.*

one qualification device or another and large numbers who have screened themselves out. This situation has led to extensive discussions about whether the applicable standards are themselves just and appropriate. Unfortunately, it is not always possible to know in advance which standards are the ones that will be exclusionary. In some cases, one set of standards has been waived only to reveal that recruitment is no less difficult or that retention of the new recruits is very low.

Regardless of the propriety of particular criteria of selection, a larger proportion of minority group youth than white youth fails to pass standards of an apparently objective nature. For example, requirements for apprenticeship such as a high school diploma, absence of a criminal record, and the passing of a competitive test in arithmetic and verbal skills will screen out large numbers of minority group applicants. Public commissions and industry bodies that have conducted searches for minority group apprentices and journeymen have often found that potential applicants were functionally illiterate or unfamiliar with concepts basic to any trade (such as standards of measurement).[40] In consequence, many programs have continued to operate with low levels of minority group participation.

There is no clear consensus on the origin of the educational deficiencies of large numbers of minority group members, nor is this the place to seek one. Kenneth Clark blames the public schools for failing to educate youth in the ghetto.[41] Whatever the cause, large numbers of minority group youth are unprepared for introduction into formal training programs without extensive revision of the nature of these programs. On the whole, construction training programs have assumed a degree of success on the part of the public school system and are not currently capable of providing enrollees with extensive remedial education.

This is not to say that there are not many persons in the minority community who are fully capable of entering and succeeding in training and employment on the same basis as anyone else. This happens often. Apprenticeship outreach programs have as their premise the existence of such a group, and they have had considerable success. Further, relaxation of certain selection

[40]See, for example, the description of the interviews held by the Rodgers Committee in New York City in Briggs and Marshall, *The Negro and Apprenticeship*, pp. 31–34.
[41]"These children, by and large, do not learn because they are not being taught effectively, and they are not being taught because those who are charged with the responsibility of teaching them do not believe they can learn, do not expect that they can learn, and do not act toward them in ways which help them to learn." Kenneth B. Clark, *Dark Ghetto: Dilemmas of Social Power* (New York: Harper & Row, 1965), p. 132.

standards for programs (age limitations, for example) often enlarges the effective number of persons available for training. In fact, the more common situation may well be the one that the outreach programs envision: "The average unemployed or underemployed black ghetto resident is not 'hardcore'. . . . Our study confirmed that, given the opportunity, blacks can enter construction work the same way whites do and learn as readily as do other men."[42] Nevertheless, considerable problems and difficulties have arisen with respect to those persons unable to meet training standards.

Similarly, problems of turnover have often been serious in special programs to employ minority group workers on construction jobs. Many blacks have been employed on projects as a result of civil rights agitation only to quit the job soon thereafter. The reasons for voluntary quitting range from dislike or unfamiliarity with the work to personality problems. But the relative lack of a tradition of craft work in the minority community may also play a part, as well as weak adaptation to industrial work discipline.[43]

Often, persons are recruited for training or journeyman work from the black community who have little attachment to the building industry and who develop very little attachment. These persons are sometimes engaged in illicit or secondary activities of many different types, involving only brief periods of regular employment.[44] The experience of contractors and unions with such persons has been unfavorable and has made the process of recruiting and training stable employees more difficult.

In sum, the social and educational characteristics of many minority group members are such as to require extensive revisions in selection and training procedures if they are to enter construction employment successfully. This circumstance adds a set of factors to the problem of achieving racial balance that is clearly not a result of overt discrimination in the industry and that must be dealt with constructively and effectively if a better racial balance is to be obtained.

Labor Market Factors

Increasing the number of minority group workers in construction is often

[42] A. L. Nellum and Associates, "Manpower and Rebuilding," report prepared for the U.S. Department of Housing and Urban Development (Washington, D.C., 1969).
[43] See Michael J. Piore, "On-the-Job Training in the Dual Labor Market: Public and Private Responsibilities in On-the-Job Training of Disadvantaged Workers," M.I.T. Department of Economics Working Paper no. 23, mimeo (Cambridge, 1968). "The ghetto labor force is the latest of successive waves of migrants from agriculture to the industrial sector, and its relative proximity to agricultural antecedents may be the root cause of the problem" (p. 28).
[44] See *ibid.* for a description of "secondary" labor markets and street life in the ghetto.

complicated by factors that do not at first seem of major importance but increase the difficulty and cost of recruitment and retention. First, minority group members often have little or no tradition of work at building trades and thereby lack familiarity with the nature of the business and its institutions. There is in many cases a reluctance to consider employment at the trades as a feasible method of earning a livelihood.[45] Further, young persons have little opportunity, except in a few trades, to become acquainted with the rudiments of a craft from journeymen in the area. To a large degree, these conditions are the heritage of past discrimination, but they also stem from the recent migration of many blacks from the agricultural South to the cities of the North and West. Because few blacks come to building industry programs on their own initiative or through the referral of their associates, it may be necessary to employ extensive recruitment efforts in order to attract them.

Second, the residential concentration of minority persons in central city areas in the North and West creates transportation problems and problems related to preferred work locales. It is often difficult to commute from center-city neighborhoods to building jobs on the periphery of a metropolitan area, although in some cities this is far less of a problem than in others. (In addition, building trades wages, when work is available, are adequate to allow a man to obtain automobile transportation.) In many cases, minority mechanics, like other workers, prefer jobs near their residence and will refuse more distant work. Because of this, ensuring the employment of any particular portion of minority group members on projects widely distributed in a metropolitan area can be difficult. Furthermore, the geographic jurisdiction of local unions is very different among the building trades. Local unions of the operating engineers, iron workers, and boilermakers may cover very large areas, often including several states. When there is no tradition of worker mobility, as in some sections of the black community, it is difficult to retain minority workers in the trade. Similar problems exist in large sections of the white community also, of course.

Third, economic conditions in the building industry affect the feasibility

---

[45]The California Advisory Committee to the U.S. Commission on Civil Rights notes "a general misconception [among blacks] of apprenticeship as something to which only the intellectually inadequate are to be relegated." U.S. Commission on Civil Rights Advisory Committee, *Reports on Apprenticeship* (Washington, D.C., 1964), p. 26. See also "Negroes in Apprenticeship, New York State," *Monthly Labor Review* 83 (September 1960): 955 (the report of a study of black apprenticeship by the New York State Commission against Discrimination).

of introducing new men to the work force. When journeymen are unemployed, it is of course difficult to find employment for trainees or new entrants to the labor force. The seasonal downturn in construction is a complicating factor in several ways. It makes it difficult to increase the hiring and training of blacks during the winter because of the availability of journeymen for jobs. Not only is there resentment from the unemployed work force, but employers prefer to hire fully qualified mechanics than others at the same rate of pay. In addition, the seasonal downturn reinforces concern for job availability in the existing work force, making its members reluctant to assist in increasing the labor supply. Finally, seasonal unemployment is as unattractive to minority mechanics as to whites, and many nonwhite journeymen and apprentices lose their jobs and leave the industry permanently in the winter months.

Construction is not only seasonal in nature but is also highly volatile in terms of the aggregate level of work opportunities. Building booms often dissipate rapidly, and programs to increase minority employment may founder with the lack of jobs.

The instability of employment is alleviated in some measure by the absence of seniority systems in layoffs and hires. In consequence, new entrants to the labor force who are good workers are as likely to be employed in poor seasons as any other workers in the industry.

Discrimination by Default

The result of the interaction of past and present discrimination, of educational and social characteristics, and of unfavorable labor market conditions is that minority group workers cannot be expected to respond in large numbers to employment opportunities in construction without special efforts by the industry. This is an unpalatable statement to some, and an excuse for failure to others, but it is a fact. In this context, the degree of progress in integrating many trades will depend primarily on the strength of their efforts to increase minority participation. In the absence of such efforts, there will be little progress in many areas of the country.

Theodore Kheel participated in an effort of Local 3 of the IBEW (New York City) in 1962 to recruit black apprentices. An extensive recruitment effort resulted in a class of 1020 apprentices, 300 of whom were either blacks (260) or Puerto Ricans (40). In November 1967, 790 apprentices graduated, 125 of whom were blacks. Reflecting upon the successful conclusion of Local 3's efforts, Kheel commented, "Since access to such jobs comes largely through the ancient apprenticeship system, the craft unions and their leadership are chargeable with 'discrimination by default' — with the failure to seek out and recruit potential apprentices among the minority community.[46]

Local 3's efforts have not been the only effective attempts by building trades unions to recruit and train minority group apprentices. In some 25 cities, local building and construction trades councils operate apprentice outreach programs funded by the federal government. These have been among the most effective such programs operated and in several cases have considerably exceeded the goals for placement established in conjunction with Labor Department funding. Many individual local unions have actively sought minority group mechanics and have brought them into the mainstream of construction activity. Other locals have often seemed content to let their fellow craft unions carry the burden of outreach and training, without doing their part.

There is really no substitute for the positive action of contractors and unions to increase minority participation in the industry. Unfortunately, there has been far less such activity than is warranted and than would be in the best interests of the industry. It is very difficult to compel unions and contractors by law or pressure, to assist imaginatively in recruitment and training efforts. They must be persuaded to do so, both by each other and by persons outside the industry. Where there is enthusiastic industry cooperation, a great deal can usually be accomplished. Where the industry is reluctant to be of assistance or is indifferent, progress is slow and halting at best.

Improving Racial Balance in Construction

Enforcing Compliance with Equal Employment Opportunity Clauses in Construction Contracts and with Title VII of the Civil Rights Act of 1964

Legal efforts to place a greater number of minority group persons on construction jobs have normally taken two routes. The first has been the introduction into the "General Provisions" sections of construction contracts of a clause or group of clauses requiring the contractor and his subcontractor to take steps to assure equal employment opportunity on the project. Both private and public owners have placed such clauses in construction contracts, but the greatest degree of imagination — if not success — has surrounded the efforts of the federal government. Essentially, the federal government has

---

[46]Theodore W. Kheel, "Increasing Employment Opportunity in the Printing and Electrical Trades," in Northrup and Rowan, *The Negro and Employment Opportunity*, p. 195.

attempted to require contractors, by the terms of construction contracts on federal and federally assisted construction jobs, to take affirmative action to place nonwhites on such jobs. What affirmative action is to consist of has not, at this writing, been finally determined.

Second, the enactment of Title VII of the Civil Rights Act of 1964 has provided a means by which government agencies may respond to complaints of racial discrimination in employment and, through the Department of Justice, may institute proceedings in federal court against those accused of violating the law. As a result, there has been a large volume of complaints and legal actions alleging racial discrimination filed against contractors and building trades unions. In addition, there has been considerable litigation arising out of charges against contractors and unions for violation of state fair employment practices laws.

In several of these cases, labor organizations have been found guilty of racial discrimination (including "pattern of discrimination" charges under Title VII), and courts have taken the membership, job referral, and apprenticeship training practices of the local union and contractors under extensive review. For example, Local 53 of the Asbestos Workers (New Orleans) was charged by the Justice Department on December 15, 1966, with a pattern and practice of discrimination. The U.S. District Court entered an injunction against the union on May 31, 1967, and the injunction was upheld by the Fifth Circuit Court of Appeals on January 15, 1969. The injunction issued was intended not only to rectify Local 53's discrimination against certain individuals but also to require affirmative action to prevent further racial discrimination.

The injunction prohibits discrimination in excluding persons from union membership or referring persons for work; prohibits use of members' endorsements, family relationship or elections as criteria for membership; ordered that four individuals be admitted to membership and nine others be referred to work; ordered the development of objective membership criteria and prohibited new members other than the four until developed; and ordered continuation of chronological referrals for work, with alternating white and Negro referrals until objective membership criteria are developed.[47]

The injunction has been successful in eliminating the pattern of racial exclusion practiced by Local 53; it has been far less successful in achieving a reasonable racial balance in the membership of the union. By the terms of

---

[47] At the time of the commencement of the suit there were 1200 men working in Local 53's jurisdiction, of whom 282 were members of the local; the others were on permit. Asbestos Workers, Local 53 v. Vogler, 59 LC No. 9195 (5th Cir. 1969).

the order, 1.4 percent of the membership of the local became black. Since that period, the percentage has increased very little. What is required to achieve racial balance is an affirmative outreach, recruitment, and training program in which the union and contractors are active and willing to participate.

A much more extensive injunction has been issued by the U.S. District Court of the Southern District of Indiana against Local 73 of the United Association (plumbers).[48] The union was found to be guilty of a pattern of racial discrimination and has been ordered by the court to perform 26 separate actions to remedy the discrimination, including actions related to membership in the local, referral to jobs, and apprenticeship. The effect of the court order is to establish objective criteria for membership, referral, and apprenticeship and to require the union and contractors to inform the minority community of these criteria and enforce them fairly. Again, it may be anticipated that the court order will result in the entrance of a few[49] minority group mechanics to the plumbers' trade and its apprenticeship programs. The numbers will not be large, however, and the court is unable, even if it so desired, to compel the local to seek and train minority group members with the effort and imagination that a significant expansion of minority group entry to construction would require.

There have, of course, been cases in which a local union, under pressure from the courts, has begun by reluctantly accepting a few black members and has then gone on to increase its minority membership significantly.[50] In circumstances of this nature, it appears that court action may break a pattern of discrimination, opening the way to considerable progress. Nevertheless, there have been few cases of this kind, and those in which there has been improvement have been predicated on the availability to the union of a program of recruitment and training effectively utilized by other trades in the area.[51] Despite the importance of court action in cases of continuing racial

---

[48] U.S. v. Plumbing and Pipefitting Industry, Local 73, 61 LC No. 9329 (S.D. Ind. 1969).
[49] The court mentioned 30 to 35 black plumbers licensed by the City of Indianapolis and allowed the union to retain its requirement that an applicant for membership have a city license. *Ibid.*
[50] This has been the outcome of the several years of litigation (beginning in late 1962) involving Sheet Metal Workers Local 28 in New York City. See Vernon M. Briggs, Jr., and F. Ray Marshall, *Equal Apprenticeship Opportunities* (Ann Arbor: University of Michigan – Wayne State University Institute of Labor and Industrial Relations, 1968), pp. 34–35.
[51] In the New York City Sheet Metal Workers case, the union has recruited blacks only through the apprenticeship route. No minority person has qualified for journeyman

discrimination, such legal action is very limited in its ability to achieve a large increase in minority participation in some trades. Outreach and training must still be performed with the cooperation of the union, contractors, and minority groups. Court action may assist in setting the stage for such cooperation; it cannot ensure it.

Contract compliance efforts are often made difficult by the general un-availability[52] in the major metropolitan areas of qualified nonwhite mechanics in many of the skilled trades.[53] The effectiveness of contract compliance efforts in actually putting nonwhite mechanics on jobs depends, of course, on their availability. Most compliance efforts have not provided mechanisms by which nonwhites could be recruited and trained other than those operating in the industry generally, nor is contract compliance an effective tool for developing such programs. Compliance can require a contractor and his subcontractors to participate actively in efforts to recruit and train nonwhites if such efforts are under way. But to require training programs that apply to only one or a group of jobs and that do not extend throughout the jurisdiction of the union involved is an ineffective means of increasing entry to the trades.

Recruitment and Training Programs for Minority Workers

In construction, manpower training and hiring and industrial relations are all organized on an areawide rather than on a project basis. Recruitment and training programs for minority workers must also be organized on an area-wide basis if there is to be a rapid increase in the pool of minority workers available for jobs in all crafts in the industry.

For a variety of reasons,[54] effective training programs in contract construction must involve the following characteristics. First, the majority of training must take place on the job. (This applies to virtually all crafts, with very few exceptions.) Construction craft work is best learned by experience,

---

status without serving his apprenticeship in the local, despite the review of the union's membership policies by the state courts. Nonwhite apprentices have been recruited largely through the efforts of the Workers' Defense League preapprenticeship training program in New York, established to serve the entire construction industry in the city. *Ibid.* Other cases of interest in the relationship of building trades locals to nonwhite mechanics include Lewis v. Ironworkers, Local 86, 61 LC No. 9364 (Wash. 1969); Central Contractors Assoc. v. Electrical Workers, Local 46, 61 LC No. 9347 (W. D. Wash. 1969); Dobbins v. Electrical Workers (IBEW), Local 212; Sheet Metal Workers, Local 36, 416 F. 2d 123 (8th Cir. 1969).

[52] Except among some trades in a few areas.

[53] "Qualified" is used here to mean only that the contractor is willing to employ the mechanic at the journeyman wage scale negotiated by the craft involved.

[54] See Chapter 7 for a detailed discussion of methods of formal training in construction.

in part because judgment in performing tasks under a variety of conditions is
an essential element of productivity. Second, there must be some training in
the theoretical aspects of a trade, which may be provided in a formal schooling environment. Third, provision must be made to supply the persons in
training with a degree of continuity of employment. In construction employment the jobsite shifts constantly, and workers must often shift employers as
well. For training to be effective, the person in training must be working, and
this may require the ability to shift employers and jobsites. Fourth, provision
should be made for a wage scale starting below the journeyman's rate and
advancing with the length of employment and skill of the applicant. Where
persons in training have received the full journeyman's scale, many unfortunate consequences have resulted, including resentment by fully qualified
mechanics at the equal rates given persons in training, lack of incentive for
the person in training to improve his skills by diligent effort, and upward
pressure on journeymen's wage scales caused by divorcing wages from productivity (in the training categories).

There are major shortcomings with regard to a project-by-project approach
to training similar to that envisioned in many contract compliance efforts.
It is very difficult to achieve two of the principles of an effective training
program with a project approach. First, providing continuity of employment
to persons in training may be very difficult. Even on large-scale jobs, particular crafts or contractors may be involved at the site for only relatively brief
periods (such as a few months) and then often only intermittently (that is, a
few days each week). Ensuring the person in training a full week's employment
and work at the craft after completion of the particular project may be very
difficult. Shifting him to another project covered by the plan may involve a
shift of employers and a loss of work during the transition that would be
largely avoidable were all jobs in an area covered by the program. Second,
achieving a less-than-journeyman rate for persons in training on a project-by-
project basis is very difficult, since such a rate requires either modification of
relevant collective bargaining agreements between contractors and unions
(normally the contractor will already be bound to an areawide set of wage
classifications and rates which will be difficult if not impossible to alter on a
project basis), or congressional action to modify the Davis-Bacon Act (where
federal funds are involved in the relevant projects), or perhaps both of the
foregoing.

The peculiar characteristics of construction jobs have led to the development of unique methods of training in which the role of labor organizations

in the training process is relatively great. Because training on a project basis is both inefficient and generally ineffective, most formal training programs (including apprenticeship) cover the entire geographic jurisdiction of a local union, along with all union contractors. Such areawide training programs can be designed to realize all four principles of successful training.

Apprenticeship programs have been adapted in several ways to the necessity of recruiting and training increasing numbers of blacks. Most importantly, programs have been set up to recruit and tutor nonwhites so that they may pass entrance examinations and other standards of admission. By 1971, more than 70 cities had outreach programs of this kind funded by the federal government and modeled after the Workers Defense League—A. Philip Randolph Educational Fund Joint Apprenticeship Program in New York City.[55]

Other federally funded programs have been established to train minority youths for several months prior to starting as an apprentice. These programs are distinguished from the WDL-type approach in that training in rudiments of the trade is provided, whereas the WDL concentrates solely on preparing persons to pass apprenticeship entrance requirements. In the normal situation, the job training component of the apprenticeship preparation need be only very limited.

In the future, it is possible that the opening of apprenticeship opportunities to nonwhites will itself serve as a stimulus to many nonwhite youths to complete high school and prepare themselves to meet the formal standards of apprenticeship as now established. At the present time, however, standards of selection that often require a high school diploma, several years' local residence, limited age ranges (normally 18 to 25), and passing of written exams in verbal and mathematical skills exclude many nonwhites,[56] even though they are objectively applied. As a consequence, many unions have in effect reduced their standards of admission and have exerted special efforts to recruit and retain nonwhite apprentices. Many union members feel that these practices are a threat to the integrity of the existing apprenticeship programs and perhaps constitute a fraud upon the nonwhite community. In the former case, the argument is that other apprentices will resent it if special provisions are made in apprenticeship training for those who are less qualified. In the latter

[55] For a description and evaluation of the Workers Defense League Program in New York and other cities, see Edward C. Pinkus, "The Workers Defense League," in P.B. Doeringer, ed., *Programs to Employ the Disadvantaged* (Englewood Cliffs, N.J.: Prentice-Hall, 1969), pp. 168–203. See also Briggs and Marshall, *Equal Apprenticeship Opportunities*.

[56] Requirements vary greatly among the trades and in different cities.

case, there is the fear that the less qualified may never become fully qualified journeymen and may not be able to obtain work on a continuing basis in the industry. There is no solid evidence to evaluate the validity of these objections at the moment. Nonetheless, in some cases where nonwhites have been accepted into apprenticeship programs without full qualifications, resentment has been minor and performance acceptable; in others, there have been difficulties.

Because of the incapacity of apprenticeship programs to provide entry to the industry in the numbers demanded by public opinion, and in some cases by public policy, special training efforts have been established in some trades and in some areas. Both the Model Cities Act of 1966 and the Housing Act of 1968 include requirements that residents of the areas affected be involved in construction carried out under the programs. Thus, Section 103 of Title I of the Demonstration Cities and Metropolitan Development Act of 1966 requires the Secretary of Housing and Urban Development to "emphasize local initiative in the planning, development and implementation of comprehensive city demonstration programs." Similarly, Section 3 of the Housing and Urban Development Act of 1968 instructs the Secretary of Housing and Urban Development to

. . . require, in consultation with the Secretary of Labor, that to the greatest extent feasible opportunities for training and employment arising in connection with the planning, construction, rehabilitation, and operation of housing assisted under such programs be given to lower income persons residing in the area of such housing.

In response to these statutory requirements, union contractors and unions sought to design a mechanism by which residents of the affected areas might receive training and work, as required, on the construction to be done in the areas in which they reside. Negotiations were conducted in 1967–1968 at the national level among international unions and contractor associations regarding an agreement to cover area residents as trainees. These negotiations were terminated in the spring of 1968. At that time, the Building and Construction Trades Department of the AFL-CIO issued a policy statement providing their local affiliates with guidelines for the negotiation of such agreements. In 1970, multitrade, areawide agreements in Chicago, Boston, and other cities were negotiated (in some cases with representatives of the black community as a third party to the agreements), based in part on these guidelines and on other policy statements issued more recently.

The essential provisions of the multitrade, metropolitan-area plans are the following:

1.

Recruitment of residents of the area for construction jobs without regard to age, education, or similar qualifications.

2.

Fully qualified mechanics to be placed on jobs at the union scale.

3.

Partially skilled mechanics to be placed on jobs as "advanced journeyman trainees," at a rate below the journeyman scale.

4.

Placement of the unskilled on jobs as "trainees" at not less than the starting apprentice rate in the craft to which they are assigned.

5.

The agreement is to be administered by two committees: a general administrative committee and an operations committee specific to each craft.

6.

The purpose of the program is "to develop fully qualified and competent craft union journeymen."[57]

In many areas, it has proved valuable to associate training programs with outreach and tutoring efforts provided by WDL-type projects. They are normally staffed by persons from the minority community, who can ensure more community support and assistance to the training program than would otherwise be possible.

Finally, many branches of the industry established training programs of one kind or another in conjunction with the federal government which were neither apprenticeship nor formal areawide nonapprenticeship efforts.[58] The most important of them were on-the-job training programs negotiated between national unions or contractor associations and the Labor Department. In toto, these programs involved millions of dollars and several thousand trainees. National programs were negotiated by the government with the Laborers, Plasterers and Cement Masons, Carpenters, Operating Engineers, Bricklayers, Plumbers and Pipefitters, and Ironworkers, among the international unions; the National Association of Home Builders and the Associated

[57]"Policy Statement and Guidelines for Special Local Agreements on Rehabilitation and Related Housing Construction Work in the Model Cities Programs," Building and Construction Trades Department, AFL-CIO, July 16, 1968.
[58]For example, Project Upgrade in Oakland, California, and Project Justice in Buffalo, New York

General Contractors, among the employees; and the National Joint Painting and Decorating Apprenticeship and Training Committee.[59]

Contracts for training were also awarded to individual employers in several trades under the JOBS program. Unfortunately, training contracts with individual employers make very little sense in construction because of the difficulty of providing continuity of training and a wide range of tasks for the trainee to learn. These contracts were very expensive in terms of cost per trainee. Generally, they were awarded for training laborers and carpenters, trades in which minority participation is high. There seems little justification for these training contracts. Federal support for training programs in construction should be awarded only to responsible employers' associations or unions, and the cost per trainee of the programs should bear a reasonable relationship to the actual cost of training and to its potential benefits to the individual. Wherever possible, public funds should cover costs of recruitment, instruction, and administration only and not supplement trainees' earnings on the job.

Informal Training

Apprenticeship is not the only route of entry to the skilled trades, and it does not have the same importance in all trades. Apprenticeship is, however, the major route of entry to the mechanical trades in large metropolitan areas and has been so for many years. The other major route to union membership in the mechanical trades is through organization of nonunion contractors and their work forces. Normally, only nonunion mechanics with sufficient skill to earn the union wage rate are retained by the contractor and are accepted into the union. In other trades and areas, entry through the permit system or by contractors hiring from the street is common. In some unions, especially the carpenters, painters, roofers, cement finishers, and laborers, turnover among the membership is relatively rapid, and entry in many years is largely outside of any apprenticeship program.

For the most part, entrance to the trades through organization, hiring by contractors off the street, and so on, is available only to qualified journeymen. Many blacks have availed themselves of this avenue. Many more whites have also used it. However, as a mechanism to integrate the trades, informal entry has two major limitations. First, it applies primarily in trades that already

---

[59] U.S. President, *Second Annual Report on National Housing Goals* (Washington, D.C., 1970), pp. 146–148.

have a better balance of nonwhite employment than others. Second, informal entry requires a high degree of skill at the trade, often picked up in suburban areas on housing work. Informal entry generally originates in sectors of the industry that, although nonunion, are nevertheless not frequented by nonwhite craftsmen. Where informal entry routes are operated in an overtly racially discriminatory fashion, they are subject to challenge in the courts and have been so challenged.[60] But informal entry routes do not provide a mechanism that can offer training to many nonwhite entrants to the industry.

Assistance to Black Contractors

Black contractors have an important role in integrating the building trades.[61] For several reasons, black contractors may be expected to employ a larger proportion of nonwhites than white contractors, although the evidence on this point is mixed. There is little indication, for example, that in the North and East the bigger black contractors employ a large number of nonwhite mechanics. Rather, they draw on the same labor pools as their white counterparts, preferring to employ the best-qualified men they can obtain, and they normally concentrate their energies more on the business and financial aspects of their operations than upon integrating the building trades work force. Contractors generally devote as little attention as possible to personnel and manpower problems, and black contractors are no exception.

There are, however, numerous small nonwhite contractors in urban areas doing residential rehabilitation and repair work. In many cases, these contractors employ one or two persons to assist them on jobs. Often, the contractor is licensed himself (especially in the mechanical trades). There are also larger black contractors, union as well as nonunion, operating primarily in the black community or in suburban areas. The enlargement of the size of these businesses and their incorporation into the mainstream of contruction will help to bring nonwhite mechanics into the trades.

It would be erroneous, however, to expect much numerically from the organization by unions of black contractors. Often the nonunion contractor will have been paying his men well below the union scale and will be unwilling to raise their pay. Rather, he will seek to obtain union craftsmen from the hiring hall because of their greater productivity. The union will customarily agree to accept as members those persons on the contractor's labor force

[60]See Dobbins v. Electrical Workers (IBEW), Local 212.
[61]In the interest of public policy, it may be desirable to assist the enterprises of black contractors for other reasons than their potential impact on integrating the labor force of the construction industry.

whom he wishes to continue to employ, at union wages, after he signs the labor agreement. But the contractor will not normally wish to keep his less productive men, regardless of their color, and is likely to let many of them go. There have been many instances in this country of unions seeking to organize larger nonwhite contractors, in part because of the attraction of their nonwhite work force, only to find that the contractor insists on replacing his old employees with the current union work force. Therefore, in most of the country a quick way to increase racial integration of the trades is not available through the organization by unions of the nonwhite employees of minority contractors. The necessity for training or upgrading of nonwhite mechanics, where large numbers of entrants are desired, continues.

Black contractors can, of course, play a significant role in attracting black craftsmen to the industry. Many problems of racial discrimination or fear of discrimination may be alleviated by the existence of black contractors. Further, black employers may have better informal access to minority persons who may be recruited for construction jobs. The fact that there will be no immediate and dramatic improvement in racial integration in the trades does not obviate the need for efforts directed at a long-term solution to these problems.

There are several ways through which the building industry can assist black contractors in improving their business position. Alternative mechanisms for performing this function are being experimented with in many areas, some with the assistance of public funds. While it is too much to expect of contractors that they assist the growth and improvement of their competitors' or potential competitors' businesses, many contractors and their associations are nonetheless providing assistance to minority contractors.

There are three primary types of assistance that other contractors and owners could provide to black contractors seeking to enter or expand in construction. First, assistance could be provided in the provision of surety (bonding) to the owner for the contractor's performance on the job. Second, capital could be provided to the business. Third, technical assistance in the estimation and bidding of jobs is of the utmost importance. Good estimators are crucial to a contractor's success. The contractor must bid a job low enough to get the award but high enough to cover his costs and make money. To determine an appropriate bid is the estimator's function. Recognition of the primacy of this function is critical. Technical assistance should also include assistance in methods of managing a business, including bookkeeping, scheduling of work, cost-control, and so forth.

Surety is normally required of a contractor on public and many private construction jobs as a condition of the awarding of a contract. Surety is not an insurance system but a third-party obligation. It is essentially the cosigning of an obligation. The surety company obligates itself, in the event the contractor fails to perform, to fulfill his contract (by engaging some other contractor). In addition to this "performance bond," a payment may also be required, by which the surety absorbs the contractor's liability to his workmen, materials suppliers, and subcontractors.

Because of the nature of surety, the company providing the bonds is extremely careful in agreeing to provide surety for a contractor. The surety normally evaluates three aspects of a contractor's operation in deciding whether or not to bond:

1.
Financial. Does the contractor have the necessary capitalization to do the job?
2.
Technical capacity. Does the contractor have the past experience to handle a job of the size and type contemplated? Sureties will very rarely agree to support contractors in a sudden dramatic increase in the size of jobs performed. Big jobs require considerable technical competence.
3.
Business management. Does the contractor have adequate cost control, a proper accounting procedure, and a good accountant?

Only if the contractor can satisfy the surety of his capacity and reliability in these several aspects of his business will he be bonded.[62] Normally, a big contractor will have an established relation with a surety in which financial statements, balance sheets, and so on are made continually available to the surety. Many small minority contractors have no business history of this nature. Often they are unable to substantiate on paper earlier jobs successfully completed.

Financial support is an important part of a business operation, and several federal and other programs have been directed at providing working capital to contractors. Yet important as capital is, technical assistance in the operation of the business is more critical.

Established contractors must provide the technical assistance. It may be done formally through an industry program, on a project basis through joint ventures, or as part of the relationship between a general contractor and a sub-

[62] See Luther E. MacKall, *Surety Underwriting Manual* (Indianapolis: Rough Notes Co., 1963).

contractor. Owners may facilitate such technical assistance in several ways, including negotiating (rather than bidding) jobs that are joint ventures between white and black contractors, agreeing to allow a general contractor to carry a black subcontractor on a job, and contacting black subcontractors to bid the owner's jobs. Often bringing new or growing firms into a job will be somewhat expensive. It is interesting that private owners are better situated to act effectively through these mechanisms than public or publicly assisted owners. Normally, competitive bidding is required on publicly assisted jobs, and the lowest responsible bidder must be selected. Consequently, opportunities for favoring minority contractors are limited. Because of this, the greatest promise of assistance to black contractors is through cooperation with larger contractors on privately financed jobs. Major private owners and local contractor associations are the most appropriate parties to establish programs of support for black contractors.

Conclusions: The Need for a Cooperative Effort

There are many means for arriving at an increase in minority employment in the building trades. The more important ones include efforts to induce the industry to employ qualified nonwhite mechanics, efforts to recruit and train nonwhite entrants, and programs to increase the number and size of minority contractors. Each of these general mechanisms may function in any number of ways, and the variety of specific programs that can be designed is infinite. The preceding pages have described briefly some of the major programs currently operating and the experience with these programs. It should be clear that there are principles that are necessary to the success of any program, and without them little can be achieved. The nature of the industry itself determines that some mechanisms offer far greater promise than others of delivering a significant increase in minority participation. In general, such programs are superior because they (1) have a training component (and thereby provide a means for new entry by nonwhites); (2) provide training in a manner consistent with the needs and practices of the trades involved; (3) extend the coverage of the plan to a sufficient volume of work to allow continuity of employment; and (4) actively involve the participation of contractors and unions in the affected trades. Programs lacking any of these elements may be expected to be of only limited value, especially in a quantitative sense.

Because there are many procedures that will help to increase minority participation, it is more important to achieve a commitment from each branch of the industry than it is to establish any particular program. But this commitment must be precisely that — a voluntary agreement to do what is necessary to achieve increased minority involvement in the trades. Such a commitment cannot be legislated or compelled by court orders or by contract provisions. Where a commitment cannot be obtained, it may be necessary for public policy to resort to requiring specific plans and programs as a less desirable alternative. Conversely, the promulgation of a specific program may prove useful if the purpose of the program is to move the industry toward a voluntary agreement. If, however, concentration by public agencies on a particular scheme is such that it effectively preempts any program based on the voluntary cooperation of the industry, then the public and the minority community will achieve less than might otherwise be obtained.

There is a widespread view in the United States that coercion, of either a legal or extralegal nature, is the most effective method for achieving social advance. While there are important and numerous instances in which resort to the law and regulations is necessary and useful, there are very definite limits to the capacity of these measures to provide more than minimum levels of progress. A more useful strategy is often to enlist the active cooperation of persons in the area involved. Compulsion may be effective where a simple, straightforward problem is at issue. Thus, if a local union has denied membership and job referral to a black journeyman, it will normally be effective for a court or other public agency to order the local union to admit and refer the individual. However, if the issue is one of recruitment and training, in which positive efforts will be required of the union leadership and members and in which a long period of time and the development of personal relationships will be needed to accomplish the public purpose, then compulsion is likely to be unsatisfactory. It is simply not possible to prepare a foolproof plan for outreach, employment, and training, especially one not at least partly dependent for success on the cooperation of present journeymen, unions, and contractors.[63] There can be no doubt, given the evidence of recent years, that positive and imaginative efforts by employers and unions will be required to increase minority group participation in the building trades — that mere non-

[63] "No man is wise enough to write words that another (particularly the thousands of business agents all over the country) cannot misinterpret or which do not contain loopholes. In the event of an agreement in good faith, the . . . [separate sides] . . . at least are trying to make it work rather than pick it to pieces." Frank Bonadio et al., *The Resolution of Jurisdictional Disputes* (Detroit: University of Michigan – Wayne State University Institute of Labor and Industrial Relations, 1958), p. 13. The author (John T. Dunlop) was speaking here of jurisdictional disputes, but his comment is equally true regarding programs to achieve racial balance in employment.

discrimination will not be enough. But such commitments from persons in the industry can come only as a result of persuasion (appropriately supported by the suggestion of direct public action if necessary) and the will of the individuals involved.

If there were large numbers of nonwhite construction craftsmen available for entrance to the building trades, making outreach, recruitment, and training unnecessary, the cooperation of the industry would be less significant, and mechanisms of legal action and contract compliance with equal employment opportunity provisions would have far greater promise of success. It is the absence of such numbers, repeatedly revealed in major metropolitan areas, that has made compulsion so frustratingly unsuccessful. Even with far more vigorous weapons of coercion over contractors and unions, little would be accomplished in most areas without outreach and training. Effective performance of these functions requires cooperation.

III

Training in Construction

7

Formal Training Programs and Entry to Construction

Introduction

Formal training programs in construction include apprenticeship, journeyman retraining, and publicly funded programs to train disadvantaged and minority group persons. Apprenticeship is the most widespread, geographically and occupationally, of the methods of formal training and the most important numerically. This chapter and the next discuss the role and performance of formal training in construction, especially apprenticeship.

The problems of formal training programs relate not so much to the total volume of entry to the crafts (in all crafts there are means of entry other than formal training) but to their role in the development of manpower for the industry. Formal training tends to provide better-skilled and more productive mechanics and to increase the capacity of the mechanic to obtain employment when the volume of construction declines. However, the particular function of apprenticeship programs in the total manpower process differs in important respects among crafts and areas, making it hazardous to generalize about their role and performance.

Most previous academic discussions of apprenticeship have erred in three major respects regarding the analysis of the building trades programs.[1] First, they have too often viewed apprenticeship as the exclusive route of entry to the industry and have discussed the programs as if they were concerned with a labor supply mechanism rather than a training device. Certainly, apprenticeship programs perform an entry function, but the relationship between apprenticeship and variations in the supply of labor to the industry is less intimate than is normally supposed and varies greatly by craft. Second, far too little attention has been devoted to the particular functions and problems of apprenticeship in the different crafts. Many generalizations about "apprenticeship" apply to only a few crafts, and many to none at all. Third, the relationship of employers to apprenticeship, involving both the economics of the training process and the participation of employers in the mechanisms of manpower planning, has been given too little attention. Many problems of apprenticeship, along with their potential solutions, lie largely with the employers.

The full-employment economy raised important questions about the future

[1] See, for example, Jack Barbash, "Union Interests in Apprenticeship and Other Training Forms," *Journal of Human Resources* 3 (Winter 1968): 63-85, and Richard A. Lester," The Role of Organized Labor," in R. A. Gordon, ed., *Toward a Manpower Policy* (New York: John Wiley & Sons, 1967), pp. 317-332. Citations to other studies are included later.

of apprenticeship and its ability to supply the volume of well-trained manpower necessary to present and future construction demand. In the late 1960s,
problems of apprenticeship recruitment and accessibility of the programs to
large portions of the potential work force assumed great importance. Problems
developed from two sources. On the one hand, a larger portion of young men
were going to college than ever before. On the other hand, the manifold problems of the secondary school system in some areas often produced young men
with poor academic qualifications. In consequence, the pool of apprenticeship
applicants in some crafts was markedly reduced. These twin problems make
it necessary for some programs to adjust considerably to the labor market
context in which they operate.

There are four basic questions at issue respecting apprenticeship in the
full-employment economy. First, how extensive need formal training be in
each of the crafts? This question involves both the content of programs and
the relative importance of formal training in the total process of entry to the
craft. Second, what is the numerical adequacy of the programs to the functions
and demands placed on them by each craft, and by what means can these
demands be met? (This issue will be dealt with in Chapter 8.) In part, this
involves the fundamental question of the relationship of the locally administered apprenticeship programs to national manpower requirements. Third,
what is the appropriate relationship of formal training mechanisms to the
general context of youth employment and training, especially to the public
school system and its products? The American apprenticeship system is in
large part a postsecondary school program (unlike the European combination
of vocational education and apprenticeship at the secondary school level),
involving men past school age and often requiring that apprenticeship applicants have a high school education. This system has excluded a large number
of men from formal training (though not necessarily employment) in many
of the crafts. Mechanisms by which formal training may be better related to
the secondary school system are now under study in most crafts. Fourth,
what are the appropriate volume, source, and control of financial resources
supporting formal training? Funds available for certain purposes largely determine the volume and character of programs in many crafts. The federal
government has increasingly entered the manpower training process in construction, mainly through its capacity to provide large quantities of money
for certain purposes. Many federal dollars have been poorly used, however.
This chapter and the next will present evidence on these basic issues.

Formal Training in Construction

The Nature of Training for Construction Occupations

Training for the building trades is intimately related to the nature of the construction process as a whole. In most cases, the craftsman's job is not narrowly defined in terms of tasks and is not performed under direct supervision. Although instructions are given as to the flow of materials and the general sequence of operations, and although the work is inspected often and in detail, the close supervision and repetitive nature of assembly line or other manufacturing operations are largely absent. In fact, to a large extent the craft structure of work is an alternative to narrow tasks and close supervision.

Craft institutions are a method of administering work.[2] The craftsman is responsible for laying out a job and performing the tasks necessary to complete it successfully in a given period of time. The standards of the trade (for example, the pace of activity and the quality of operations) regulate the performance and flow of work. Craft administration of production is an alternative to what may be called the bureaucratic method of administration, which depends upon detailed supervision and unchanging procedures. Craft administration performs the same functions as bureaucratic administration, but in construction, craft administration is the more rational alternative in view of the industry's economic and technical characteristics. No two projects are exactly the same (often they are very different), and the flexibility of market demand for construction is quite marked. Further, firms will often have projects at widely separated geographic sites, projects whose location and nature may change over short spans of time. The maintenance of close supervision and continuously functioning centralized communication with each member of the work force is likely to be prohibitively expensive. In the words of one observer, "craft administration . . . differs from bureaucratic administration by substituting professional training of manual workers for decentralized planning of work."[3] For the most part, craft administration is an efficient response to the peculiar circumstances of the construction industry.

Training for craft occupations in construction is designed to produce a journeyman who is able not only to perform certain tasks under supervision but to supervise himself to a large degree. The journeyman is trained to perform much of the supervisory and planning functions that in other industries

[2] A. L. Stinchcombe, "Bureaucratic and Craft Administration of Production: A Comparative Study," *Administrative Science Quarterly* 4 (1959): 170.
[3] *Ibid.*, p. 175.

are the role of management. In addition, many journeymen become foremen, supervisors, or inspectors, and the training provided in many apprenticeship programs is designed to prepare men for these functions. The journeyman is expected to understand the fundamentals of his craft as well as how to perform specialized tasks; he may be asked to lay out work from blueprints and to supervise his own performance on the job. Training of this nature, while somewhat lengthy and expensive, also tends to reduce the firm's costs for close supervision and detailed scheduling of work.

While the role of the journeyman in self-supervision and scheduling is general to the crafts, there are significant differences among them in other elements of skill. In some trades, skill consists largely of the ability to perform a difficult physical task for several hours a day at an acceptable pace. A man unable to maintain the pace of work is unable to earn the wage. Bricklaying, painting, and roofing are trades in which the physical task is especially important. In some trades, skill consists largely of knowing several specialties that make up the trade and the capacity to lay out and perform a job. The work is less physically demanding and the pace of work less important than in other crafts. Carpentry and the pipe trades are primary examples.[4] In still other crafts, skill is largely manipulative in nature and involves the ability to operate machinery safely and efficiently. The operating engineer is perhaps the best example of a machinery-oriented craft. Physical effort and pace of work, knowledge of specialties, ability to plan the work, and the capacity to operate equipment vary in their relative importance to the different crafts, but to some extent they are common to all. Experience on previous jobs and judgment as to how to perform a task are also important elements in all trades[5] — certainly more important than the theoretical acquaintance with the elements of the craft that might be obtained, for example, in a vocational school.

Training methods in construction reflect the characteristics of the production process just described. They also reflect the nature and desires of labor and

[4] For a full description of job content and training in the pipe trades (plumber pipefitter, and sprinklerfitter), see Purdue Research Foundation, "A Study of the Need for Educational and Training Adjustments in Selected Apprenticable Trades," xerox (prepared for the U.S. Department of Labor, Manpower Administration, by Alfred S. Drew, Lafayette, Ind., 1969).

[5] The importance of the initiative and judgment of the individual craftsman differs with the degree of specialization of the firm and the extent of jobsite supervision exercised by management. Very specialized and tightly supervised firms do not require the full capacities of a journeyman. However, there has been, in the last two decades at least, no *general* trend in the industry toward more specialization and more careful supervision of work, although some branches of the industry exhibit these characteristics.

management institutions in the industry, but these influences are of secondary importance. Both the importance of on-the-job training and the role of related instruction in apprenticeship programs and in the more recently developed nonapprenticeship training programs are adaptations, more or less successful, to the technological and economic conditions of the industry. The structure of training is related to the craft structure of production in the industry; it is designed to produce craft journeymen, not semiskilled operatives. The content of training programs has been adjusted to the competitive conditions of the industry and to the risks of intermittent employment. Along with the structure and content of training, the relative role of employers, unions, and the public school system in the operation of programs has developed in response to the conditions of production in the industry. Any proposals for reform or alteration of existing training arrangements must initially confront the realities of the production process and the employment relationship.

There is in fact a conflict of interest between construction management and the work force regarding the scope of training. While training for much of the labor force must be broad enough to encompass demands on the fully skilled craftsman, there are nevertheless many jobs available at some times to specialists or to the partly skilled. The breadth of training and general competence of journeymen in a trade is related strongly both to the capacity of the individual workman to secure employment (especially in slack labor markets) and to the ability of the trade as a whole to command a negotiated wage scale. Semiskilled workmen cannot maintain relatively high rates of pay over time except in unusual circumstances. In consequence, the building trades unions tend to favor broader training than employers often feel is necessary.

Job content and breadth of training in construction are determined not only by technology but also by industrial relations considerations. In many cases, the content of jobs and training are issues of negotiation between contractors and unions. Jurisdictional claims define the boundaries of a craft, and apprenticeship programs define training breadth. Technology generates a range of options for job structures that, when combined with the characteristics of the labor force, results in a choice of job structure. Where employees are organized, the union exerts influence on the decision as to job structure.[6]

[6] See James G. Scoville, "Concepts and Measurements of Manpower and Occupational Analysis," mimeo (prepared for the U.S. Department of Labor, Office of Manpower Research, Washington, D.C., 1969), pp. 72 ff., for a theoretical examination of the relationship between job content, training breadth, wages, employer behavior, and workers' preferences. Some aspects of Scoville's work suggest anomalies in the con-

The building trades unions have normally resisted reduction of the range of skills associated with a craft, believing that narrower jobs (that is, greater specialization) tend to limit employment opportunities and undermine wage structures.

The Structure of Formal Training

Apprenticeship Apprenticeship is an old name for a changing institution. During the past three decades there has been a substantial evolution in the methods and content of training provided. Years ago, apprenticeship involved little more than informal on-the-job training. Modern apprenticeship involves a systematic program of instruction, including the following elements:

1. A formal syllabus or course of instruction.
2. On-the-job training.
3. Related instruction off the jobsite.
4. Indenture to a joint labor-management committee responsible for the apprentice's progress.[7]

In 1937, the National Apprenticeship (Fitzgerald) Act established federal apprenticeship policy in the United States.[8] The Bureau of Apprenticeship and Training of the Department of Labor was created to administer this act through technical assistance and general promotion of apprenticeship. In addition, minimum standards were set up for the registration of apprenticeship programs, which include a minimum starting age of not less than 16; a schedule of work processes that the apprentice will learn on the job; 144 hours per year of organized instruction in technical subjects related to the trade; an increasing wage schedule; supervision of on-the-job training and adequate training facilities; evaluation and records of the apprentice's progress on the job and in class; cooperation by both employers and employees; recognition of successful completion of a program; and training without regard to race, creed, or national origin.

---

struction context: for example, that narrower jobs are associated with increased wages (p. 102). In general, Scoville's work is very perceptive and gives promise of future direct applications to the empirical analysis of certain crafts.

[7] It is interesting in this context that the International Labor Organization, in a survey of construction training in the developing countries completed in 1969, distinguishes among modern apprenticeship, traditional apprenticeship, and institutional (only) training; it strongly favors the first of these as the best mechanism for imparting construction skills. International Labor Organization, *Construction Skills* (Geneva: CIRF Publications, 1969), p. 84

[8] The literature on apprenticeship is voluminous. For a broad discussion, see U.S. Department of Labor, *Apprenticeship: Past and Present* (Washington, D.C., 1969).

State apprenticeship councils have also been set up in about thirty states which have more than three-fourths of all the registered apprenticeship programs. These councils, where they exist, administer the programs in their own states in accordance with the federal standards set forth earlier.

The routine administration of individual apprenticeship programs in the construction industry is through local joint apprenticeship committees (JACs), composed of an equal number of representatives from the union (usually rank-and-file members or business agents) and from management (usually an executive from a local contractors' association and a few individual employers). The local JACs usually set up specific standards for their apprenticeship programs and often direct the programs. There are JACs in most building trades on the national level; they suggest standards that are ordinarily followed by the local JACs and advise them on ways to improve their programs.

The apprenticeship programs are normally financed by assessing the employers — whether or not they use apprentices — a few cents per hour for the man-hours of labor they employ. These funds may be used to pay an apprentice coordinator, to cover administration and record-keeping costs, for advertising, to finance job-related instruction by paying instructors' fees and by buying tools and texts, and sometimes even to pay apprentices who are in school full time.

Selection of apprentices is made by the JAC. An applicant must meet minimum standards, which vary from state to state and from craft to craft. Most building trades require a high school education, the most noteworthy exceptions being the plasterers and cement masons, who often require only an eighth or ninth grade education. In addition, there are residence and U.S. citizenship requirements in many crafts. There are minimum and maximum age spans for starting apprentices, ranging from 17 to 30, but usually about 17 or 18 to 25, with some exceptions made for veterans. Since the enactment of the Federal Civil Rights Act, an applicant is frequently given an aptitude test, on which he sometimes has to achieve a minimum score.

The applicant who has met the minimum qualifications already discussed may then be interviewed by the JAC and ranked according to various criteria the JAC considers relevant. After selection, apprentices enter a program, typically three to five years long, that includes on-the-job training and related class instruction. Starting pay is usually half the journeyman wage, increasing over the term of apprenticeship to the full journeyman wage. An interesting exception is the program recently initiated by the operating engineers. The operating engineers' apprentices receive the full pay for the piece

of equipment they are operating, advancing to more difficult pieces of equipment and higher pay as they move through apprenticeship.[9]

Nonapprenticeship training In some branches of construction, training of a
nonapprenticeship nature is provided for new entrants to the labor force.
The operating engineers have long used the work classification "oiler" as a
means to introduce new men to the industry. In some areas, other trades
utilize helpers as a means of training and entry for young men.

Federal legislation has called for the employment of disadvantaged persons
and of area residents on certain types of federally assisted housing (especially
in Model Cities areas and urban housing programs). Many residents of these
areas do not possess the skills necessary for employment at the journeyman
rate, and they are often ineligible for apprenticeship by virtue of age, academic
background, or other disqualifications. In response to this situation, unions
and contractors in many areas have now begun to establish formal, nonapprenticeship training mechanisms which bear a close resemblance to
apprenticeship, involving intermediate wage rates and formal on-the-job
training and related instruction.[10]

In some cases, certain of the building trades unions and employers have
contracted with the federal government to provide training to minority group
workers and disadvantaged white youths. The efforts of the operating engineers
under the Job Corps program and of the carpenters under the Labor Department's Manpower Development and Training Act are notable examples. The
national Association of Home Builders has obtained a federal contract to train
carpenters. Many local contractors' associations and individual contractors have
conducted government-financed and -supported programs either to introduce
new men to the industry or to upgrade the skills of the existing labor force.

In some cases, effective training is provided in vocational secondary schools.
Normally, graduates of these programs enter apprenticeship. It should be
recalled that the formal educational standards of some branches of the industry
are high. Perhaps as many as 20 percent of union electricians in some areas
are college graduates.

Journeyman upgrading In recent years, programs to upgrade and enrich the
skills of the existing labor force have been developed in some sectors of the
industry. In part, they are necessary to keep journeymen abreast of changing

[9] The exact structure of apprenticeship programs varies among the crafts. For a description of the programs in the pipe and electrical branches of the industry, see Sumner H.
Slichter, J. J. Healy, and E. R. Livernash, *The Impact of Collective Bargaining on Management* (Washington: Brookings Institution, 1960), pp. 91–98.
[10] See Chapter 6.

technology and work requirements. These programs are financed jointly by
union and management or are funded entirely by employer cents-per-hour-
worked contributions and jointly administered under a trust fund arrangement.

The International Training Fund (ITF) of the plumbing and pipefitting
industry is perhaps the most elaborate and extensive journeyman training
scheme. The ITF was negotiated in 1956 between the United Association and
the National Constructors' Association. It makes funds available for capital
equipment, tools, materials, and supplies used in training, for supplemental
payments to instructors, and for text materials. The ITF supplements, financially and technically, training programs administered by local joint training
committees in cities and towns. It supports apprentice programs as well as
journeyman programs.

The training facilities available, programs in operation, crafts involved, and
methods of financial support differ across the country. It is clear, however,
that more attention is now being given to training than ever before, and that
the scope and quality of these programs will increase in the coming years.

Union Interests in Formal Training

It has been fashionable among some observers to see apprenticeship (and,
by implication, other formal training programs) primarily as a device by
which labor organizations limit the supply of labor to the construction
industry. Because union members can be shown to have an interest in restricting entry to the trade, thereby creating artificial scarcities, it has been assumed
that they both seek to do so and are fairly successful at it.[11] In Chapter 8
it is shown that there are many routes of entry to construction employment
other than formal training. A previous chapter has showed that formal training
is not the only means of acquiring training in construction.[12] Thus, although
formal training may serve to some degree as a means of restricting the
supply of labor, it is at best a very incomplete method. The interest of
unions in apprenticeship arises from other, potentially threatening aspects of
training. Apprenticeship can be many different things. An apprenticeship program may be a mechanism of formal training by which a young man learns a
craft, becomes proficient at the work, and is thereby enabled to seek employment on the same footing as other trained men. Apprenticeship may also be
a sort of trial period, during which an apprentice serves out his time before he
receives the journeyman rate.[13] Finally, apprenticeship may be only a lower

[11] See fn. 1.
[12] See pp. 171-172 for a description of informal training programs in construction.
[13] In construction, the journeyman's card is not a job guarantee unless the worker can

wage classification for unskilled men working as helpers and receiving little or no training.

Labor unions have been very concerned to prevent apprenticeship from acquiring this last-mentioned role. Unless the union is able to insure that apprenticeship is a valid training mechanism, not a source of cheap labor, it will be largely unable to maintain negotiated wages and conditions for journeymen. It is primarily this circumstance that has given union leaders their historic concern for regulation of the structure of apprenticeship programs and their operations.[14]

Apprenticeship programs in which organized labor participates are primarily a means of formal training rather than a source of cheap labor. It is the union, with the joint apprenticeship committee (if one exists), that enforces the training obligations of contractors where enforcement is necessary. The union also bargains with employers over the number of apprentices to be trained. The union and employers consider both the requirements for supervision and the volume of work in the trade in establishing the numbers that can be trained. In some cases, the number of apprentices taken is considered by employers to be too low for the health of the industry, and in this sense the unions may be charged with attempting to regulate the supply of labor through apprenticeship. Though regulation of the number of apprentices remains a problem in some crafts and areas, the most objective appraisal of the issue of restrictions on apprenticeship and other rules was made by Haber forty years ago:

Before the unions can be expected to relinquish their restrictive practices, some assurance must be given that the workers will not be required to bear the entire cost of industrial changes and will be protected against the hazards which exist in the industry. In other words, what is needed as a first requisite toward more efficient operation is stabilization — stabilization of wages, of employment, of working conditions. Unless these are assured, to talk of eliminating rules which have their inspiration in unstable working conditions is to overlook the cause and to deal only with the effect.

---

perform on the job. There are few seniority provisions, and contractors may hire and lay off men largely at their own discretion. Because of this, an apprentice who learns little during his training may have difficulty obtaining employment.

[14] Richard Scheuch, "The Labor Factor in Residential Construction" (Ph.D. thesis, Princeton University, 1951), quoted a *Wall Street Journal* issue of the 1930s as saying that " 'Builder Gale Bradford of Evansville, Indiana . . . at one time . . . had eighty-five bricklaying apprentices and only five journeymen, but was soon faced with demands that he speed the promotion of apprentices to journeymen.' " Commenting generally on this problem, Haber noted, "If employers will flood the trade with 'green hands' and young boys, in order to train a labor supply sufficiently plentiful to defeat the labor organizations in the next dispute, the unions will restrict entrance to the trades and regulate strictly the number of apprentices." William Haber, *Industrial Relations in the Building Industry* (Cambridge: Harvard University Press, 1930).

To many contractors it is still a question whether stabilized employment, fewer restrictive rules and higher individual efficiency are better than uncertainty of employment, restrictive rules and lower efficiency.[15]

Entry and Formal Training for Construction

Entry of Youth to Construction

It is highly misleading and inappropriate to interpret statistics on formal apprenticeship as indicating the volume of entry to construction, even among youth. Actual numbers of new entrants are much larger than enrollment in apprenticeship. In fact, the industry has recruited what may be termed its "fair share" of the nation's young manpower. The proportion of young men entering construction is comparable to the relative size of the industry in the economy and has been so for years. Yet a very large number of these young men are not given formal training and are only marginally attached to the industry's work force.

For example, a special survey for 1968 found that approximately 9.5 percent of all males employed in the United States (on an annual average basis) were employed in construction.[16] During October 1968, among all employed males 20 to 24 years of age, enrolled or not enrolled in school, 9.6 percent were employed in construction. Of young men who were enrolled in school, 5.2 percent were employed in construction, compared to 10.7 percent of those not enrolled. Younger age groups not enrolled in school show even higher percentages employed in the industry. Among employed males 16 to 17 not enrolled in school, 12.7 percent were in construction, compared to 2.4 percent of those who were enrolled. Among all employed young men 16 to 24 years of age not enrolled in school, 10.9 percent (or 544,000) were employed in construction. By far the largest number of young workers in con-

[15] Haber, *Industrial Relations in the Building Industry,* p. 511. A further question, of course, is the degree to which unions are successful in their efforts to regulate apprenticeship and ensure that training takes place. Foltman concludes that "thus far it would appear that unions are having limited success attaining their apprentice training objective." F.F. Foltman, "Public Policy in Apprenticeship Training and Skill Development," in U.S. Congress, Senate, Committee on Labor and Public Welfare, Subcommittee on Employment and Manpower, *Selected Readings in Employment and Manpower,* vol. 3, *The Role of Apprenticeship in Manpower Development: United States and Western Europe,* 88th Cong., 2nd sess. 1964, p. 1125.

[16] These data are from the Current Population Survey and include as employed in construction all wage and salary employees of contractors, unpaid family workers, and the employees of public agencies doing construction work.

struction were 20 to 24 years of age (450,000 of the 643,000 total, enrolled
and not enrolled in school).[17]

The number of young male workers in construction far exceeds the
number of registered apprentices reported by the Bureau of Apprenticeship
and Training. On December 31, 1968, the BAT reported, there were 132,512
persons in training in registered apprenticeship programs in all the building
and construction trades. Many apprentices are known to be in unregistered
programs of varying quality (perhaps as many as in the registered programs).[18]
but even doubling the number of registered apprentices and counting completions (which totaled only 100,000 in the previous five years) would not
account for the 643,000 young men reported working in construction in
October 1968. It is important that the Current Population Survey reports
are from a month (October) in which fully 55 percent of all males 16 to 25
years of age were enrolled in school.[19] Clearly, the summer employment
of school-age youth in construction does not explain the difference between
the figures on youth employment and formal training in the industry.

The construction industry is also doing a better job of recruiting both
high school graduates and dropouts than is commonly supposed. Apprenticeship programs have in some cases experienced difficulty finding applicants,
a circumstance often attributed to the attractiveness to high school graduates of white-collar occupations. Yet in October 1968 fully 9.6 percent
of employed male high school graduates of the class of 1968 (33,000 men)
and 11.4 percent of the class of 1967 (38,000 men) were at work in con-

[17]Elizabeth Woldman, *Employment Status of School Age Youth,* October 1968, U.S.
Bureau of Labor Statistics Special Labor Force Report no. 111 (Washington, D.C., 1969), reprinted from *Monthly Labor Review* 92 (August 1969): 23–32. Racial data are less extensive.
Of males 16 to 21 years of age not enrolled in school in October 1968, 12.7 percent of
those employed worked in construction, including 5.1 percent (17,000) of the nonwhite
males and 14.1 percent (279,000) of the white males in that group. In October 1967,
the figures were very different, with 11.8 percent (42,000) of the nonwhite males and
only 11.5 percent of the white males aged 16 to 21 and not enrolled in school employed
in construction. U.S. Bureau of Labor Statistics, Special Labor Force Report no. 98.
   A similar nationwide survey taken during October-December 1968 showed 10 percent each of employed white and black males aged 14 to 24 and not enrolled in school
as employed in construction. Of those enrolled in school, 4 percent of white males and
3 percent of black males were employed in construction. U.S. Department of Labor,
Manpower Administration, *Career Thresholds: A Longitudinal Study of the Educational
and Labor Market Experience of Black Youth*, vol. 1, Monograph no. 16 (Washington,
D.C., 1971), p. 87.
[18]See John F. Henning (then Undersecretary of Labor), "Apprenticeship Data: Questions
and Answers," in Senate, Subcommittee on Employment and Manpower, *The Role of
Apprenticeship,* 88th Cong., 2nd sess., 1964, p. 1184.
[19]Woldman, *Employment Status of School Age Youth,* October 1968.

struction.[20] Among high school graduates of any year aged 16 to 21 who were not enrolled in college, 10.8 percent (153,000 men) were employed in construction.[21] The industry remains able to recruit for employment, though perhaps not for formal training, a proportion of high school graduates not in college (together with those in college but working) equivalent to its importance in the male labor force generally. The *non*college male population has, of course, been expanding numerically at the same time that it has been declining as a proportion of the total numbers in the young age groups.[22]

The formal requirements of many apprenticeship programs are such that young high school dropouts are effectively ineligible for entry. In many cases, high school graduation or a high school equivalency is required for admission to a program. Yet in October 1968, 13.1 percent (120,000 men) of all employed male dropouts aged 16 to 21 were in construction. Of male dropouts aged 16 to 24 who last attended school in 1968, 10.2 percent (11,000) were working in construction, and of those who last attended school in 1967, 11.3 percent (20,000) were in construction.[23] Apparently many young men enter the industry without high school degrees, either by obtaining high school equivalencies, through apprenticeship programs not requiring graduation, or by means other than apprenticeship.

Finally, many more young men apparently work in the industry in the course of a given year than estimates of annual average employment by age groups would indicate. The seasonal fluctuation in employment is high, and turnover among young workers is presumably fairly high as well, although no data specifically on turnover in construction are available.

In summary, there is no indication statistically of great difficulty in recruiting young men to work in construction. Rather than being an industry of old men, in 1960 the median age in construction was close to the all-

[20] Vera C. Perrella, *Employment of High School Graduates and Dropouts,* October 1968, U.S. Bureau of Labor Statistics Special Labor Force Report no. 108, reprinted from *Monthly Labor Review* 92 (August 1969): 36–43. The bases for these percentages exclude young men 16 to 24 enrolled in post-high school study and not employed. Persons enrolled in school and employed are included.
[21] Woldman, *Employment Status of School Age Youth,* October 1968.
[22] There are no general data available on employment of college-trained men in the building trades. Some crafts (especially the electricians) seem to have a fairly high proportion of college men in their membership. The current formal training mechanism for college-trained men is presumably a shortened and modified apprenticeship program. Adjustment of formal training to attract college dropouts and graduates may play a role in meeting the manpower needs of some crafts in the future.
[23] Perrella, *Employment of High School Graduates and Dropouts,* October 1968.

industry median age of men (approximately 40),[24] and it almost certainly fell later on as employment conditions in the industry improved. By the late 1960s, the industry employed a greater proportion of young men than its relative importance in the total employment picture warranted. Yet estimates of the numbers of persons in formal training in construction reveal that most young men cannot be in formal programs and probably have had little or no exposure to them. The real problems of entry to construction relate not to the numbers of young men recruited and working but to the adequacy of the training mechanisms. It may be that formal training in construction now accounts for a larger proportion of total entry than in the past; the evidence is scarce. Nonetheless, there is considerable room for expansion and improvement in the role that formal training plays in entry. The analysis of apprenticeship training that follows must be understood in this context. The issue is not the volume of entry to construction but the role that apprenticeship training is to play in the total volume of entry.[25]

Manpower Planning for Formal Training

A decentralized planning process Formal training is provided only to a minority of the young persons who find employment in construction. In large part this results from major shortcomings in the process by which decisions are made concerning the number of men to be accepted into formal training. More than any other characteristics of apprenticeship programs (for example, length or wages paid), the failure of apprenticeship to train large numbers is a failure of the planning process.[26]

Planning of a formal nature associated with apprenticeship programs involves the responsibility for adjusting apprenticeship training to construction labor market conditions and is delegated primarily to joint apprenticeship committees at the local level. In most crafts, there is no formal mechanism at the national level for assessing the changing relationship of manpower demand and supply, although national unions often exhort their locals to be less conservative in providing training opportunities. Very rarely are nonapprenticeship routes of entry considered as an element of the manpower process at any level of the industry. In consequence, the training and entry of manpower

---

[24] U.S. Bureau of Labor Statistics, *Seasonality and Manpower in Construction,* Bulletin no. 1642 (Washington, D.C., 1970).
[25] By 1975, for example, over 2 million males will reach the age of 18 each year. If construction continues to obtain recruits from noncollege youth as it has in recent years, some 160,000 18-year-olds may be expected to be available to construction annually. See U.S. Bureau of the Census, *Illustrated Projections of the Population of the United States,* Current Population Reports Series, 1970–1971 issues.
[26] See Chapter 4 for a discussion of manpower planning in construction in a broader context than that of formal training.

into the industry is largely haphazard, and the relationship of the volume
of training and entry to numerical needs is often coincidental.

The national standards of most apprenticeship programs delegate responsibility for manpower planning to the local joint apprenticeship committees.
In the sheet metal trade, for example, the local joint apprenticeship committee
has the duty "to determine the need for the new apprentices, with due regard
to present and future needs of the trade."[27] In carpentry, it is the responsibility
of the local joint committee to "conduct surveys to determine the needs for,
and the availability of, apprentices in the local area," and the ratio of apprentices to journeymen is to be based on a study of the locality's present and
future need for journeymen.[28] Similarly, for the electricians, lathers, and
other trades (with two exceptions — the operating engineers and the plasterers),
the responsibility for determining the number of apprentices is delegated to
local groups and is to be made in light of local conditions, without review or
suggestions by the national joint committee.

This localized manpower planning process has introduced a conservative
bias of considerable importance into the numbers formally trained. Employment conditions in construction show more variation in most local areas
than they do in the nation as a whole.[29] For this reason, adjusting training
to the ability of the local area to provide employment continuity normally
produces a smaller volume of entry than employment conditions on a wider
geographic scale would justify. With trained men unavailable, labor shortages are often met with semiskilled, temporary journeymen. A variety of
problems arise for both contractors and unions from this process, but little
has been done to improve it.

It was pointed out earlier that the operating engineers provide for the direct
involvement of the national authorities in the manpower planning process.
The national apprenticeship standards of the engineers delegate the responsibility for determining the numbers trained to local joint committees, but
they allow the national joint committee to request review of the "program
provisions and ratios of local union programs in order to insure an adequate
manpower supply and to meet the demands for apprentices."[30] While only

[27]Sheet Metal Industry, National Joint Apprenticeship and Training Committee, *National Apprenticeship and Training Standards for the Sheet Metal Industry* (1965 ed.) p. 16.
[28]Carpentry, National Joint Apprenticeship and Training Committee, *National Carpentry Apprenticeship and Training Standards* (1967 ed.), pp. 2, 5.
[29]See D.Q. Mills, "Factors Affecting Patterns of Employment and Unemployment
in the Construction Industry" (Ph.D. thesis, Harvard University, 1967).
[30]Operating Engineers, National Joint Apprenticeship and Training Committee, *National
Apprenticeship Standards for the Trade of Operating Engineer* (1963 ed.), pp. 2–3.

one or two crafts make formal provision for the involvement of national authorities in planning, other trades exhibit considerable informal national involvement. A common theme of international convention addresses by national union leaders is that locals must train enough manpower to meet existing and anticipated needs. In the same way, contractors' association representatives exhort both unions and contractors to recruit and train apprentices.

Thus, the role of the national unions in the manpower development process is not simply one of restricting entry. On the contrary, the interests of the unions, as well as of the contractors, require training enough men to meet expected labor demand. Speaking to the painters convention in August 1969, President C. J. Haggerty of the Building and Construction Trades Department, AFL-CIO, said,

. . . we would really have to move fast to meet the demand and man the work. So I would urge that we look at this realistically and begin to step up the size of our apprenticeship classes . . . Remember, we can only command our present wage levels as long as we dominate the labor market with adequate numbers of better skilled workers with a higher productivity factor.[31]

The department's and international unions' concern about the adequacy of the manpower supply reflects the importance to each union of controlling the work in its trade jurisdiction. Where a union is unable to supply workers to man projects, it may lose its work jurisdiction to nonunion men or to men of another union. In order to achieve an adequate labor supply, international unions will sometimes join with employers in an attempt to stimulate training at the local level. Recently, for example, the National Bricklaying Joint Apprenticeship Committee has begun to urge local JACs to increase dramatically the number of bricklaying apprentices. The national JAC has encouraged the shortening of apprenticeship terms by giving apprentices credit for previous experience at the trade,[32] a procedure long sanctioned by the international but perhaps too little used by local JACs.

The role of the international union in establishing formal training programs is important. The internationals encourage locals to establish formal apprenticeship programs where they do not exist and provide technical assistance in their development. The International Training Fund of the pipe industry is used to encourage local unions to establish and improve both apprentice and upgrading programs. Recently, the United Association (plumb-

[31] *Engineering News-Record,* August 28, 1969, p. 109.
[32] *Ibid.,* January 1, 1970, p. 51.

ers and pipefitters) has negotiated an affirmative action training program with the National Contractors Association (a Joint National Manpower Committee involving the UA and the NCA which has been in operation for several years developed this program). The program provides for trainee wage classifications and for Labor Department financing. The international union embodied elements of the training agreement in a national agreement with the NCA, so that it is binding on all local affiliates of the union. This sort of imposition of a formal training program by the international union is unusual in most branches of the industry.

Manpower planning at the national level in not sophisticated. In the usual case, when an imbalance in the availability of labor relative to demand is noted at the national level, local unions and employers are urged to increase apprenticeship. There are no formal efforts to allocate training responsibilities among geographic regions or local unions and employers. Each local area is left to pursue its own understanding of its role in the national process. Normally, the national authorities will intervene in particular localities only under very unusual and serious conditions. And unusual and serious local conditions do not always bring national involvement.

The technology of the local planning process The responsibility for manpower planning is at the local level, but in most cases it is exercised in a very primitive manner. Decisions as to the number of apprentices to be trained are based mainly on the recent employment experience of current apprentices and journeymen and on informed expectations regarding employment conditions in the year ahead. Little or no attention is paid to either the long-run (more than a year ahead) prospects of the trade and area or the requirements of any geographic area or type of construction outside the jurisdiction of the local union or district council involved. For example, where homebuilding is unorganized, the changing manpower requirements of residential construction are not considered in manpower planning by the JACs, despite the interaction of the labor markets in the residential and nonresidential sectors of the industry.

The analysis of labor market conditions and trends made in the planning process is often very limited. The large volume of data available on construction plans, building permits, and other potential indicators of manpower demand is normally not consulted. The lack of manpower analysis by the JACs has not gone unobserved:

Although committees play a vital labor market function, they do not seem to possess detailed records or information in that area. Most committees can give accurate figures on how many apprentices they have and how far along apprentices are in their indentures. They apparently pay no attention to completion rates or to the other means of entrance to their trade. More importantly, they do not usually have information on employers who are training apprentices, who have in the past trained apprentices, or who have not trained apprentices but are able to do so. Such basic labor market information would probably be helpful as a criterion for estimation future demands for apprentices in their area.[33]

At the suggestion of national authorities, some JACs have begun to maintain records on the employment experience of journeymen and apprentices in their areas.[34] The source of these data is often the records of jointly administered health, welfare, and pension funds. These records provide a more accurate picture of past economic conditions in the trade than the personal impressions of members of the JACs or the apprenticeship coordinators. However, they are of little direct use in estimating future requirements.

Joint apprenticeship committees are reluctant to accept more apprentices than they believe can be employed.[35] In the absence of reliable estimates numbers of young men given formal training. Other observers have understood and commented on this situation,[36] but there has been little discussion of the means by which the manpower planning process and the methodology of projections can be improved. A substantial effort must be devoted to providing better planning tools to local JACs and to explaining and encouraging their use (see Chapter 4).

The role of the government in planning At present, the manpower planning

[33] A.C. Filley and K.O. Magnusen, "A Study of Registered Joint Apprenticeship Committees in Wisconsin Building Trades," in *Research in Apprenticeship Training* (Madison: University of Wisconsin Center for Studies in Vocational and Technical Education, 1967), p. 86.

[34] Samuel M. Burt, *Industry and Vocational-Technical Education* (New York: McGraw-Hill, 1967), p. 421.

[35] See Buck Baker (Director, National Joint Apprenticeship and Training Committee for the Electrical Construction Industry), "Training in the Electrical Contracting Industry," in Senate, Subcommittee on Employment and Manpower, *The Role of Apprenticeship,* 88th Cong., 2nd sess., 1969, p. 146.

[36] See Herbert A. Perry, commenting on Filley and Magnusen, "Joint Apprenticeship Committees in Wisconsin," p. 98: "This paper reinforces my contention that trade unions generally dominate apprenticeship in the building and construction industry, and until the industry becomes more stabilized, and more is known about labor market conditions, future skill needs, and how to predict them, we cannot expect unions to help much in effecting change." Furthermore, virtually all discussions of manpower forecasting and planning in private industry are concerned with the problems of firms and industries with relatively stable workplaces and work forces. Little or nothing is known or said about planning for formal training in casual labor markets. See, for example, Arthur W. Slatzman, "Manpower Planning in Private Industry," in Arnold R. Weber et al., eds, *Public-Private Manpower Policies,* Industrial Relations Research Association Series (Madison, Wisc., 1969), pp. 79–100.

process is almost exclusively in the hands of employers and unions. The public role in apprenticeship amounts to little more than promoting the extension of high-quality apprenticeship programs by providing related instruction through the public school system.[37] From time to time, federal authorities insist that the volume of manpower being trained is inadequate, and public officials exhort the industry to recruit more manpower.[38] In some cases, these exhortations are based on thorough studies of labor market conditions, but they are usually construed as political pronouncements, especially since the industry is often not consulted or involved in the preparation of the background studies. Finally, federal analyses are normally not expressed in terms specific to craft and area, the actual units of the planning mechanism. In consequence, national studies are not a basis for action in the industry.

Unions and employers are perhaps less concerned with consumer interest in avoiding delays arising out of manpower shortages than they might be. The consumer tends to benefit in the short run from actions that will increase the supply of labor and other resources, limit cost increases, and lower the price of construction through competition. Yet such short-run actions may destabilize the industry and tend over time to make it less efficient and perhaps even more costly. An understanding of this process is usually limited to persons who are quite familiar with the industry, few of whom are in the federal government, so that longer-range benefits are likely to be ignored in the political processes of government. In consequence, there may be real and continuing conflicts of interest between the government and elements of the industry, particularly the unions. At this time, the process of manpower development through formal training rests firmly in the industry's control, with government agencies performing little more than an advisory function.

The volume of formal training accomplished by the industry is a result both of the numbers recruited and of the effectiveness of the training process itself. The planning process already discussed is primarily concerned with the numbers to be recruited. The effectiveness of the training process is currently dependent on the promotional activities of public authorities on

[37]See, for example, Martha F. Ritchie, "An Assessment of Apprenticeship," in Senate, Subcommittee on Employment and Manpower, *The Role of Apprenticeship,* 88th Cong. 2nd sess., 1964.
[38]See, for example, a speech by James D. Hodgson (then Undersecretary of Labor) to the Construction Employers National Legislative Conference, reported in *Daily Labor Report* (Bureau of National Affairs), no. 41 (March 2, 1970), pp. A3–A4, and Assistant Secretary of Housing and Urban Development Samuel Simmons's speech to the Michigan Building and Construction Trades Council Legislative Conference, *ibid.,* no. 43 (March 4, 1970), pp. A6–A7.

behalf of registered programs.[39] The public interest in the volume and effectiveness of apprenticeship training might suggest to some that the public should play a larger role in all aspects of formal training in the industry. At present, apprenticeship regulations in the union context are developed with explicit consideration of the interests of employers, apprentices, and the current work force.[40] The public interest is presumably some combination of the interests of these groups, and of the consumers (the government itself is a major consumer of construction) as well. In the United States, the public interest is not directly represented in the administration of apprenticeship except in an advisory capacity to joint apprenticeship committees at the national or state level.

Certainly, the most conservative interests represented are those of the current journeymen (represented by the union, while both the joint apprenticeship committee and the union represent the interests of the apprentices). The building trades are replete with tales of the reluctance of many journeymen to accept the training of new entrants. In part, the conservatism of current journeymen reflects a conflict over the possession of a restricted group of employment opportunities, although concern with job opportunities is not limited to the building trades, nor is it the only objective of the journeyman mechanics or their unions. However, in the United States the importance of the unions in the planning and training process does introduce a strongly conservative influence in determining the volume of training. In some countries, the influence of unions is minimized.[41]

Employers and public officials often assert that only the interests of the public, employers, and apprentices are appropriately considered in the training process. It is thought to be better to exclude the journeymen, because of their intimate concern with the number of men working at the trade. Yet, beyond the practical impossibility of such exclusion in this country, there are also strong reasons in favor of the continuing representation of journeymen in the training process. First, there is a direct relationship between the

---

[39] A registered program meets certain criteria of the state or federal agency concerned with apprenticeship training.

[40] John T. Dunlop, *Industrial Relations Systems* (New York: Holt, Rinehart & Winston, 1957), pp. 229–234, has listed provisions normally appearing in collective bargaining agreements in skilled crafts, not only in this country but abroad, which deal with apprenticeship, including (1) indentures; (2) ratios of apprentices to workmen; (3) wages to be paid apprentices; and (4) relationship of vocational education in the schools to apprenticeship entry and advancement. It is not only in the United States that apprenticeship is a subject of collective bargaining.

[41] *Ibid.*

success of current journeymen in obtaining a livelihood and the availability of new entrants or trainees. Second, where training is primarily conducted on the job, the failure of journeymen to cooperate can make the program ineffective. Clearly, the representation of journeymen in the planning and training process is both necessary and appropriate. The problem is to reach a desirable balance of interests among employers, journeymen, and the public in the flow of new manpower to the industry.

Industry elements often say that it is unwise to train apprentices in the presence of unemployed journeymen. The presumption is that under these conditions an apprentice will either be without work himself or will displace another man. This position is not inappropriate from the point of view of the public interest. The government as well as private industry seeks an economically efficient allocation of the work force. A situation of considerable unemployment may represent an inefficient overinvestment in training. Thus, it is not inappropriate to limit job training to avoid such surpluses. The real issue is how to adjust entry to employment expectations and, therefore, how to obtain accurate predictions. Where the industry consistently underestimates employment, serious shortages may result. The government and private industry have an important role in developing accurate estimates on which to base planning.

When industry groups refuse to respond reasonably to employment expectations, taking into account uncertainties and differing interests, then public action beyond the informal function is appropriate. Unfortunately, the federal government has consistently projected higher levels of employment in the industry than have occurred. Had federal projections been heeded, overinvestment in training, greater unemployment, and perhaps lower wage scales would have resulted. Workers are not perfectly mobile, and it is a disservice to the economy and to a man to train him extensively for prolonged un- or underemployment.

In summary, the structure of the planning and training mechanism in apprenticeship largely excludes the public authorities. In so doing, it has probably functioned more conservatively than otherwise. Public authorities (educators, manpower analysts, and elective or appointive officials) have sought to influence the planning process by manpower forecasting and exhortation. This public role has been poorly performed, which has limited the success of the training process in meeting national needs. This in turn has produced a general reluctance in the industry to provide public authorities with a greater role in the manpower process. Effective performance of an advisory and leadership role by the government would help to support claims for a more extensive public part in planning and training.

Adjusting Apprenticeship Programs to the Educational Context

Apprenticeship and secondary schools An important additional factor contributing to the surprisingly low proportion of new entrants to construction who receive formal training is the requirement of certain levels of academic achievement as a condition of acceptance into apprenticeship. Most but not all apprenticeship programs require that an applicant demonstrate a secondary school education. In some cases, a high school diploma (or an equivalency certificate) and written aptitude tests are required. In others, completion of some grade of secondary school (such as the eighth) is necessary. Unfortunately, many students fail to finish secondary school or finish it with only low levels of achievment. These young people are often excluded from apprenticeship because of poor academic performance. Many do enter construction employment, but generally without access to formal training programs. The use of academic achievment in secondary schools as a screening device for apprenticeship would be less of a problem if the inadequacies of secondary schooling were more evenly distributed throughout our population. Unfortunately, ghetto and rural secondary education is generally far less adequate than the education provided in white urban or suburban areas.[42] Apprenticeship programs that use secondary school performance as a standard of admission tend to perpetuate the effects of the breakdown of our public school system in many areas.

The number of young men who drop out of high school or who graduate with low levels of academic achievement is quite large. The National Advisory Commission on Vocational Education estimates that in an average year 700,000 young people drop out of the nation's schools before graduating.[43] In 1968, there were 1,663,000 dropouts (male and female) aged 16 to 21 in the labor force, 22 percent of whom were nonwhite.[44] There are few statistics regarding the actual (tested) academic achievement of either dropouts or graduates, but not all high school graduates perform at acceptable academic levels. For example, in New York City in 1963, the Rodgers Committee interviewed

[42]See, for example, Kenneth B. Clark, *Dark Ghetto: Dilemmas of Social Power* (New York: Harper & Row, 1965). The ability of students in the less-favored areas to perform well on the job is often not reflected in their academic achievement.

[43]National Advisory Commission on Vocational Education, *Second Report, Vocational Education Amendments of 1968, Public Law 90-576* (Washington, D.C.: Department of Health, Education, and Welfare, 1969), p. 2.

[44]*Statistical Abstract of the U.S., 1969* (Washington, D.C., 1970), Table 158.

several hundred black and Puerto Rican applicants for apprenticeship. The committee report commented,

One of the greatest eye openers to this committee was the apparent abandoning of many youths in our school system. Most of the committee was shocked that boys who were graduates of our vocational high schools or who had at least two years of these schools could not spell such words as "brick," "build-ing," "carpenter," etc. or could not add inches and feet . . . . It is quite apparent that they are the products of a social system that pushed them through the earlier grades of school without insuring that they had the basic tools neces-sary for a minimal academic education.[45]

Nor can the apprenticeable trades normally be learned in the vocational schools. On-the-job experience remains the most significant element of the training process. Further, the mechanization of construction has increased the costs of simulating on-site conditions in the school to such a degree as to be prohibitive in many crafts. In consequence, successful completion of voca-tional education normally leads not into the journeyman's classification but into apprenticeship.[46]

Only in a few crafts have apprentice applicants been too few in number to fill the available positions. In most trades, there are waiting lists of ap-plicants for apprenticeship. Should programs be dramatically expanded, these lists might be exhausted, but at this time the age and educational re-quirements of apprenticeship simply shorten lists of applicants too numerous for the openings. Thus, problems of exclusion associated with entry standards are significant in their distribution of openings among applicants rather than numerically. Basing apprenticeship upon successful completion of the public school system tends to exclude those for whom the schools have provided the fewest opportunities.

It is instructive in this context to compare the apprenticeship system in this country with its counterpart in Western Europe. In America, apprentice-ship is a postsecondary school system of training, but in Europe it is a part of vocational schooling. In this country, apprenticeship has only tenuous connections with the public school system through related instruction. In Europe, apprenticeship is an integral part of the process of schooling. In fact, apprenticeship performs considerably different functions here than it does abroad and is really a very different system of training. In Europe,

[45] "Report of the Building Industry of New York Referral Committee" [the Rodgers Committee], quoted in Vernon M. Briggs, Jr., and F. Ray Marshall, *Equal Apprentice-ship Opportunities* (Ann Arbor: University of Michigan–Wayne State University Insti-tute of Labor and Industrial Relations, 1968) pp. 32,34.

[46] See Slichter, Healy, and Livernash, *The Impact of Collective Bargaining,* p. 67.

apprentices are boys 14 to 18 years of age. The apprentice is expected to finish his on-the-job training and be a skilled worker at 18. The apprentice in Germany, for example, receives no wages but is paid an educational allowance that is intended only to aid his parents in supporting him.[47] Further, the apprentice must, by law, attend a vocational training school for eight hours each week until he reaches age 18. Programs in the other Western European countries are similar with respect to both the age of apprentices (14 to 18) and the lack of reliance on previous academic achievement as a requirement for apprenticeship. The American apprentice, however, is generally an older person and has behind him a more extensive academic education. It may well be that the average apprentice trained in this country is a more fully trained, more skilled workman than abroad. Certainly, the on-site construction industry in the United States has a more highly specialized, far more highly paid work force than in Europe. The contribution of post secondary school apprenticeship in this country to the quality of the American work force has been of great significance, so that a shift to the European model is not called for. Yet the problem of providing access to apprenticeship or other formal training for American youths who have done poorly in secondary school remains serious.

Improving the relationship of apprenticeship to schooling There are two aspects of the relationship between apprenticeship and secondary schooling that are now of considerable importance. First, the government has been greatly concerned about the difficulty of indenturing the educationally disadvantaged (often minority group members) in most of the building trades. Second, elements of the industry have been concerned at the apparent lack of interest in apprenticeship by graduates of the public school system. The government has sought to find means to provide formal training (apprenticeship or otherwise) to the disadvantaged. The industry has sought the upgrading of vocational education within the public school system and has attempted to influence guidance counselors and teachers in favor of the blue-collar occupations. Upgrading of vocational education in central cities and rural areas would tend to further both purposes.

Currently, vocational education is under extensive review. Vocational programs have generally been underfunded and poorly structured.[48] Voca-

[47] James R. Wason, "Apprenticeship and Youth Employment in Western Europe: An Economic Study," in Senate, Subcommittee on Employment and Manpower, *The Role of Apprenticeship,* 88th Cong., 2nd sess., 1964, p. 1311.

[48] National Advisory Commission on Vocational Education, *First Annual Report* (Washington, D.C.: Department of Health, Education, and Welfare, 1969), pp. 1–2; also, G.S. Rajan, "A Study of the Registered Apprenticeship Programs in Wisconsin" (Ph.D. thesis, University of Wisconsin, 1966), p. 115.

tional schools run few programs in the building trades, and nonvocational school shop courses are normally not directed toward construction. Most vocational education courses offered are in auto mechanics or machine shop, while many schools offer little vocational education or none at all.[49] There are, however, many courses involving some elements of carpentry, painting, and other crafts. There are perhaps 700 vocational education programs that include masonry, of which 300 are bricklaying only.[50] In some states, materials manufacturers or contractors have developed training programs in the various trades for vocational schools. Often these programs supply men to the nonunion sector of construction.

There is no reason why vocational training in the construction crafts could not be improved and expanded if the government appropriated the necessary funds and called on the industry for the necessary expertise.[51] All apprenticeship programs provide a mechanism for crediting a beginning apprentice for skill developed elsewhere against his period of apprenticeship.[52] Improved vocational education programs might increase the exposure of students to the crafts and shorten the period of on-the-job training necessary to become a journeyman. There is little likelihood that vocational training in the schools can replace a period of two or more years of on-the-job training in creating a fully trained mechanic. Improved vocational schooling prior to apprenticeship can, however, supplement the apprenticeship process.[53]

The government has experimented recently with several mechanisms by which to increase the opportunity for the disadvantaged to receive formal training in construction. Preapprenticeship training programs have operated in several crafts and in many geographic areas.[54] Other government-spon-

[49] J.J. Kaufman, "The Role of Vocational Education in the Transition from School to Work," in Weber et. al., *Public-Private Manpower Policies.*

[50] Bill Roark, Director of Mason Relations, Structural Clay Products Institute, Washington, D.C.

[51] During the late 1960s, several persons at Ohio State University, supported by an Office of Education grant, produced in cooperation with industry groups a new technical-vocational curriculum for junior high school students in construction. See *The World of Construction* (Bloomington, Ill.: McKnight and McKnight, 1970). This project indicates what can be accomplished to improve vocational education through the cooperation of government, industry, and academic institutions.

[52] In some crafts, this provision is widely ignored, and the apprentice may be made to serve a full term regardless of his previous skill at the craft.

[53] Observers often argue that the essential role of education, including vocational education, is not specific training at all, but "to provide youth with those basic attitudes which will inculcate in them a desire to learn on a life-time basis." J. J. Kaufman, "The Role of Vocational Education," p. 191.

[54] For favorable analyses of preapprenticeship programs, see George Strauss, "Related Instruction: Basic Problems and Issues," in *Research in Apprenticeship Training*; and J. S. McCauley, "Increased Apprenticeship Opportunities through Pre-Employment

sored programs have involved special outreach and tutoring mechanisms such as those embodied in the Model Cities training programs. Most such programs have been instituted as a means for increasing the participation of minority group members in crafts. Because of the educational disadvantages of many minority group youths, special programs have been necessary.[55] Finally, the government has sponsored formal training for the "hard-core" disadvantaged. Many of the people trained under such programs have been in the laborers' and helpers' classifications.

In summary, vocational education can be improved and special programs developed for dropouts and other educationally disadvantaged youths in order to apprentice a greater number of people in these groups. Too often in our society, young people are academically handicapped less through their own fault than through the failures of the public schools. Because apprenticeship in this country is a post-secondary school program, special efforts must be made to close the gap that often exists between secondary school and formal job training. All elements of construction and all crafts should participate in these efforts. Programs must be developed that are specific to the circumstances of each craft. For example, the bricklayer and carpenter may cooperate in expanding and improving courses offered in vocational and academic high schools and simultaneously seek to improve recruiting for their crafts in the schools. The mechanical trades may consider participating in cooperative work-schooling programs for high school youths and extending to the economically disadvantaged the summer work opportunities that are offered to many students. In any case, the problem is to improve the interface between secondary schooling and formal training in construction, not to pursue the unlikely objective of replacing formal on-the-job training with vocational schooling.[56]

Financing of Training

Training costs in construction are normally borne by four separate parties: the individual apprentice, his employer, a joint union-employer committee, and the public. Costs have been distributed in this manner since the enact-

---

Training," in *ibid*. A. L. Nellum and Associates, in "Manpower and Rebuilding," a report prepared for the U.S. Department of Housing and Urban Development (Washington, D.C., 1969), were far more negative in their evaluation.

[55] See Chapter 6 for a more extensive discussion of these programs.

[56] See Foltman, "Public Policy in Apprenticeship Training," p. 1117, for an analysis of apprenticeship that considers its replacement by vocational education in the schools.

ment of the Fitzgerald Act in 1937, but the exact nature of financing and the distribution of costs among the different parties vary by craft and area. The apprentice (actually apprentice, helper, or other classification) bears part of the cost of his training in earnings foregone by virtue of a rate of pay below what he might earn elsewhere. If the apprentice's productivity is in fact equal to his wages, the lower rate simply eliminates any cost to the employer. When the apprentice's productivity exceeds the wage, the apprentice bears the cost of training directly. Productivity varies with the apprentice, the particular job, supervision, and other aspects of the production process; however, apprentice wages are not determined individually but on an area-wide basis as negotiated wage classifications.[57] In some cases, apprentices are tested initially and placed at a wage classification commensurate with their qualifications relative to journeymen.

The employer bears the cost of training in two ways: (1) the cost of supervision of the apprentice; and (2) the difference between the productivity of the apprentice and his wage (if productivity is below the wage). Productivity depends, of course, not just upon the apprentice's skill but also upon his pace of work and damage to equipment and materials, if any. In some crafts, employers pay wages to apprentices for time spent in related instruction.[58]

Joint union-contractor bodies bear the cost of administration and promotion of programs. In some cases, members of the joint committees have financial support; in others, time is donated by each of the members. Often the joint committees are financed by cents-per-hour contributions from all contractors employing men in the craft, for each hour worked. In other cases, the union and the contractors' associations jointly finance the committee or the union does it alone.[59] Jointly administered training funds to which employers contribute were authorized by the Landrum-Griffin Act in 1959 but are treated as trust funds, with the trustees accountable for the fund's revenues. Generally, the financing of apprenticeship training started out on a very limited basis, involving primarily the discharge of administrative costs. Currently, however, many funds employ full-time apprentice coordinators to assist in administering the programs. In some branches of the industry, training funds have been established on a national basis. Finally, public support for apprenticeship is provided through federal and state bureaus of

[57]Employers sometimes pay apprentices more than the minimum rate set by collective bargaining agreements.
[58]Burt, *Industry and Vocational-Technical Education,* p. 421.
[59]Filley and Magnusen, "Joint Apprenticeship Committees in Wisconsin," p. 86.

apprenticeship and training. The bureaus provide technical assistance to the parties and promote apprenticeship programs. The public school system provides facilities and teachers for related instruction, though many crafts either supplement public funds or establish programs totally their own.

The distribution of costs among the parties varies over the period of training. Thus, it is commonly conceded that the apprentice in most crafts constitutes a net drain on the employer during his first six months, that is, his productivity is below his wage.[60] Later, the wage of the apprentice may more closely approximate his productivity, until in his final months of training he may be the full equivalent of a journeyman while the employer still compensates him below the journeyman scale. Farber has attempted to estimate the relative distribution of an apprentice's productivity over time for the different crafts.[61] First approximations of the relative cost of apprenticeship to employers and apprentices may be obtained in this fashion.

Apprenticeship may be appropriately analyzed as an investment expenditure by both the trainee and his employer. The apprentice accepts wages below what he might obtain elsewhere in return for the higher wages anticipated when he becomes a journeyman. Similarly, the employer may "invest" in training an apprentice in order to obtain a skilled man. The foregone earnings of the apprentice relative to his expected future earnings determine the advisability of the investment. Because training is usually general in nature, not specific to the firm, it is commonly cheaper for a contractor to hire men trained by other firms than to train them himself.[62] In fact, contractors

[60]See Henning, "Apprenticeship Data: Questions and Answers," p. 1189, and Charles F. Hanna, "Expanding Apprenticeship Opportunities," in Senate, Subcommittee on Employment and Manpower, *The Role of Apprenticeship,* 88th Cong., 2nd sess., 1964, p. 111.
[61]David A. Farber, "Construction Apprentices and Construction Workers: A Study of Worker Mobility," mimeo (1968).
[62]Theoretically, a firm should refuse to bear the cost of training men in generally applicable skills; thus, one would expect the costs of training in construction to be borne entirely by parties other than the contractors. Empirically, this is not the case. Presumably, however, if a small burden of training cost rested on the employer, a larger number of men would be trained. See Scoville, "Concept and Measurements of Manpower," for a theoretical analysis of the incidence of training costs. It is interesting that Scoville's model suggests that in an organized (unionized) labor market, "workers cost share [of the total training costs], job and training breadths would all be greater than in a disorganized labor market." Rather than using organization strength to shift training costs to employers, Scoville believes the unions "would be willing to assume costs in order to safeguard control of the work for their members" (p. 134). In fact, unions do shift the incidence of training costs in part onto employers by enforcing training standards. Second, control of training is not equivalent to job control except when formal training is the only route of entry to the trade. Scoville's theoretical work is suggestive but requires further adjustment to particular empirical situations.

often resist hiring apprentices when journeymen are readily available. Also, apprentices are too often the first men laid off.

In terms of actual expenses, the public currently bears little of the out-of-pocket cost of apprenticeship. Hanna anticipated that in 1964 California would spend $130 per year per apprentice (including related classroom instruction, promotion, and administrative expenses) — considerably above other states' expenditures.[63] Using California figures as an upper limit, it is possible to estimate that total state expenditures on apprenticeship have not exceeded $10 to $15 million in recent years. Federal expenditures are far smaller. However, the federal government spends far larger sums on training programs in construction under the Department of Labor manpower programs. By early 1970, expenditures were at the rate of more than $30 million per year, with a presidential directive to expand the rate of these expenditures by 50 percent over the next five years.[64]

The training expenditures of private industry are very large. A rough estimate of the receipts of joint apprenticeship committees and other training funds suggest that their upper limit would be $120 million and their lower limit about $40 million.[65] There are no estimates of the forgone earnings of trainees, nor of the cost of training to individual employers. But there is no doubt that the total cost of training to apprentices and employers far exceeds these figures. In 1968, for example, the total shortfall of apprentice wages from the journeyman scale for the year probably exceeded $300 million.[66]

Proposals to increase the number of trainees in construction often focus on financial incentives to employers.[67] These proposals sometimes include

[63] Hanna, "Expanding Apprenticeship Opportunities," p. 1109.

[64] "Statement by the President on Combatting Construction Inflation and Meeting Future Construction Needs," mimeo (issued by the White House on March 17, 1970), p. 5.

[65] Author's estimates, based on a contribution of 0.5 percent of the wage bill to a joint fund and adjusted for probable coverage. See, for example, the statement of Fred B. Irwin, Assistant to the President, IBEW, in Senate, Subcommittee on Employment and Manpower, *Role of Apprenticeship,* 88th Cong., 2nd sess., 1969, p. 1154.

[66] Author's estimates. Assuming average union hourly wage of $5.43 (U.S. Bureau of Labor Statistics, *Union Wages and Hours: Building Trades, July 1, 1968,* Bulletin no. 1621, Washington D.C., 1969), an average apprentice rate of 70 percent of the journeyman scale, 1600 hours of work in the year, and 126,000 registered apprentices in training (U.S. Bureau of Apprenticeship and Training).

[67] See, for example, Foltman, "Public Policy in Apprenticeship Training," p. 1131 "Some way should be developed to provide some form of financial assistance to employers who train skilled workers." In addition, several federally financed training programs in construction have involved subsidies to contractors who pay the journeyman rate to trainees.

the suggestion that employers be reimbursed for the costs of training. There are major shortcomings of any such scheme. First, it may be prohibitively expensive if conducted on a wide scale, The availability of federal money for training may cause reductions in the contributions of private parties, resulting in tremendous costs to the government. Second, enforcement of training provisions in government contracts for construction is almost impossible. The dispersion and number of jobsites, occupations, and employers create tremendous problems of monitoring. Further, employers have an incentive to pocket federal training cost reimbursements and use trainees as semiskilled or unskilled help. Normally, the union or the joint committee enforces training responsibilities, but is futile to suggest that the federal government spend large sums of money with no enforcement safeguards except the language of the training contract.

Informal Routes to Learning the Trades

Persons without formal training in construction occupations sometimes pick up a trade in one way or another. Learning methods include experience in the armed forces, summer work, observation, and trial and error. In some trades, these informal mechanisms are institutionalized — for example, improvers in the asbestos workers, oilers in the operating engineers, permitmen among the ironworkers, and summer employees among the electricians. In some cases, the informal routes feed into formal apprenticeship programs or journeyman upgrading programs. In others, men may become journeymen without ever obtaining formal instruction. In some crafts (especially the engineers and the laborers), different wage rates paid for different machines facilitate the informal learning process, for a man may move up the scale by learning to operate more complicated machines.

Union membership is not normally denied to men who have mastered the craft, no matter how they learned it. The requirements for union membership differ considerably among the crafts but do not, according to the national constitutions, require the applicant to have completed an apprenticeship. In most trades, an examining board meets to review the competence of men applying for membership, and if the men are accomplished at the craft, they may become members.

For example, Section 158 of the constitution of the United Association (plumbers and pipefitters) provides the following:

Every applicant for membership as a journeyman in a Building and Construction Trades Local Union or a Combination Local Union (Building and Construction Trades Branch) must be a skilled craftsman and his application must contain information as to his experience and/or training. These qualifications must include:

1. That he has had a minimum of at least 5 years actual practical working experience in the plumbing and pipefitting industry.

2. That he is of good moral character.

3. That he passes a satisfactory examination as to his skill and ability as a Building and Construction Trades journeyman, conducted by the Examining Committees of the Building and Construction Trades Local Union or by the Building and Construction Trades Branch of a Combination Local Union.

In many areas, apprenticeship is virtually the only method of obtaining five years' experience in the unionized sectors of the plumbing and pipefitting industry. But a nonunion mechanic may apply for membership and by demonstrating his experience and his skill be accepted into the union. In fact, locals of the United Association normally augment their membership largely through the organization of previously nonunion mechanics.[68]

The Painters, on the other hand, provide that a man may be admitted to the brotherhood if he has had three years experience in the trade and is able to command the journeyman rate of pay.[69] The Bricklayers insist that any applicant for membership be qualified at one of the branches of the trade (including bricklaying, cement masonry, plastering, and so forth) and provide that "no applicant for membership shall be black-balled except for incompetency."[70]

Most trades attempt to control the informal instruction of learners on union jobs, in part for fear of flooding the trade with partially trained mechanics. Control of training is intimately associated with maintenance of the journeyman rate of pay. Further, partially trained mechanics are often difficult to place in jobs and constitute a source of dissatisfaction in the union. Control may be exercised by any one of a variety of means. The most important means of limiting the entry of learners is the enforcement of the journeyman's rate of pay for all men working at the trade except apprentices. Another mechanism is to deny membership in the local to semi- or unskilled

[68] For a description of the informal training of pipeline welders in the nonunion sector of construction, see Bernie Graves, "Breaking Out: An Apprenticeship System among Pipeline Construction Workers," *Human Organization* 17 (Fall 1958): 9–13.

[69] Brotherhood of Painters and Allied Trades, *International Constitution,* Sections 88 and 213.

[70] Bricklayers, Masons, and Plasterers International Union, *International Constitution* Article XII, Section 1.

mechanics. Less common provisions include prohibitions against members' training persons other than apprentices.[71]

In summary, all the crafts attempt to regulate the training of men in the unionized sectors of construction. In some crafts, apprenticeship is enforced as virtually the only means of training. In others, less formal means of training are permitted or even facilitated by special wage provisions, issuance of working permits, or other mechanisms. For the most part, however, during the past two decades the crafts have been relying more and more on apprenticeship as the only means of training (formal or informal) in the union sector. All crafts do provide for the admission to union membership of men who have picked up the trade in one way or another, including work in the nonunion sectors. Learning a job nonunion remains a major route of entry for mechanics to the unionized sector of construction.

During the late 1960s, attention in some trades was directed to formalizing the training component of what have in the past been primarily informal methods of learning in the union sector. Thus, the Operating Engineers have established formal apprenticeship programs in many areas to replace the informal training provided by the oiler classification. The Electricians are now establishing a two-year apprenticeship program to produce residential wiremen, in an attempt by the union to organize residential work. The Ironworkers have considered institutionalizing a means of entry to membership in local unions through the work permit system for men who are initially qualified in a narrow range of skills. Finally, as an element of affirmative action to increase minority group participation in the crafts, most unions are now considering the establishment of formal training mechanisms outside the apprenticeship programs. In most cases, these mechanisms will include additional wage classifications of trainees and advanced trainees. The training programs established should include on-the-job instruction and related education, as in apprenticeship programs.

In the future the increasing formalization of training associated with the nonapprenticeship means of learning a trade promises to increase the supply of better-trained mechanics to the industry.

---

[71] For example, the Bricklayers' constitution reads as follows (Article XVIII, Secion 3): "Members of subordinate unions who further the interests of firms, corporations, manufacturers, public or private schools by teaching laborers, convicts, or any persons other than regular indentured apprentices the trade of masonry shall be subject to a fine for the first offence of not less than $100 or more than $500."

8

The Numerical Adequacy of Apprenticeship Programs

The Role of Apprenticeship

Evaluating the numerical adequacy of apprenticeship to future manpower needs in construction is a complex task, involving not only quantitative measurements and expectations but also the use of informed judgment. Since the number of apprentices trained is not an indication of the total volume of manpower entry to construction (other sources of entry are also of great importance), measurement of the number of apprentices against expected demand and replacement needs is appropriate only under restrictive assumptions. Instead, the numerical adequacy of apprenticeship programs must be evaluted in light of the role desired for apprenticeship in the total volume of entry to a craft. Furthermore, apprenticeship training performs somewhat different functions in different crafts, and although most crafts promote apprenticeship as the best mechanism of training for a young man, it is dominant in only a few trades.[1] Apprenticeship appears to supply a core of key journeymen, foremen, supervisors, and even contractors in most trades [2] In this sense, it can be as much a management training mechanism as a means of training the work force itself.

Evaluation of numerical adequacy is also hampered by the poor quality of many apprenticeship statistics, including the lack of data specific to the construction industry and the lack of figures on formal training in unregistered programs. Also, the quality of registered apprenticeship varies considerably among crafts (and among areas in the same craft), so that aggregate numerical measures, even by craft, conceal considerable differences in the extent and

---

[1] A survey conducted in April 1963 demonstrated the varying importance among the crafts of formal training (including technical school training, apprenticeship, and training in the armed services) as a means of learning the occupation. U.S. Department of Labor, *Formal Occupational Training of Adult Workers*, Manpower/Automation Research Monograph no. 2 (Washington, D.C., 1964). The percentage who learned the craft through formal training differed as follows:

Brickmasons, stonemasons, and tilesetters	44.7
Carpenters	31.1
Electricians	72.9
Excavating, grading, and road machinery operators	11.2
Painters	27.8
Plumbers and pipefitters	55.0
Tinsmiths, coppersmiths, and sheet metal workers	70.9
Cranemen, derrickmen, and hoistmen	17.5

[2] A study of apprentices who completed their programs in 1950 found that by 1956 some 20 percent were employed as supervisors and another 10 percent were contractors. U.S. Bureau of Apprenticeship and Training, *Career Patterns of Former Apprentices*, Bulletin T-147 (Washington, D.C., 1959).

value of the training provided. Thus the numerical adequacy of apprenticeship programs must be related to the role of apprenticeship training in each
craft and to the quality of the programs provided. On the basis of certain information and assumptions regarding the role of apprenticeship in each trade,
it is possible to evaluate the degree to which variation in national employment
conditions for each craft is reflected in the volume of apprenticeship and to
test hypotheses regarding the effect of economic conditions on registrations,
completions, and cancellations in programs. From the research presented in
this chapter, it is clear that apprenticeship programs in the various crafts respond differently to economic conditions and that in most crafts the volume
of entry to and exit from apprenticeship training is, in the short run, remarkably insensitive to economic conditions nationally for the particular craft.
Yet long-run imbalances between formal training and the need for manpower
do cause adjustments to be made in the direction of enlarging programs or
improving their qualitative performance. Because the problems of programs in
the crafts vary considerably, the types of adjustments vary as well.

The Statistics on Apprenticeship

The Quality of the Data

Statistics regarding apprenticeship in this country have been subjected to
critical examination by other researchers,[3] but I will mention their major
limitations as a prelude to the analyses that follow. First, there are few statistics available on the number of apprentices in construction, as opposed to
the total number of registered apprentices in the building and construction
crafts, many of whom are apprenticed in firms or institutions that are not in
the building and construction industry. There is certainly some movement into
construction of apprentices trained outside the industry, but the degree to
which this occurs is unknown. Virtually all apprenticeship statistics for the
building trades, therefore, are overestimates of the numbers being trained in
construction itself. Second, it is not possible to obtain good estimates of the
number of nonregistered apprentices, either in aggregate or by craft. In part,
the unreliability of estimates on unregistered apprentices is a result of the
great variation in the quality of these programs. Many so-called "apprenticeship" programs are no more than low-wage unskilled work. Nevertheless, the
volume of training in unregistered programs has been estimated to be as high

---

[3]See especially Phyllis Groom, "Statistics and Their Limitations," pt. 3 of "An Assessment of Apprenticeship," *Monthly Labor Review* 87 (April 1964): 391-395.

as that in registered programs.[4] Third, major revisions have occurred in the reporting system, which have made time-series data less than perfectly continuous in several periods.[5]

The quality of estimates of the number of employed journeymen is not much better than the apprenticeship data. There are no data available on employment by craft in *contract* construction, and unpublished Current Population Survey estimates of employment by craft in all construction include employees of government construction agencies as well as of contractors. Certainly, no data are available that give us a measure of the number of highly skilled construction mechanics — the men apprenticeship training is designed to produce and replace.[6]

The Ratio of Apprentices to Journeymen

Statistics are available on the ratio of apprentices in training to active journeymen by craft, and examination of these data provides important insights into the operation of apprenticeship programs in the different crafts. Data are available from two sources. First, the Bureau of Labor Statistics each year surveys building trades unions in 52 cities with populations (in 1950) of 100,000 or more. The unions are requested to report the ratio of apprentices working, apprentice completions in the preceding twelve months, and journeymen who have become inactive (due to accidents, death, or retirement) in the preceding twelve months to the number of active journeymen. These data are available for most crafts annually since 1950. Second, the Bureau of Apprenticeship and Training compiles estimates of the number of apprentices in training, registrations, completions, and cancellations annually, by craft, for the entire nation. These data may be related to national employment estimates by craft to obtain apprentice to journeyman ratios.

Analysis of the BLS 52-city data shows considerable variation by trade in the ratios of apprentices and completions to active journeymen.[7] Generally,

4 John F. Henning, "Apprenticeship Data: Questions and Answers," in U.S. Congress, Senate, Committee on Labor and Public Welfare, Subcommittee on Employment and Manpower, *Selected Readings in Employment and Manpower*, vol. 3, *The Role of Apprenticeship in Manpower Development*, 88th Cong., 2nd sess., 1964, p. 1184.
5 F.F. Foltman and L.S. Tunkel, "National and State Apprenticeship, 1960–1966: Up to Data or Out of Date?" in *Research in Apprenticeship Training* (Madison: University of Wisconsin Center for Studies in Vocational and Technical Education, 1967), p. 128.
6 See, for example, Sumner H. Slichter, J.J. Healy, and E.R. Livernash, *The Impact of Collective Bargaining on Management* (Washington: Brookings Institution, 1960). Discussing the distinction in the census between skilled workers and others, the authors comment, " . . . but many so-called 'carpenters' are only saw and hammer men, many 'painters' are just brush hands . . ." (p. 62).
7 This analysis is limited to the period ending in 1968 by the nonavailability of data for later periods.

the electricians, roofers, and sheet metal workers show relatively high ratios of apprentices and apprenticeship completions per 100 active journeymen (see Table 19). The painters and carpenters show relatively low ratios of apprentices (and completions) to active journeymen. However, the types of apprenticeship programs that yield similar performance in terms of apprentices per 100 active journeymen are very diverse. Thus, the electricians', sheet metal workers', and roofers' programs, while similar in quantitative performance, are very different in operation, and circumstances unique to each of the crafts result in a similarity in numerical performance that is largely coincidental.

The electricians' and sheet metal workers' programs each take four to five years and require high school graduation or equivalency, plus competitive examinations, for admission. These apprenticeship programs are normally closely monitored ones in which the apprentice's progress is periodically evaluated and in which related instruction is very important to his success. The roofers' program is a three-year apprenticeship, in which acceptance requirements are much less stringent (a high school diploma is generally not required), and much of the successful completion of apprenticeship depends on the trainee's willingness and ability to remain in a very difficult and exhausting job. Turnover in the roofers' craft and in apprenticeship programs is very high, and a large ratio of apprentices to journeymen is necessary to sustain the supply of manpower in the trade. Employment in construction among electricians and sheet metal workers has grown slowly over the past two decades, and the completion rates of apprentices have generally exceeded journeyman loss rates, allowing for growth in the trade through apprenticeship as well as through other sources. The employment of roofers has been largely stationary, with high rates of journeyman losses largely compensated for by high rates of apprenticeship training and completion.[8]

The relatively low ratios of apprentices to journeymen among carpenters and the failure of completions to match journeyman losses reflect the somewhat stagnant employment conditions for carpenters in the post–World War II period and the great importance of informal entry to the trade. It became clear by the mid-1960s that the role of apprenticeship in meeting manpower demand in carpentry was declining, and international union officials began to exhort local unions to increase the volume of apprenticeship. A major prob-

[8] For employment estimates by craft, 1960–1966, see John T. Dunlop and D. Q. Mills, "Manpower in Construction," in *Report of the President's Committee on Urban Housing: Technical Studies,* vol. 2 (Washington, D.C., 1968), p. 285.

Table 19.   Ratios of Active Apprentices, Apprenticeship Completions, and Journeyman Losses to Active Journeymen by Craft, 52 Major Cities, Selected Years

	Average Ratio of Apprentices per 100 Active Journeymen[a]		Apprenticeship Completions per 1000 Active Journeymen[b]		Journeymen Losses per 1000 Active Journeymen[c]	
	1950–1964	1965–1968	1950–1964	1965–1968	1950–1964	1965–1968
Asbestos workers	n.a.	20.5	n.a.	41.5	n.a.	27.2
Bricklayers, marble, terrazzo, mosaic, stone, and tile workers	7.4	5.3	25.7	10.8	19.7	19.5
Carpenters (including soft floor layers and millwrights)	4.3	4.4	7.2	4.8	15.7	14.2
Electricians	13.2	12.4	32.0	27.3	20.6	28.0
Ironworkers (including rodmen)	5.0	6.3	16.7	15.5	21.5	23.0
Lathers	n.a.	7.0	n.a.	18.2	n.a.	26.0
Painters, glaziers, and paper-hangers	3.3	4.2	7.9	8.8	22.6	24.2
Plasterers and cement masons	6.8	4.3	19.3	9.0	21.4	20.5
Plumbers and pipefitters	10.2	11.3	19.3	16.0	20.8	23.5
Roofers	12.3	12.7	33.3	28.2	29.0	32.0
Sheet metal workers	12.7	12.7	27.9	25.2	15.5	17.2

Source: U.S. Bureau of Labor Statistics surveys of building trades unions in 52 cities with 1950 populations of 100,000 or more.
[a] Ratio of number of persons working under apprenticeship agreements to number of journeymen working or available for work on July 1 of the specified year.
[b] Ratio of number of persons completing prescribed apprentice training during the previous twelve months to the number of active journeymen on July 1 of the specified year.
[c] Ratio of number of journeymen who became unavailable for work because of death, permanent disability, or retirement during the previous twelve months to the number of journeymen active on July 1 of the specified year.

lem with increasing the volume of apprenticeship training in carpentry appears to be the unwillingness of general contractors in many areas to employ carpenter apprentices. Possible reasons for this situation will be discussed later.

The painters' program suffers from problems very similar to those of the carpenters. The programs for both painters and glaziers are normally three years in length, with certain specialties (especially dry-wall taping) requiring only two years to complete. Informal entry remains very important in painting, and apprenticeship programs provide only a small part of the trade's manpower.

The limitations of these data make it difficult to use them for analytic purposes in certain crafts. First, considerable confusion is introduced by the aggregation of separate crafts into wider categories. Thus, the apprenticeship programs for plumbers and pipefitters, painters and glaziers (and tapers), plasterers and cement masons, and structural and reinforcing ironworkers are quite separate, often existing in largely distinct branches of the industry and involving, especially in the large cities, separate local unions and contractors. Aggregation of the data tends to suppress any distinctions between the performance of the separate programs and makes analysis hazardous. As an important example, the standards and performance of apprenticeship programs in cement masonry and plastering are quite separate, and the employment experience of the two crafts has been very different in the past two decades. Employment of plasterers in construction declined by 43 percent from 1950 to 1960, while employment of cement masons rose 130 percent.[9] The apprenticeship programs in the two crafts have reflected this employment experience, but the aggregation of data masks the difference in performance. Second, the journeyman membership of many trades includes specialties that are not normally apprenticed and the inclusion of which in the journeyman estimates causes the ratios of apprentices to journeymen in each craft to be underestimated. The situation is especially marked for the bricklayer and ironworker. In many bricklayers locals, marble, terazzo, stone, and tile workers are a significant portion of the journeyman membership, and rodmen (who place reinforcing rods in concrete) are a major proportion of many ironworkers locals.

Using these data with circumspection, it remains clear that apprenticeship in the pipe trades is an important route of entry but that it normally does not exceed replacement needs. Instead, a large proportion of entry to the big city locals is through organization of previously nonunion shops. The ironworkers,

[9] Ibid.

for whom apprenticeship entry also does not exceed replacement needs, continue to experience rapid variations in local demand and to meet increases in demand through the mobility of their membership and the use of the permit system. Apprenticeship programs in the ironworkers' craft are used primarily to replace losses among journeyman members of the locals, not to meet needs for short-run expansion.

In virtually all crafts, the relatively rapid expansion of employment in the mid-1960s led to a decline in the ratio of apprentice completions to journeymen and to increases in the ratio of apprentices in training to active journeymen. Similarly, losses of journeymen rose proportionately as employment expanded and the pace of work (especially overtime) increased. In virtually all crafts, apprenticeship volume lagged behind the economic growth of the later 1960s, and classes are only now being expanded to meet the new conditions.

It is also instructive to compare journeyman-to-apprentice ratios in the large cities with national estimates. The two sets of data are not perfectly comparable, since the BLS survey covers only 52 large cities and union programs. The national data represent all registered apprentices and all employment, union and nonunion.

In general, over the past two decades the national ratio of journeymen to apprentices has been higher than the 52-city ratio for four trades: carpenters, painters, plasterers, and roofers (see Table 20). On the whole, this reflects the confinement of large-scale, formal apprenticeship in these trades to the larger cities, but the large nonunion sector of these trades and the existence of semi-skilled specialty workers in the carpentry and painting industries must also be taken into account. For the pipe trades, bricklaying, and electrical work, national and major city ratios are much the same. For the electrical and pipe trades, this is explained by the strong nationwide apprenticeship programs; for brickmasonry it reflects a program that is national in scope but somewhat weak in recent years in most areas. In two crafts, the ironworkers and sheet metal workers, the 52-city journeyman/apprentice ratios exceed the national ratios. This result is apparently a consequence of the poor quality of the statistics. Apprenticeship data for the national level of all trades includes apprentices in industries other than construction, and those figures are especially large for sheet metal and structural iron erection. The national employment (or journeyman) estimates are specific to construction, so that the national ratio of journeymen to apprentices is probably a significant understatement.

Table 20.   Ratio of Employment at the Trade to the Number of Apprentices in 52
Selected Cities and Nationally, Selected Years

	1952	1958	1962	1966
Bricklayers				
Selected cities[a]	10.6	13.6	19.5	16.3
Nationally[b]	23.8	11.9	18.6	17.6
Carpenters				
Selected cities	23.1	27.7	20.9	22.9
Nationally	38.3	29.4	28.7	27.9
Electricians				
Selected cities	8.4	7.0	8.5	8.3
Nationally	9.7	7.7	8.2	8.2
Ironworkers				
Selected cities	14.0	16.4	23.0	16.5
Nationally	30.9	9.3	6.7	7.7
Painters				
Selected cities	37.0	28.3	25.8	22.8
Nationally	98.9	70.4	53.3	52.5
Plasterers and cement masons				
Selected cities	10.6	13.3	19.5	23.3
Plasterers				
Nationally	24.8	24.5	22.0	26.9
Cement Masons				
Nationally	51.4	31.4	37.1	39.4
Plumbers and pipefitters				
Selected cities	9.6	9.7	10.2	8.6
Nationally	12.6	8.7	8.4	9.0
Roofers				
Selected cities	6.8	8.4	7.9	8.5
Nationally	29.4	23.8	25.9	19.2
Sheet metal workers				
Selected cities	7.7	7.9	8.0	8.0
Nationally	5.1	2.9	4.2	4.2

[a]Computed by the U.S. Bureau of Labor Statistics on the basis of data collected from the building trades.
[b]Computed by the author from U.S. Bureau of Apprenticeship and Training data on the number of registered apprentices in training in each craft and the author's estimates of employment in the building trades. See John T. Dunlop and D.Q. Mills, "Manpower in Construction," in *Report of the President's Committee on Urban Housing: Technical Studies,* vol. 2 (Washington, D.C., 1968), p. 285.

To sum up, data regarding the relative volume of apprenticeship and employment reflect very different circumstances among the various crafts. In some crafts, apprenticeship plays a relatively small role in replacing journeyman losses and meeting additional manpower demand. In other crafts, the programs are a major route of meeting employment growth. In some trades, programs have been numerically stagnant or declining in recent years; in others, they are stronger than before. Finally, in some crafts apprenticeship is largely confined to the major cities; in others, the programs are national in operation. In all cases, evaluation is based on the application of qualitatively informed judgment to data of varying accuracy and usefulness.

Apprenticeship Adequacy Rates

Most researchers have attempted to evaluate apprenticeship by measuring the volume of apprenticeship training against expected future demand for construction labor. The problems in construction of estimating what has been called an "adequacy rate" are considerable, owing largely to the paucity of occupational employment data.[10] Researchers using various concepts of adequacy to evaluate training in the industry have issued dire warnings of the supposed inadequacy of apprenticeship periodically for many decades.[11] Yet the industry has managed to increase its volume of output without markedly increasing its volume of training.

Several authors have made quantitative estimates of the adequacy of apprenticeship to manpower needs. Haber and Levinson argue that even in the peak years of apprenticeship completions (1950-1951), only about half the necessary journeymen were being produced.[12] The *Manpower Report of the President* for 1963 contained a series of estimates of the percentage of additional journeymen required by 1970 that would be supplied through apprenticeship at current rates of completion. The estimates ranged from 3 percent for painters to 36 percent for electricians. The industry, particularly the Building and Construction Trades Department of the AFL-CIO, challenged these estimates, chiefly on the grounds that certain underlying assumptions

---

[10]The first part of this section depends heavily on Howard G. Foster, "Labor Supply in the Construction Industry: A Case Study of Upper New York State" (Ph.D. thesis, Cornell University, 1969), pp. 198–204.

[11]See, for example, Paul Douglas, *American Apprenticeship and Industrial Education* (New York: Columbia University Press, 1921); William Haber, *Industrial Relations in the Building Industry* (Cambridge: Harvard University Press, 1930), pp. 130–132; and Slichter, Healy, and Livernash, *Impact of Collective Bargaining*, p. 102.

[12]William Haber and Harold M. Levinson, *Labor Relations and Productivity in the Building Trades* (Ann Arbor: University of Michigan Bureau of Industrial Relations, 1956), pp. 82–85.

concerning rates of growth and productivity increases were unwarranted.[13]

Strauss has suggested two ways to calculate adequacy rates.[14] The first relates apprentice completions in each craft to the estimated number of openings created by attrition and net growth as projected for the 1965–1975 decade by the Bureau of Labor Statistics. The second relates completions to actual changes between 1950 and 1960 according to census figures. The overall results are similar in both cases. The range of rates was found to be between 8 and 57 percent, with the mechanical trades typically at the high end.

Most attempts at calculating apprenticeship adequacy rates fail to recognize that apprenticeship fulfills a different function in different crafts. Foster conceived of apprenticeship in all crafts as designed to produce only the core of workers who must be able to read blueprints and fill other highly skilled functions. He then offered an admittedly crude way of isolating the number of most-skilled men and assessing the success of apprenticeship training in supplying that number.[15]

There are, however, very serious limitations to this method. First, while Foster has used openings for craftsmen only in construction, the apprenticeship data used are for all industries. Thus, there is an overestimate of the relative volume of training in several crafts, especially the electricians and sheet metal workers. More important, there are no direct measures of the key group in any trade. Foster's attempt to relate the key group to the proportion of men employed fifty weeks or more is largely nonsense. For several trades, such as those most affected by seasonality, this method yields far too low a proportion of key men in the work force. Thus Foster's adequacy rate is highest for bricklayers and ironworkers (and is greater than 1) — a conclusion that no one closely familiar with the industry would support without major qualifications. Alternatively, the fifty-week measure generates a key group percentage of 71.8 for the electricians — a figure so high that it reduces the concept of a "key" group to absurdity.[16] In fact, there is no reason to believe that the key group can be directly measured from any statistics currently available. Nor is the function of apprenticeship in all trades only to provide for a key

[13] Senate, Subcommittee on Employment and Manpower, *The Role of Apprenticeship*, 88th Cong., 2nd sess., 1964, pp. 1157–1179.
[14] George Strauss, "Apprenticeship: Problems and Policies," mimeo (1968), quoted in Foster, "Labor Supply in the Construction Industry," p. 200.
[15] See Allan F. Salt, "Estimated Need for Skilled Workers, 1965–75," *Monthly Labor Review* 89 (April 1966): 368.
[16] In fact, however, an important segment of what Foster and others mean by the key group is conceptually excluded from his measurement, for all managerial personnel above the foreman level are excluded from the employment series Foster uses. In some trades, the role of apprenticeship in training supervisory personnel is very marked.

group of men. Certainly in the sheet metal, electrical, and pipe trades apprenticeship is a major mechanism of training and entry for much more of the work force than the key man concept would suggest.

A more useful approach (suggested by Foster) might be to relate the proportion of current journeymen who have served apprenticeship to the expected future manpower demand by craft and to the expected (or current) rate of apprenticeship training. Projections of manpower demand like those used by Salt[17] and Dunlop and Mills[18] and estimates of apprenticeship training by craft will suggest whether current apprenticeship training falls further behind future requirements than in the past. Perhaps, however, the greatest practical difficulties relate to obtaining accuracy in the manpower projections with which apprenticeship volume is to be compared.

In any case, adequacy rates have not yet been refined to the necessary degree of conceptual and quantitative accuracy to be useful for national policy making. Flows of manpower are too important and the availability of data too limited at the national level to justify reliance on adequacy rates. The concept of a measurable adequacy rate for apprenticeship could be of considerable assistance to local joint apprenticeship committees, however. Most JACs have access to information regarding local labor conditions that would allow intelligent use of the adequacy rate as a planning tool. JACs might estimate demand and replacement needs and compare them with alternative volumes of apprenticeship training. A particular adequacy rate or range of rates might be suggested to local JACs by national leaders, and the number of new apprentices might thereby be determined on a more rational planning basis. But no matter how it is worked out, any adequacy rate, to be useful, would have to be based on local conditions.

Apprenticeship Volume and National Economic Forces

The Impact of National Economic Conditions on the Total Number of Apprentices
The volume of apprenticeship training depends in large part on employment conditions in the crafts and on expectations regarding these conditions. While local employment conditions are the relevant ones, nevertheless they are affected by national economic conditions in many areas, and it is possible that apprenticeship volume, in each craft and in aggregate, responds to the

[17]Salt, "Estimated Need for Skilled Workers, 1965–75."
[18]Dunlop and Mills, "Manpower in Construction."

national economic position of the craft or industry. If apprenticeship programs were responsive to national conditions, concern with the localized control of programs might merit little attention.

David A. Farber has investigated the relationship between total apprenticeship volume in the building trades and national economic conditions. He has found what he considers to be "striking . . . relationships" between certain economic variables and the number of entering apprentices in construction.[19] The inverse relationship between new apprenticeship registrations and the volume of unemployment is said to be especially important. Farber suggests that

if . . . the basic parameters of apprenticeship are in fact fundamentally responsive to the general state of the economy and the particularistic forces of supply and demand in the job market, we may conclude that labor unions may at best only influence the apprenticeship system. Perhaps we may eventually conclude the number of apprentices entering an occupation is a function of demand for labor.[20]

Unfortunately, the response of apprenticeship programs to national economic conditions is spotty at best, and the expected relationships among apprenticeship volume and economic variables are difficult to demonstrate statistically. In fact, the apprenticeship programs of the different crafts react quite differently to changes in the national employment and wage position of the individual crafts. The creation of statistical models of the programs is still in its infancy, and for many purposes they are so far not very revealing. Farber, for example, argues primarily from visual inspection of data plots or from simple correlation coefficients. Multiple regression models, in which fairly complete specification of the apprenticeship process is attempted, provide less support for the relationship between apprenticeship volume and economic conditions.

It is possible to obtain useful models of the number of apprentices in training, however. A regression of the average total number of apprentices in training between January 1 and December 31 of each year from 1952 to 1968 against the construction average annual unemployment rate, the construction unemployment rate of the previous year, average annual employment in contract construction, and the ratio of average annual hourly earnings in contract construction to those in all nonagricultural industries generates a multiple regression coefficient (R^2) of 0.9442 (the F ratio is significant at 1 percent),

[19] "Construction Apprentices and Construction Workers: A Study of Worker Mobility," mimeo (July 1968), p. 32.
[20] David A. Farber, "Apprenticeship in the U.S.: Labor Market Forces and Social Policy," *Journal of Human Resources* 2 (Winter 1967): 84.

but a Durbin Watson statistic falling in the questionable range (d.w. = 1.5775), indicating possible serial correlation in the residuals of the equation. The coefficients of both unemployment variables and the employment series are statistically significant in the equation, but the relative wage variable is insignificant, and the introduction of an industry turnover rate[21] fails to improve it.

Annual percentage changes in the total number of apprentices are also related to construction unemployment and employment. However, models specifying the male (age 20 and over) unemployment rate rather than the construction rate perform somewhat better. These regressions indicate that changes in average annual employment in contract construction are associated with increases in apprenticeship of 8.5 percent of the employment increase, or 85 apprentices for each additional 1000 jobs, assuming that unemployment conditions are unchanging. The impact of employment conditions is relatively small. An increase of 1 percent in average annual employment generates, other things being equal, an increase of 1.05 percent in the total number of building trades apprentices in training (that is, the elasticity of apprenticeship to average annual employment at the margin is greater than 1). Therefore, it appears that for the most part the relative importance of apprenticeship in supplying manpower to the industry would not be expected to decline in periods of rapid expansion of employment, although it may do so in certain crafts.

Statistical analyses of apprentice registrations, cancellations, and completions are disappointing. Regressing total new registrations annually on the construction average unemployment rate, average annual employment, and relative average hourly earnings (contract construction versus all nonagricultural industries) indicates a significant statistical relationship between total registrations and the contract construction employment variable. Increases in employment appear to stimulate increases of apprenticeship registrations numbering approximately 2 percent of the increase in employment. Models of percentage changes in new registrations using unemployment, employment, wage, and turnover variables are statistically insignificant. The much-discussed relationship between new registrations and the unemployment rate (in con-

[21] Construed as the ratio of total employment in contract construction (as reported to the Social Security Administration) to annual average employment in contract construction (estimates compiled by the BLS). The ratio indicates the number of persons employed in the industry at some time during the year to the annual number of positions (jobs) filled in the industry. Farber stresses the importance of this industry turnover rate in his analysis.

struction or for males generally) does not appear significant when employment changes in construction are explicitly considered in the regressions.

Models of the completions process are not much more useful. The annual
number of completions (all building trades) is weakly related (positively) to
the unemployment rate and positively related to employment conditions (an
increase in average annual employment in contract construction has been
associated with an increase in apprentices' completions of 1 percent of the
employment increase). Models of percentage changes in completions are
without statistical significance.

The annual total number of apprentice cancellations (due to military service, dropouts, and so on), 1952–1968, does not appear statistically related
to unemployment rates, employment in construction, relative wages, or
turnover rates, when studied in a multiple regression framework. The percentage change in cancellations is, however, negatively related to changes in
current-year unemployment rates. When the construction or male unemployment rate rises, the percentage decline in cancellations tends to be marked
(approximately 8 points decline in cancellations for a single point rise in the
unemployment rate). The percentage change in cancellations is also negatively
related to changes in the contract construction turnover rate. Possibly this
result is not behavioral, for one would expect that, taking employment and
unemployment changes into consideration, the rate of cancellations would
increase rather than decrease when turnover rises.

**The Impact of National Economic Conditions on the Number of Apprentices
in Each Craft**
Existing data also allow investigation of the statistical relationships among
national economic variables specific to the different crafts. The average annual
number of apprentices in training (1952–1968) in each of 6 crafts was examined in relation to the number employed at the craft, the unemployment
rate among males 20 to 24, and the national average construction journeyman's rate for all trades.[22] Theoretical expectations were that the number of
apprentices in training would be positively related to employment in the
craft nationally, positively related to the youth unemployment rate (the
greater this unemployment rate, the larger the pool of manpower likely to
apply for apprenticeship programs, assuming that employment conditions in
the craft hold constant), and positively related to each craft's relative wage
position. Tests were made for the programs of the carpenters, electricians,

[22]These series were compiled from annual issues of the U.S. Bureau of Labor Statistics'
Union Wages and Hours: Building Trades, which provide summary data.

bricklayers, plumbers and pipefitters, painters, and sheet metal workers. The electricians' program showed a strong response to employment conditions in the trade (an increase in employment tended to produce an increase in apprentices in training of 13 percent of the employment increase). Other variables were statistically insignificant in the electricians' case. In no other craft were apprentices in training closely related to the volume of employment at the trade nationally. The plumbers' and pipefitters' and sheet metal workers' programs appeared responsive to the size of the intercraft relative wage differential but to no other conditions. The painters' program showed a statistically significant *negative* relationship to employment in the craft nationally.

Annual registrations in the various crafts were regressed against employment, wage relatives specific to the craft, and the young male unemployment rate. The number of new registrations was significantly related to these variables only for the electricians' program. Let

y = number of new registrations, electrical apprentices, 1952–1968,

x_1 = employment of electricians in construction,

x_2 = unemployment rate, males 20 to 24 years of age,

x_3 = ratio of the hourly wage rate for electricians in contract construction to the electricians' rate in basic steel (an interindustry wage comparison),

n = number of observations,

yielding

$$y = 0.0441x_1 - 0.3019x_2 - 5.4865x_3$$

       (.05%)   (.05%)   (5%)   (– significance level)

$R^2 = 0.8876$, $F(4,12)$ is significant at 1%, $n = 17$, and d.w. = 2.4242 (no serial correlation).

The positive relationship of electricians' registrations to the employment of electricians nationally is encouraging, but the negative relationships to the two other variables are disappointing. Apparently, more complex mechanisms than the ones reflected in these national averages of unemployment rates and wages are involved. In no other craft were the equations relating new registrations to national economic conditions at all successful.

Differencing the registrations equations to eliminate serial correlation generated a successful equation for the painters. Changes in new registrations for painters were positively related to employment changes (a regression coefficient of 0.045) and positively related to changes in the unemployment rate. (The equation showed an $R^2 = 0.4883$; F significant at 5 percent; d.w. = 2.0272, no evidence of serial correlation; and $n = 16$.)

Percentage changes in registrations provided evidence that carpenters' registrations were related positively to percentage increases in employment. The elasticity of apprenticeship registrations to employment changes in carpentry was 2.17. Models constructed for the other crafts (bricklayers, plumbers, and sheet metal workers) were in all cases unsatisfactory.

Completions in the several crafts were studied in relation to registrations in the craft k years before (where k was the term of apprenticeship appropriate to the craft), an index of employment stability in the craft in the k years of each apprenticeship term, and the construction unemployment rate. Only for the bricklayers were completions closely related to registrations in previous years. (The regression coefficient was 0.48046, other variables insignificant; $R^2 = 0.8874$; $F(3,8)$ significant at 1 percent; and d.w. = 2.1428, no evidence of serial correlation; $n = 12$). The 5 other trades gave no statistical evidence of the effect of previous registrations or economic conditions on apprenticeship completions. Similarly, percentage changes in completions were strongly and positively related to percentage changes in registrations k years previously only for the bricklayers among the 6 crafts.

In summary, apprenticeship programs in the separate crafts generally respond poorly to national economic and employment conditions in their crafts. Only in the electricians' program do the number of apprentices in training and new registrations reflect the changing fortunes of employment in the craft nationally, though there is some evidence of responsiveness in the painters' and carpenters' programs as well. National economic conditions in each craft do not appear to affect the number of men in training, registrations, or completions in any other craft studied. Thus, however responsive apprenticeship programs may be to alterations in local economic conditions, they appear to respond poorly to current national needs.

There is, of course, the basic question as to why apprenticeship should be expected to respond to changes in national economic conditions. Ultimately, programs are adjusted to a period of long-run rising demand (as they were in the late 1960s in most trades), but it is important to know that this process is not automatic — that national industry leaders cannot ignore the operation of local apprenticeship programs in the belief that economic conditions alone will induce an adequate volume of formal training in the industry nationally. Rather, efforts must be made to keep apprenticeship programs in step with manpower demand, and national authorities must exert leadership by taking the necessary initiatives.

Adjustments in the Volume of Apprenticeship in Several Crafts

Despite the housing depression, construction volume as a whole remained high in the late 1960s. In consequence, apprenticeship in many crafts fell behind the national demand for manpower. Full-employment conditions placed considerable strains on apprenticeship programs, and there were widespread demands for adjustments and reforms. In some crafts, the problems of apprenticeship were more difficult than in others, but all crafts made and continue to make efforts to improve the performance of their programs. The particular problems and the methods of adjustment adopted in several selected crafts are described in the following pages.

Briefly, the electricians, sheet metal workers, and plumbers and pipefitters greatly strengthened the structure and content of their programs and experienced waiting lists of apprenticeship applicants.[23] In many localities, these crafts have been quite conservative in the number of apprentices they are willing to indenture. Demand conditions in many areas continue to suggest increases in the numbers trained. The pipe trades and electricians have both developed special formal training programs recently to facilitate the training of new manpower. Thus by 1969 the number of registered apprentices in training in each of these crafts reached its highest point in two decades.

The ironworkers experienced rapidly improving employment conditions in the late 1960s, but too often local unions met increasing demands through the permit process rather than through formal training. Should the use of permits and the acceptance of permitmen into membership continue, it may dilute the strong role that apprenticeship has achieved as a means of entry to the ironworkers' jurisdiction since the early 1950s.

The operating engineers responded to the expansion of employment in their craft with the development of formal apprenticeship (since 1958) and with continued efforts to expand apprenticeship programs among the local unions. The role of apprenticeship in the operators' craft is increasing, and the numbers in training are rising.

The carpenters' programs lagged behind the demands for workers in their jurisdiction, and many unions accepted a relatively large number of non-apprenticeship entrants, even in the larger cities where apprenticeship has

[23] Battelle Memorial Institute, "Final Report on an Evaluation of the United Association's Apprenticeship Training Program" (prepared for the United Associated by D.N.McFadden et al., Columbus, Ohio, 1968).

traditionally played a major role. In many areas, employers were unwilling to employ carpenter apprentices, and the recruitment of apprentices among young people was difficult. In response, the national union and employers began negotiations on ways to make apprenticeship more attractive to young men through devices such as shortening the program and improving related instruction. Some local unions threatened to include provisions in collective bargaining contracts requiring employers to hire apprentices. By 1969, as a result of these efforts, the number of carpenters' apprentices had begun to rise rapidly.

The bricklayers have been faced with problems somewhat akin to those of the carpenters. From a high of almost 15,000 registered apprentices nationally in 1958, the number of apprentices in training fell to less than 9000 in 1967 and expanded only slightly thereafter. Apparently the decline in the number of apprentices was due to difficulty recruiting men and to the continued reluctance of journeymen to train new men in the face of the pervasive and extreme seasonal pattern of employment in the craft. The national union and contractors sought to increase the numbers of apprentice applicants by increased recruiting in vocational high schools. Local unions were exhorted by the national union to apprentice more youths, and the brick industry as a whole has taken a series of steps toward reducing the seasonal pattern of work.

The painters' program declined in numbers after the mid-1960s and was widely criticized among employers and some local union representatives. Both the length and quality of the program remain at issue. Many persons have become painters without formal training. These men are a source of manpower to employers when demand conditions require expansion of the work force. But increasing wages in many major cities have made poorly trained men less attractive to contractors, and the competition for apprenticeship-trained mechanics is great. In this environment, employers who invest in apprenticeship training often have difficulty retaining their men, so that the employer investment in apprenticeship declines. Major reforms in the program are under discussion by painting industry leaders. Meanwhile, the number of apprentices in training is rising slowly.

Methods of Increasing the Number of Apprentices

Whether or not the number of apprentices in a particular craft should be expanded is an issue involving current and projected needs for fully trained mechanics. The role of apprenticeship in the different crafts and the mechanisms by which the number of apprentices is determined have been discussed earlier. Similarly, I have examined the numerical performance over time of apprenticeship generally and in each of several crafts. Assuming now that conditions in a craft warrant increasing the number of apprentices, there are several ways in which a craft might proceed, although recruitment may not be the only problem it will face if it wants to obtain and keep a larger number of young men.[24]

In some cases, crafts have long waiting lists for apprenticeship openings, and the process of increasing numbers simply means accepting more applicants into apprenticeship classes. In other crafts, it may be difficult to recruit men for apprenticeship, to retain apprentices through the term of their training, or to get employers to hire apprentices at all. A small number of apprentices is not always the result of union restrictions on the numbers trained.[25]

Rottenberg has pointed out that the economics of the apprenticeship process are as important in many cases as arbitrary limitations on the number of apprentices or apprentice/journeyman ratios.[26] Other authors had pointed out that the number of apprentices in training often fell below the number allowed by the apprentice/journeyman ratio in each craft and argued that these ratios were therefore not restrictive. Rottenberg demonstrated that

[24]The problem of retaining apprentices (that is, minimizing the dropout rate) is often as important as increasing recruitment. There have been few studies of the problem of dropouts, but see U.S. Bureau of Apprenticeship and Training, *Dropouts from Apprenticeship* (Washington, D.C., 1960). Most of the discussion in the text on making apprenticeship more attractive to potential recruits would apply as well to minimizing dropouts.

[25]Disputes over the number of apprentices have occurred in this country for many years. Frederick L. Ryan, *Industrial Relations in the San Francisco Building Trades* (Norman: University of Oklahoma Press, 1936), recorded long-term disputes between the unions and employers in San Francisco from 1900 to 1920 over supposed union restrictions on the number of apprentices. Apprentice shortages during the period 1921–1923 were generally blamed on the unions. But, Ryan concludes, "the belief that union restrictions were alone responsible for the shortage of mechanics has been thoroughly disproved" (p. 150). In New York City, the Building Congress discovered in 1920 that the unions were not directly responsible for shortages and made considerable improvements in the administration and structure of the programs. By the mid-1920s, the Apprenticeship Commission of the New York Building Congress had increased the number of apprentices significantly. Haber, *Industrial Relations in the Building Industry*, pp. 466–469. Even with insufficient evidence, some authors still attack the unions as the sole source of the problems of apprenticeship. See Jack Barbash, "Union Interests in Apprenticeship and Other Training Forms," *Journal of Human Resources* 3 (Winter 1968): 76.

[26]Simon Rottenberg, "The Irrelevance of Union Apprenticeship/Journeyman Ratios," *Journal of Business* 34 (July 1961): 384–386.

where the relative wages of the apprentice (vis-à-vis the journeyman) and the length of apprenticeship were established by union and contractors, these conditions, if unattractive, might discourage youths from applying for apprenticeship, so that limitations on the total number trained would remain academic. Further, if the union participated in the determination of the wages and length of training of apprentices, then these conditions of employment might limit the number of apprentices as effectively as more direct means. Hence, the fact that the number of apprentices fell below the number allowed did not indicate that employers were unwilling to hire apprentices. It could as easily indicate a lack of applicants.

In reality, cases are observed in which any of the possible causal factors may be at work. The number of apprentices may be what it is because of restrictions on the total number admitted (often the situation today in the mechanical trades), because of the unattractiveness of apprenticeship to young men (the case in some trowel trades in some areas), or because of the unwillingness of employers to hire apprentices (often now the case with carpenters' and painters' programs, for example). In the last case, unemployed apprentices testify to the contractors' unwillingness to hire.

Rottenberg is correct, or course, in emphasizing the importance in some situations of the economic conditions attached to apprenticeship. But he lists only the length of the program and the structure of apprentice wages (vis-à-vis journeyman wages) as significant aspects of the economic conditions. Equally important are the wages paid an apprentice relative to his capacity to earn at other jobs and the lifetime expected earnings in the craft as compared to alternative sources of livelihood. Furthermore, for the purpose of the apprentice's own comparison, relative *earnings* over some period of time (such as a year or more) may be more important than relative wage rates alone.

Technical note: Factors affecting the desirability of apprenticeship

Assume that the number of applicants for an apprenticeship program rises with the earnings offered the apprentice over his term of apprenticeship relative to earnings in other occupations open to the applicant (see Graph 1). Assume also that the number of applicants rises as the expected lifetime earnings in the apprenticeable craft rise relative to those in alternative occupations, other things being equal (see Graph 2). Now assume that the number of applicants rises as the ratio of apprentice earnings over the term of apprenticeship to journeyman earnings (at the same craft) rises (see Graph 3). Note that the position of the curve in Graph 3 depends on the values of the relative earnings variables listed in the two previous relationships. For example,

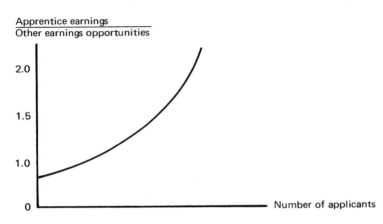

Apprentice earnings
─────────────────────
Other earnings opportunities

Graph 1.

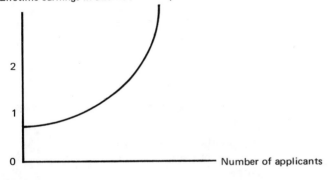

Lifetime earnings in apprenticeable occupation
──
Lifetime earnings in alternative occupation

Graph 2.

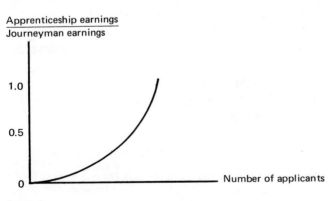

Apprenticeship earnings
─────────────────────────
Journeyman earnings

Graph 3.

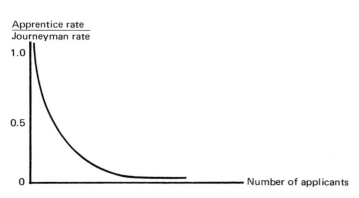

Graph 4.

the higher the relative earnings of apprentices to those in other occupations, the farther to the right (that is, the larger the number of applicants) the curve in Graph 3 will lie. Alternatively, the position of each of the three curves is contingent on a position of the other two.

The willingness of employers to hire apprentices depends solely on the relative earnings of apprentices and journeymen. The employer will hire apprentices so long as the ratio of their value productivity (net of all costs except wages) to journeymen's value productivity exceeds the ratio of the apprentice's to the journeyman's hourly rate of pay (see Graph 4).

The higher the relative hourly rate of apprentices to journeymen, the more attractive apprenticeship will be to applicants with the position of this curve contingent on relationships described in the three preceding graphs. Plotting the applicants (supply) curve against the contractor's willingness to hire apprentices (demand) curve will identify, on the two axes, respectively, a relative apprentice to journeyman hourly wage rate and a number of applicants hired which will tend to exist in a free (hiring) market (see Graph 5). Thus, at relative wage y_1, a number of applicants x_1 will be hired as apprentices.

Neither labor nor management will, in the organized sector of the industry, allow a freely fluctuating market in apprentices.[27] Rather, the relative apprentice-to-journeyman wage is established by the collective bargaining agreement, and the number of apprentices hired is allowed to fluctuate with shifts in the demand and supply of applicants (except where limitations on the total number of apprentices are established).

From this discussion, it is clear that there are various means by which to

[27] If the apprentice wage rate were allowed to fluctuate freely, it would undermine the basic purpose of removing wages as an element of competition among employers for projects.

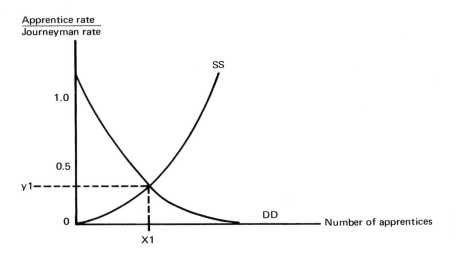

Graph 5

increase the number of applicants and/or apprentices hired. The most efficient method will depend on the relative elasticity of the supply of applicants to changes in the several variables affecting the number of applicants. The magnitude of these supply elasticities are empirical matters that have not received attention from economists. Yet they are critical to such issues of public policy as the best means for increasing formal training in construction (assuming that an increase is warranted). It is likely, for example, that where the quantity of apprentices demanded exceeds the quantity supplied at the established relative hourly rates of apprentices and journeymen, an increase in earnings in construction relative to other industries could generate a considerable increase in the number of apprentice applicants without affecting the apprentice/journeyman relative wage. Certainly the recent dramatic increases in construction wage rates in many areas have increased the attractiveness of apprenticeship to many young men.

The Role of Employers in Apprenticeship
The role of employers in hiring and training apprentices is at least as critical as the role of the unions in the operation of these programs. In many crafts, small employers rarely train apprentices; the middle-size firms sometimes train, but very large firms are often national contractors operating only temporarily in the area and do not train. The result is that only a small proportion of employers eligible to train (by size and length of time in the busi-

ness) actually employ apprentices.[28] Employers cite several reasons for their unwillingness to train apprentices, including the costs involved, the intimacy of contact with the union over apprentices, lack of business, and lack of applicants.[29] In some crafts, employers willing to hire apprentices are so rare that the joint apprenticeship committees do little more than indenture whomever an employer agrees to train.

Several methods of inducing employers to train larger numbers of apprentices have been suggested. An obvious solution is to adjust the economics of the process in the employers' favor by increasing the differential between the journeyman's rate of pay and the apprentice's rate. Unfortunately, a more common method is to allow the employer to avoid certain requirements of the training process by using the apprentice as a laborer or semiskilled man, thereby increasing his productivity to the employer. This procedure seriously weakens the training process itself. Finally, suggestions have been made that employers be required to hire apprentices. This might be done as a provision in a collective bargaining contract, or by law on public works projects. In California, legislation has been enacted requiring a ratio of one apprentice to five journeymen on all public works projects.[30] President Nixon's construction manpower message (March 17, 1970) directed federal agencies "to include a clause in construction contracts that will require the employment of apprentices or trainees on such projects."[31]

Requiring contractors to employ apprentices on public projects is subject to the weaknesses inherent in any project-by-project approach to training in construction. Essentially, there may be little training provided on the job and no provision for continuity of employment if employers will not hire the same number of apprentices on nonpublic work. However, because these apprentices will be registered and will be able to work on any job at the apprentice rate, employment opportunities on private work may be wider than if the

[28] "As of 1961, some 24,000 Wisconsin employers had the potential to train apprentices in all occupations, but only 2000, or 8.2 percent, participated in apprentice training." G. Soundara Rajan, *A Study of the Registered Apprenticeship Program in Wisconsin* (Madison: University of Wisconsin Center for Studies in Vocational and Technical Education, 1966), p. 91.

[29] *Ibid.*, p. 207

[30] "California Law Called 'Featherbedding,' " *Engineering News-Record,* November 28, 1968, p. 140.

[31] "Statement by the President on Combatting Construction Inflation and Meeting Future Construction Needs," mimeo (Washington, D.C., March 17, 1970), p. 5. This proposal had also been advanced by F. F. Foltman, "Public Policy in Apprenticeship Training and Skill Development," in Senate, Subcommittee on Employment and Manpower, *The Role of Apprenticeship,* 88th Cong., 2nd sess., 1964, p. 1133; and Charles F. Hanna, "Expanding Apprenticeship Opportunities," in *ibid.*, p. 1112.

trainee rate applied only to public projects. In essence, proposals to require employment of apprentices on public work are a mechanism to shift training costs to the taxpayer through the price of public construction. Perhaps this is not inappropriate, though construction has normally distributed training costs relatively heavily to the apprentice and his employer, and only in small part to the owner.

The Length of Apprenticeship

The length of apprenticeship programs is continuously subject to criticism for what are apparently quite varied reasons. Some observers feel that the programs are too long in light of the skill and information they impart.[32] Others may believe that the length of the programs discourages young persons from applying to them and thereby reduces the manpower available to the industry. In fact, the length of apprenticeship is only one of the characteristics of apprenticeship programs that determine their attractiveness to applicants as well as to contractors (who must agree to employ apprentices). Certainly as important to potential applicants as the length of a program are the initial wages paid, the pattern of stepped increases in wages, and the expected earnings upon completion. The length of a program can be manipulated with these other characteristics to increase its attractiveness to young men where programs are undersubscribed because of shortages of applicants.

Where programs do not lack for applicants, and where wages normally closely approach the journeyman scale in the last year or so of apprenticeship, it is difficult to see why shortening a program is of great importance. "No harm is done if a few additional months are devoted to apprenticeship. . . . On the other hand, reducing the period of training to less than is essential for mastery of the skill and knowledge of the trade results in a permanent loss to the apprentice."[33] A major exception to this may occur, ironically enough, when employers resist hiring apprentices and are encouraged to do so by a briefer period of training. The briefer period may allow a larger portion of the total training an apprentice receives to be given by one or two employers,

[32]See, for example, A.L. Nellum and Associates, "Manpower and Rebuilding" (report prepared for the U.S. Department of Housing and Urban Development, Washington, D.C., 1969), p. 11. "One year of efficient skills training should bring any inexperienced man to the status of a fully employable journeyman in most of the trades we looked at."
[33]Charles F. Hanna, discussion of Filley and Magnusen, "Joint Apprenticeship Committees in Wisconsin," *Research in Apprenticeship Training,* p. 102.

rather than several, thus lessening the difficulty of finding employment for apprentices.

Apprenticeship programs vary in length. Of 25 programs in the building and construction industry listed by the Department of Labor,[34] 6 were of four or five years, 15 of three years (or three to four years, and 4 of two years (or two to three years). Formal training in specialties may be of even shorter duration (for example, some painters locals have established eight-month training programs for drywall tapers).

The length of programs is also adjusted according to the experience, if any, of the applicant. All programs provide for granting credit for previous experience. In some crafts and some areas (particularly the electricians and sheet metal workers), these provisions are too often ignored. In other cases, programs rarely last the two to three years provided in the national standards because apprentices are promoted to journeyman scales whenever they can show they have the qualifications. In the special training programs developed for equal employment opportunity purposes, it is customary to provide that the formal length of programs does not preclude earlier advancement as individuals' qualifications warrant.

In many crafts, the fundamental purpose of the period of apprenticeship is not to require that an apprentice serve out his time but quite the opposite. The purpose is to insure that a man does not indefinitely remain an apprentice — he must either learn the craft and find work as a journeyman when the apprenticeship period is over, or he must leave the industry.

A Look Ahead

There is currently a formal training policy in each of the construction crafts in the United States. Apprenticeship programs are the major component of formal training, but they are supplemented in the crafts by various combinations of upgrading, retraining, and/or affirmative action training programs. The standards of training in each trade are established nationally, but the administration and control of programs are at the local level. The programs primarily provide on-the-job training. In many crafts, they have undergone or are now undergoing considerable revision and restructuring.

The preceding review of the current status of formal training in the construction crafts suggests the following response to the four basic issues raised in the introduction to Chapter 7. Apprenticeship programs involving on-the-

[34]See Senate, Subcommittee on Employment and Manpower, *The Role of Apprenticeship,* 88th Cong., 2nd sess., 1964, pp. 1197–1215.

job training and related instruction must be continued, should be jointly administered wherever possible, and should attempt to produce a fully trained journeyman. The basic objective of unions and contractors in formal training is to develop fully trained mechanics familiar with the major aspects of the craft, competent to earn the journeyman rate of pay and to provide supervision and training to others. The content, length, administration, and requirements of programs must be continually reevaluated in light of these basic objectives. In most crafts, the standards of apprenticeship have been reviewed and reissued periodically; such continual updating is important. The standards of training should not be reduced simply because in some areas they are hard to attain. Moreover, comprehensive and high-quality training need not be associated with any particular length of program or requirements for admission. There are many ways in which programs may be operated more efficiently and the instruction process improved. No convincing arguments have been presented for replacing apprenticeship generally with programs of lessened content or off-the-site instruction (such as vocational education in a school) as the primary means of formal training in the construction crafts.

The process of planning for manpower training to meet manpower demand and supply conditions requires considerable improvement, however. First national industry authorities need to be much more active in suggesting the volume of training appropriate to local programs and in monitoring their performance. Second, the federal government must assist the industry with improved forecasts of manpower demand, disaggregated by craft, area, and sector of construction and developed in cooperation with industry representatives. Only projections with these characteristics can be of assistance in the manpower planning process. Third, local authorities in the industry must obtain more extensive data regarding the manpower situation in their jurisdiction and engage in a more sophisticated analysis of the role of formal training in the craft in their area and its appropriate volume. National authorities should assist local groups in improving the planning process.

There are serious problems in every craft concerning the relation between formal training programs and the public school system. In some crafts, the rewards of training and the demand for apprentices by contractors are so large that long lists exist of applicants awaiting apprenticeship openings. Over the years, these crafts have responded by raising the entrance standards for apprenticeship until the disadvantaged are largely excluded from the programs. In these cases, adjustments must be made in apprenticeship requirements or separate training programs established in order that disadvantaged youth not be denied the opportunity for formal training. In other crafts, relatively high admission requirements are associated with few applicants rather than many. In those crafts, means of increasing the exposure of high school students to the crafts are under development. Especially important may be finding ways to make direct contact with high school teachers and guidance counselors. In some cases, it may be necessary to reduce standards for admission or to provide remedial education in association with apprenticeship. Increasing the wages of apprentices may serve as an incentive to applicants, so long as employers will hire apprentices at the new rates of pay.[35] A final group of crafts have had trouble recruiting apprentices mainly because of the nature of the work performed. In tight labor markets, young men often prefer jobs that have greater stability of employment and are less physically difficult and hazardous than some of the building trades. Improvements in the conditions and stability of work in these trades should facilitate recruitment.

Currently, only a few crafts can be said to be training apprentices in the volume necessary to meet the requirements for well-trained men that some economists and government spokesmen insist will occur in the future. Because expectations for a boom in housing are strong, projected employment increases for masons, carpenters, and painters are especially large.[36] Yet the apprenticeship programs in these trades are in special difficulties at the present. Nor does it appear that much can be done to improve the capacity of apprenticeship in general to anticipate major increases in manpower demand. Apprenticeship training invariably responds to local employment conditions with a lag that results both from the period of training necessary to complete a program and from a conservative bias in the expectations of future conditions widely shared among workers, union representatives, and some contractors. Construction booms appear in the separate branches of the industry with great rapidity, and collapses occur with equal speed. It is extremely difficult to train apprentices in advance of a sudden expansion in employment, even if it is foreseen. Thus instability of job opportunities limits on-the-job training, in spite of future needs.[37]

---

[35] In some apprenticeship programs, the structure of apprentice wages appears to have moved either so high that employers do not hire or so low that young men do not apply. Adjustments in the relative distribution of training costs between employer and apprentice are appropriate in light of labor market conditions but are rarely made on this basis.
[36] Dunlop and Mills, "Manpower in Construction," p. 268.
[37] A potential resolution (but without practical importance in current conditions) of the paradox of how to provide on-the-job training now for jobs that will materialize only in the future has been suggested in some trades. Were entry to the trades actually limited to apprenticeship, so that men entering as replacements or in the normal course

of job turnover in construction were required to enter only through formal training, then a well-trained supply of manpower could be developed around which future expansions in employment could occur. Because unions are now legally restricted from denying entry to persons because they have not completed joint apprenticeship programs, legislative action would be necessary to accomplish this. In the current context of public concern over union domination of the hiring process and union control of the manpower supply, any such legislative action is difficult to imagine. Other proposals, such as requiring contractors on federal work to hire apprentices, will affect the numbers hired in only a few crafts and areas and will provide little or no additional training.

IV

Public Policy and
Construction

9

The Special Problems
of Housing

Introduction

Few sectors of American industry have ever been so criticized by public officials and private observers as the housing industry in the late 1960s. The industry was condemned as technologically backward, economically inefficient, and so bound by past practice as to be unable to adjust to the needs of a modern economy.[1] Business firms and unions in the industry were held accountable for cost increases in housing and falling production volume. A total reorganization of the industry was called for to meet the nation's need for housing. Included in the bill of particulars presented against the industry were charges of ineffective management, rising labor costs, and restrictive practices by unions.[2] These factors were said to be driving up the price of housing and excluding consumers from the market. Some observers were candid enough to admit that other factors also contributed to the decline in housing production, but inefficient organization of the industry and the activities of the unions were cited in virtually all cases as major factors contributing to the industry's low rate of production.[3]

In fact, the problems of the housing industry arise less from the activities of builders and organized labor than from the impact of national economic policy. The characteristic technology and organization of the industry are themselves responses to a highly unstable product market whose instability is largely attributable to actions of the national government and preferences of consumers. This chapter will explore the structure of the housing industry and try to show how it has been formed by the economic environment. Initial sections describe the operation of business firms, the labor market, and the role of unions. A further section discusses the prospects for industrialized housing in this country and the response of organized labor to industrialized

[1] See, for example, Albert G. Dietz, "Dramatic Steps in Construction," *Boston Herald Traveler,* May 4, 1969; Wolf von Eckardt, " 'Renewed Hope' Faces Grim Realities" (first of a series), *Washington Post,* October 27, 1968; and the comments of several participants in "Housing: Mass Industrialization" (13th Urban Design Conference, Harvard Graduate School of Design and the National Urban Coalition, May 6–8, 1970).

[2] See, for example, Secretary of Housing and Urban Development George Romney's testimony before the Joint Economic Committee of Congress in *Daily Labor Report* (Bureau of National Affairs), no. 32 (February 17, 1971); also Sylvester Petro, "Unions, Housing Costs and the National Labor Policy," *Law and Contemporary Problems* 32 (Spring 1967): 319–348; John Herbers, "Romney Reports Review of Policy," *New York Times,* February 5, 1968; and "Housing Boom Is Near, but So Is a Ceiling," *Business Week,* December 21, 1968, pp. 71–72.

[3] See, for example, the report of the President's Committee on Urban Housing, *A Decent Home* (Washington, D.C., 1969), and the report of the National Commission on Urban Problems [the Douglas Commission] (Washington, D.C., 1969).

building. However, it is not possible in a single chapter to give a full description of the residential construction industry in the United States. Instead, I
will use these pages to place the industrial structure and labor relations of
housing into the context of the economy as a whole and to illuminate the
major determinants of the industry's performance.

The Housing Industry

Specialization of Firms

Housing production is not a single industry but a group of largely separate
elements having in common only the end use of the product as dwelling units
of one type or another. The most important part of the industry by volume
is the production of single-family homes, but even within this sector there is
great diversity among builders. First, there are the large tract builders who
assemble and develop land and produce and sell houses on their own account.
The firms in this business are variously referred to as merchant builders or
operative builders. They range in size from small partnerships or sole
proprietorships doing only a few units a year to large corporations building
several thousand units annually distributed over many sites. A second group of
single-family builders (including some merchant builders) construct homes on
contract with buyers. Apartment construction, like single-family home construction, is also composed of largely separate major parts — principally the
building of low-rise, garden-type apartments and high-rise apartment buildings.
The technologies of high-rise and garden-type construction are quite different, but because the processes of financing, land development, merchandising,
and project management are much alike, it is not uncommon to find
individual firms doing both. Another section of residential construction
involves the rehabilitation of existing housing units, either for rental or resale,
or the remodeling of homes for their owners.[4] Yet another sector developed
in the 1960s as the federal government began to sponsor the construction of
housing units for particular groups in the population. By the end of the 1960s,
several hundred thousand units a year were being constructed under a
variety of programs.[5] Methods of development and financing in these pro-

---

[4] See Allen F. Jung, "Price Variations among Home-Remodeling Contractors," *Journal
of Business* 34 (January 1961): 52–56. Jung identified three types of contractors doing
remodeling: general contractors, carpentry contractors, and remodeling specialists
(who often subcontracted much or most of the work).
[5] These programs were given various numerical designations from the appropriate sections
of the enabling legislation; for example, 221(d)(3), FHA Section 235, 221(h). Also
important were various "turnkey" programs for public housing. See U.S. President,
First Annual Report on National Housing Goals (Washington, D.C., 1969), pp. 17–26.

grams present peculiar problems to builders and have rapidly become a special section of the residential construction industry. Finally, vacation homes, or second homes, became a significant portion of the industry in the 1960s, involving a large group of firms.[6] While there was a considerable degree of specialization among builders in these sectors of residential construction, it was also common to find a single firm engaged in several activities simultaneously.[7]

For the most part, this diversity in the specialization of residential building firms arises from the fragmented market for new housing. There is in no sense a single housing market but rather a group of largely independent submarkets reflecting the demographic characteristics of buyers or renters and their preferences as to location and conveniences. Housing has become as much a method of providing consumer services as a means of shelter.[8] Thus builders are necessarily concerned with major aspects of consumer demand, such as installed appliances, lot characteristics, neighborhood qualities, and so forth.

It is not surprising, therefore, that many builders are less construction firms than developers whose method of operation is to subcontract all or most of the actual construction of the dwelling units. Subcontracting is most pronounced in the high-rise sector of the industry, but it is common in all sectors, including single-family homebuilding, especially among the larger contractors.[9] Subcontracting may involve not only special trades (for example, mechanical, plumbing, and electrical), but carpentry, painting, and masonry as well. Many residential builders operate much as general contractors, doing the basic trade work (carpentry, general labor, masonry) themselves and subcontracting the specialties. Some builders, particularly in the single-family sector, do electrical, plumbing, and mechanical installations, as

[6] See U.S. Department of Commerce, *Second Homes in the United States*, Series H-121, no. 16 (Washington, D.C., 1969).

[7] Many builders are engaged in business activities other than residential construction, especially real estate operations (for example, land development and sales). See Michael Sumichrast and Sara A. Frankel, *Profile of the Builder and His Industry* (Washington, D.C.: National Association of Home Builders, 1970). This document, based largely on a 1969 survey of the membership of the NAHB, is the best source extant on the structure of the residential construction industry.

[8] By 1969, 39 percent of new housing sales in the United States included air-conditioning units in the sales price, 89 percent included cooking ranges, 9 percent included refrigerators, and 51 percent dishwashers. *Ibid.* (figures from U.S. Bureau of the Census, C25-69-13), p. 21.

[9] In 1969, 40 percent of homebuilders reported subcontracting 75 to 100 percent of all construction costs; only 12 percent subcontracted less than one-quarter of construction costs. *Ibid.*

well as painting and roofing. Small-volume tract builders are especially likely to do a wide range of construction work themselves.[10]

Residential builders, considered separately from their subcontractors, are generally small firms,[11] especially when measured by employment. Builders replying to the National Association of Home Builders 1969 questionnaire had, on the average, 2.8 executive personnel, 3.4 office employees, 3.4 salesmen, and 25 construction employees (2 supervisors, 8 carpenters, 5 masons, 3 painters, and 7 laborers) whom they employed full time year-round. However, the median number of construction workers employed was only 8, a figure that would be more likely to be near the national mean on the basis of a random sample.[12]

The discussion so far has been restricted to what may be called the conventional construction industry. Conventional construction involves the assembly or fabrication at the project site of the structure and subsystems (for example, mechanical and electrical) of a dwelling unit. But many units are also shipped largely prefabricated. The mobile home industry is the foremost example of prefabricated housing, but the manufactured home has also been an element of the industry. Manufactured homes are shipped to the

[10] For information on subcontracting in residential construction, see Battelle Memorial Institute," Final Report on a Study of Recent Developments in the Residential Construction Industry and Their Effects on Small Homebuilders" (prepared for the Small Business Administration by Edward E. Laitila et al., Columbus, Ohio, 1969); John P. Herzog, *An Analysis of the Dynamics of Large Scale Home Building* (Berkeley: University of California Press, 1962); U.S. Bureau of Labor Statistics, *Labor and Materials Requirements for Private One-Family House Construction,* Bulletin no. 1404 (Washington, D.C., 1964), and *Labor and Materials Requirements for Public Housing Construction,* Bulletin no. 1402 (Washington, D.C., 1964).

[11] There are no statistics available from the government regarding the total number of firms engaged in residential building. Marsh Trimble, publisher of *Professional Builder*, which conducts an annual survey of the number and activities of residential builders, estimates there are some 100,000 firms in the industry. "The home building industry is a highly complicated industry. A house or apartment development takes many months — if not years — to complete. It requires extensive planning and preparation work, including zoning and financial arrangements, and coordination with scores of building contractors and other specialists. As a result the business of the small individual builder might very well move along in fits and starts — in terms of completed housing units, he's very active one year, but dormant or virtually out of business the next." *Washington Post*, May 23, 1970.

[12] Some 8885 builders replied in usable form to the questionnaire. It is likely that the response was more heavily weighted toward large builders than a randomly chosen sample would have been. See Sumichrast and Frankel, *The Builder and His Industry*, pp. iii, 201.

The lack of a census of residential builders is unfortunate. The 1967 census included a separate category for operative builders (numbering 13,237 firms and 72,305 employees), but many homebuilders were undoubtedly classified as general contractors or real estate firms.

project site from a factory nearly completed but requiring assembly or installation at the site. For the most part, manufactured homes have been of the wooden panel variety. During the 1960s, the production of these units became a significant element of total housing production.

Market Instability and the Housing Industry

Fluctuations in the volume of residential construction Considerable instability of market demand has been a major characteristic of residential construction in this country.[13] There have been four major cycles in the volume of residential construction since World War II, and significant shifts in the composition of residential construction occurred during these cycles. The expansion and contraction of the industry in the period between World War II and the Korean War was the most pronounced of these cycles, but the cycle that took place in the late 1960s was of only slightly lesser impact.[14]

Furthermore, during the 1960s there was a substantial shift in new housing construction toward apartment construction. The decline of 1966 had been across the board in new housing, but the recovery was concentrated in apartments. From 1966 to 1969, the annual rate of new starts in single-family houses rose only 4 percent, but in buildings with five or more units it rose 75 percent. Single-family units fell from 65 percent of all starts in 1966 to 54 percent in 1969, and multiunit starts rose correspondingly. Similarly, the geographic location of starts shifted. In the upturn that followed the decline, the West (hardest hit in 1966) recovered most strongly; the Northeast did not recover at all. In the course of the 1960s, housing construction shifted markedly to the South and West, especially to Florida, California, and Texas. Because housing is a largely localized industry, small-area fluctuations in demand are very important to producers. And as the historic pattern would suggest, the variability of housing was much more pronounced in many local areas than national data reveal.[15]

[13] See Miles L. Colean, *American Housing* (New York: Twentieth Century Fund, 1944); also Leo Grebler, "Stabilizing Residential Construction," *American Economic Review* 39 (September 1959): 898–910, and *Housing Issues in Economic Stabilization Policy* (Los Angeles: National Bureau of Economic Research, 1960).
[14] From 1963 to 1966, new housing starts declined almost 30 percent. A partial recovery occurred in 1967 and 1968, but volume slipped again in 1969 and 1970. In late 1970 and 1971 a strong recovery took place.
[15] For example, between 1965 and 1966, permits issued for new housing units fell 22 percent nationally but rose in six states. Permits issued fell almost 50 percent in California but only 10 percent in Florida. Even more dramatic changes occurred in metropolitan areas. In Los Angeles–Long Beach, California, permits issued for new units declined 60 percent from 1965 to 1966 and 86 percent from 1963 to 1966. The data cited in this section are from various issues of *Construction Review* (monthly of the U.S. Department of Commerce, Business and Defense Services Administration).

Impact of instability on the size and efficiency of builders Market instability associated with economic conditions has hindered the growth of large-scale production enterprises and thus blocked the development of a more efficient homebuilding industry. Construction in general and homebuilding in particular are dominated by small firms. In large part, the predominance of small-scale production is not a result of technological processes but of characteristics of market demand. The housing development and construction process itself is subject to economies of scale (that is, larger-volume firms tend to have lower unit costs than smaller firms). Unfortunately, the larger size so well adapted to the technology of construction is poorly adapted to market conditions and may in fact be very risky for business concerns. In consequence, the efficiency and economy of the homebuilding process suffer.

It has been pointed out by many authors that economies of scale exist in virtually every element of the residential development process.[16] First, larger firms are better able to acquire land in advance of price increases and are able to accumulate parcels of significant size. As land near urban centers grows increasingly scarce and costs rise, the ability to inventory land becomes an important advantage. While small firms are not financially unable to purchase land in large quantities, they must be very careful not to tie up too much of their asset structure in land. Large firms have a proportionately greater advantage in this aspect of the development process.

Design may also be handled better by larger firms, since they are able to keep a staff of architects and engineers and to interface the design and costing processes with a view toward economical design.

Accurate estimation of construction costs is a critical element in bidding for jobs as well as for economical and profitable operation. Larger firms are able to maintain full-time estimators, allowing a greater volume of bidding and costing out of negotiated or own-account projects and, more importantly, providing greater accuracy in cost estimates. Small firms may have considerable difficulty with the estimation process and may be effectively limited to small-volume and certain special types of work, because they do not have access to good estimators.

Normally, larger firms are able to take advantage of large-lot purchases of materials and the savings that result. Larger homebuilders commonly purchase

[16]See for example, Battelle Memorial Institute, "Recent Developments in the Residential Construction Industry"; Sherman J. Maisel, *Homebuilding in Transition* (Berkeley: University of California Press, 1953); and Herzog, *Large Scale Home Building.*

direct from the factory, which is considerably less expensive than purchasing retail.[17]

The building process is also characterized by potential economies of scale, especially in large developments. There has been considerable documentation of the cost savings of repetition in construction,[18] and though estimates of the volume of financial advantage differ (and will certainly differ by type of project), the value of large-scale operation is well established. Further, large-scale builders are better able to work out stable arrangements with groups of subcontractors, which offer the builder considerable advantages in cost control, scheduling, and quality of work received. Small builders are often unable to establish ongoing business relationships with subcontractors and are subject to higher costs as a result.

Larger size allows a firm to achieve firmer cost control over operations than is possible for most small firms. Experienced bookkeepers and computerized accounting facilities provide more than proportional benefits to larger firms in the form of close control of monetary flows through the firms. Such controls would tend to make large firms more profitable than others.

Finally, even manpower development may be facilitated for larger firms. It is easier to retain experienced employees when work is available during all seasons of the year and continuously enough to allow permanent employment relationships. The cost of training may be recovered when the flow of work is stable enough to allow firms to retain employees. Larger firms, by maintaining a large volume of work and a year-round schedule, may achieve labor cost savings beyond those associated with returns to repetition of tasks at a single jobsite or on a given type of work.

Continuity of work is the sine qua non of the large firm, but in construction continuity is very difficult to achieve. The exigencies of the market are such as to make dependence on a large and continuing flow of work hazardous to the firm. Not only do seasonal downturns occur, but there are localized and national building cycles as well. Builders must be able to shift the geographic locus of work and even the type of construction they do as local markets are spoiled by overbuilding or demand-induced declines. In residential

[17]There is some dispute regarding this point. Maisel stresses the importance of volume purchases, while the Battelle report considers the small builder's disadvantage in this respect to be rather minor.
[18]See United Nations, Economic Commission for Europe, *Effect of Repetition on Building Operations and Processes on Site* (report of an inquiry undertaken by the Committee on Housing, Building and Planning, New York, 1965), and David C. Avid, *Manpower Utilization in the Canadian Construction Industry*, National Research Council Technical Paper no. 156 (Ottawa, 1963).

work, periodic crises of national scope occur with the tightening of monetary and credit conditions.

Thus the very aspects of size that generate economies of scale may become liabilities to the firm in an uncertain market. Because of the extreme uncertainty of construction and especially homebuilding markets, the growth of large firms is limited. For example, the specialization of staff and functions that generates economies of scale also limits the flexibility of the firm in shifting to alternative types of activity. Many small firms weather depression in the construction market by drastically reducing operations or even shutting down entirely. Such shifts are not easily achieved by large organizations, and they may be inordinately costly. The less risky mode of operation is normally to restrict the growth of business during favorable market conditions. Even in the absence of market stability, larger firms would come to dominate a competitive market if building cycles were long enough to allow full development of economies of scale. Normally, they are not.[19]

In order to maintain themselves in a declining market, larger firms must absorb a greater proportion of local markets or shift into other geographic or product markets.[20] Larger firms may be less well adapted to geographic shifts than small firms, especially in an industry in which *localized* building codes, manpower practices, zoning, and other requirements are prevalent.

Because of the small size of firms, their number, and their diversification, the residential building industry finds itself inextricably bound into the building and construction industry generally. In many instances, it is the importation of practices from the broader construction context into residential work that creates the appearance of inefficiency and stagnation. Building codes, technological developments, and manpower practices borrowed from non-residential building impose additional inefficiencies and costs on residential work. To a large degree, homebuilders and developers constitute a large industry that is not in control of its own destiny. Subcontractors may be primarily oriented toward nonresidential work and available to residential contractors only at costs that reflect their nonspecialized nature. In areas

[19]The residential building cycle in the United States has averaged less than five years from peak to trough since World War II.
[20]Sumichrast and Frankel, *The Builder and His Industry,* comment, "The diversification of builders into other construction related (and into many nonconstruction related) fields is in direct response to the nature of the construction industry. The striking short-term changes in volume, caused by the frequency of changes in money flow into capital investment as well as the interruption of construction production caused by seasonal investment and market demands, forced builders to enter many fields of construction activity rather than commit themselves to one type of operation" (p. 15).

in which homebuilding is unionized, collective bargaining contracts are often negotiated without the effective participation of residential builders, and their peculiar interests are not well protected.

There can be little doubt that a more stable market in housing would tend to return greater discretion and control over his industry to the homebuilder. The number of subcontractors fully specialized to his work would be enlarged. Manpower could be trained and retained in his industry, codes might be more easily adjusted to meet his particular problems, and technological developments and managerial expertise could be improved.

Monetary policy and housing Instability of total volume of housing demand and shifts in its composition are largely the result of federal monetary policy. During the mid-1960s, for example, in an attempt to control rising prices in the economy, the Federal Reserve Board restricted growth of the money supply and allowed interest rates to rise to unprecedented levels. The impact of a restrictive monetary policy on housing construction (especially single-family homes) was dramatic. Rates of new residential construction fell to very low levels (especially by the standards of the National Housing Goals enacted in 1968) and remained there for several years.[21]

A consensus has developed among economists on the mechanism by which stringent monetary policy affects housing. First, increases in interest rates raise the carrying charges on mortgage loans. An increase of 1 percent in the interest rate (for example, 6 percent to 7 percent) adds the equivalent of a 13 percent increase in construction costs to the purchaser's monthly payment on a new unit.[22] Second, increasing interest rates raise the cost of construction loans to builders and thereby increase the construction costs of new housing. Third, savers react to changes in the structure of interest rates by shifting deposits among thrift institutions, with the usual result of lessened credit for housing mortgages. Therefore, both prices and availability of credit move to reduce or expand new home construction. Finally, monetary changes impact new housing rather rapidly. Maisel noted that "on average, a change in monetary conditions affects the rate of starts (of new housing) six months later."[23]

[21] There have been mortgage feasts as well as famines. The early 1960s were such a feast. There was, if anything, too much mortgage credit. Bad loans were made and the quality of credit declined. See Saul B. Klaman, "Public/Private Approaches to Housing," *Law and Contemporary Problems* 32 (Spring 1964): 250–265.

[22] On a $15,000 unit with a 40-year mortgage. *A Decent Home*, p. 120.

[23] Sherman J. Maisel, "The Effects of Monetary Policy on Expenditures in Specific Sectors of the Economy," *Journal of Political Economy* 76, no. 4, pt. 2 (July–August 1968): 796–814.

Housing construction responds strongly and quickly to monetary policy. It is therefore a major economic stabilizer. In fact, it may well be the only one. To cite Maisel once more, "We know that most econometric studies of the past covering state and local expenditures, inventories, outlays for consumer durables, and other consumption have attempted without success to relate changes in monetary variables to expenditures."[24] Maisel's detailed analysis of the impact of monetary policy on specific sectors discusses only housing and other fixed investment. Unfortunately, the impact of monetary policy on nonresidential fixed investment is less direct and certain than it is on housing, for interest rates must be high relative to expectations regarding future rate levels and also to expected increases in costs of construction in order to retard nonresidential construction. Rising interest rates will retard nonresidential construction in conjunction with certain business expectations; with others, they may accelerate it. In sum, housing appears to be the central (or exclusive) thrust of monetary policy. Thus, to shelter housing construction from monetary policy is to make it ineffectual. This path is clearly unacceptable, for it would tend to result in inflation uncontrollable by monetary policy.

Some economists have sought to make a virtue of necessity. Brownlee argues that "the residential construction industry . . . is relatively well qualified to fluctuate in opposition to . . . disturbances in the general level of demand."[25] After all, the argument runs, housing uses relatively unspecialized labor, little fixed capital investment, and mobile entrepreneurs. This description of the industry is of course largely accurate. Homebuilding has adapted as much as possible to extreme flexibility in market conditions and is now fairly well specialized as an economic stabilizer. There has been no alternative. But the nation has had to accept considerable costs associated with this policy, including (1) inefficiency in an industry that has been required to maximize flexibility, not production, and (2) the relegation of new housing production to a very low position in our national system of priorities. Less reliance on monetary policy (as it currently operates) in order to stabilize the economy might avoid these costs.

An essential problem of housing policy is thus to seek mechanisms by which the impact of monetary policy may be effectively transmitted to other sectors of the economy. Proposals to shelter housing from money market controls

[24] *Ibid.*, p. 802.
[25] Oswald Brownlee, "The Effects of Monetary and Credit Policies on the Structure of the Economy," *Journal of Political Economy* 76, no. 4, pt. 2 (July–August 1968): 792.

without transferring its effect to other sectors are certain to continue to be ignored because their effect must be to undermine monetary policy.[26] It should certainly be possible to develop methods of achieving a shift of monetary impact to other sectors.

In conclusion, increased housing construction in the current inflationary context can be achieved only by (1) shifting from monetary means of controlling inflation to other means with a more general impact on the economy or (2) developing mechanisms of shifting the impact of monetary policy to sectors other than housing. In the end, both methods would naturally involve shifts among sectors in the allocation of national productive capacity.[27]

The Labor Market in Residential Construction

Operation of the Labor Market

Among construction firms, homebuilders stand in an unusual relation both to the construction and to the nonconstruction labor markets. When labor markets in construction are generally loose, homebuilders may experience little difficulty in recruiting well-trained, qualified workers. Normally, homebuilders prefer to hire such workmen, not only because training construction workers is a lengthy and expensive task, but also because competent and experienced men require less supervision and expose the employer to fewer risks. When labor markets in construction are tight, however, the homebuilder is often the first to have to accept partially or poorly trained workmen or to recruit and train new men. To some extent he is in a better position than most builders to do this effectively. Homebuilding is often unorganized or poorly policed by business agents.[28] When lesser or unskilled men are hired,

[26] See, for example, the report of the National Commission on Mortgage Interest Rates (Washington, D.C., 1969).

[27] See the testimony of Lester C. Thurow, "Adequate Housing Policies," in U.S. Congress, House, Committee on Banking and Currency, *Emergency Home Financing: Hearings on H.R. 136964, H.R. 14639, H.R. 15402, and H.R. 11,* 91st Cong., 2nd sess., February 3, 1970, pp. 61–67.

[28] Residential work is not widely unionized. It is impossible to know the exact extent of unionization in homebuilding, but it appears to be small and on balance decreasing. Except in certain large cities, homebuilding (largely confined to suburban areas) is generally nonunion. Homebuilders themselves and concrete, carpentry, and masonry subcontractors are normally nonunion. Electrical and plumbing subcontractors have often been union, but the volume of nonresidential work in the late 1960s kept many union contractors from doing homebuilding work. Loss of control over homebuilding has motivated several international unions to express concern about organization in the residential sector. See Chapter 1.

they are more likely to be paid a wage commensurate with their productivity than they would under a union scale. When both construction and the economy generally face manpower shortages, the situation may be especially difficult for homebuilders. Certainly, wages in homebuilding would be expected to rise rapidly in the face of such shortages. When there is pressure to keep costs down — especially from a sales standpoint — the manpower "crunch" may be quite severe. Thus, at any time there are at least three major determinants of the manpower situation (in terms of shortages or surpluses in homebuilding): the state of the construction labor market, the state of labor markets generally, and the current relative structure of wages, fringes, and working conditions in homebuilding and other construction.

Short-run adjustments to labor shortages have taken many forms in residential construction in the past. The methods used include recruitment of partially trained men from outside construction, job redesign, and changes in the product, among others.[29] Generally these methods are haphazard and costly. An extensive period of high labor demand in residential construction — with demand for labor at high levels elsewhere[30] — will require adjustments of a more fundamental sort, involving improvements in manpower training and utilization.

Manpower Utilization and Development

Methods of manpower utilization and of training are poorly developed in residential construction. Apprenticeship and journeyman upgrading programs in nonresidential construction provide construction with the core of skilled men necessary to the operation of the industry. The residential sector of the industry conducts only a minor portion of these programs. Residential construction is also characterized by considerable seasonality in employment and presumably by a generally high level of intermittency of employment (although data are not available to measure intermittency in residential employment separately from construction as a whole).

[29]See D. Q. Mills, "Manpower in Construction: New Methods and Measures," in Industrial Relations Research Association, *Proceedings of the Twentieth Annual Winter Meeting* (Madison, Wisc., 1967) pp. 269–276.
[30]There was at the beginning of the 1970s a general expectation that the decade would be characterized by a large-scale expansion of residential construction in conjunction with a high-employment economy. See, for example, Sumichrast and Frankel, *The Builder and His Industry,* pp. 7–11. Sumichrast and Frankel relied extensively on Henry B. Schechter, "Estimates of Housing Requirements for the Coming Decade," a paper presented at the Federal Statistics Users Conference, November 20, 1969. See also U.S. Bureau of Labor Statistics, *Patterns of U.S. Economic Growth*, Bulletin no. 1672 (Washington, D.C., 1970).

The problem of underutilization of labor is of major importance in residential construction. Probably no other source of labor offers such promise of meeting the future needs of the industry for manpower as improved methods of utilization of the existing labor force.[31]

There is, apparently, very little formal training of workers by employers in residential construction. In 1969, for example, a survey of the membership of the National Association of Home Builders found that only 11 percent of members responding participated in any local manpower training programs.[32] Nor is it likely that the small subcontractors prevalent in residential building participate in formal training programs any more than the builders themselves. Unfortunately, there are no data on the number of workers trained by homebuilders or their subcontractors, but it is likely to be quite small relative to the total level of employment in the industry. Where formal training does occur in residential work, it is generally provided either by large nonunion tract builders or by union homebuilders in cooperation with a jointly administered (labor and management) apprenticeship program covering both residential and nonresidential work.

Little formal on-the-job training is done in residential construction because of the difficulty of providing training on a single-firm basis.[33] In most areas of the country, special efforts would be required to assemble an employers' group to coordinate trainees' activities and to establish financial incentives for firms' participation in training programs. There are some instances in which homebuilders' associations provide formal training in the basic trades, often with federal financial assistance. Programs established by single employers, with or without federal support, have not generally been successful in providing training.

Men working in residential construction have been trained by a variety of methods other than formal on-the-job instruction. Some learn skills in voca-

---

[31] The problem of intermittency and methods of dealing with it are very well described in a study authorized by Title IV of the Manpower Redevelopment and Training Act; see "Seasonal Unemployment in Construction: Report and Recommendations of the Secretary of Labor and the Secretary of Commerce to the President and Congress," mimeo (Washington, D.C., 1969).

[32] Builders of single-family houses reported 10 percent participation; builders of multifamily units only reported 14 percent participation. Small-volume builders reported 8 percent participation; medium-volume, 13 percent; and large-volume, 18 percent. Sumichrast and Frankel, *The Builder and His Industry*, pp. 199–200.

[33] See Chapters 7 and 8 for a discussion of the structure of formal training programs in construction.

The discussion of work rules in this section is devoted to residential construction but would apply in most cases to construction generally.

tional education in the schools, other from friends and relatives, others by picking up the work informally on the job, and still others in formal training in nonresidential construction or in the military. These methods, without supplementary formal training on the job, generally produce not a well-qualified mechanic but a semiskilled worker. Since the semiskilled man is not often able to command the rate of pay of nonresidential work, which is usually unionized, he does residential work. The nonunion character of much residential work, with its wide range of pay rates, makes it possible for the industry to operate with a largely semiskilled work force. It also enables the builder to avoid the expense of training by hiring whoever is currently available at whatever rates are mutually agreeable.

Unions and Restrictive Work Practices

Restrictive practices frequently have been cited as affecting productivity in homebuilding.[34] The list of these practices is a conglomerate one; it includes restrictions on the use of machines and hand tools, on the use of tools by foremen, and on the activities of shop stewards; regulations concerning the employment of apprentices, jurisdictional requirements, the pacing of work, subcontracting, the honoring of picket lines, wildcat strikes, and hazard pay; provisions for cleanup, coffee breaks, and lunch breaks; requirements concerning crew size, call-in time, wage scales and overtime, hiring arrangements, standby workers, and the storage of tools and clothing; and provisions affecting layoffs and promotion, travel time and maintenance allowances, and job classifications and premium pay. This list ranges from the provisions of work and work practices — normally the subject of collective bargaining — to informal practices and illegal work stoppages. There is little systematic and comprehensive information on these subjects and on their actual effects on productivity. There have been few, if any, objective surveys of the actual extent of such practices and their cost effects throughout the country and by locality.

The concept of a restrictive practice is often ambiguous and elusive. A crew size rule may be seen as a safety rule by some and a restrictive practice by others. There are genuine differences among workers and employers over the pace of work, the existence of health hazards, flexibility in administering work rules and craft assignments, the normal quality and skill of the work

---

[34] See William Haber and Harold Levinson, *Labor Relations and Productivity in the Residential Construction Industry* (Ann Arbor: University of Michigan Bureau of Industrial Relations, 1956).

The discussion of work rules in this section is devoted to residential construction but would apply in most cases to construction generally.

force and acceptable variations from this norm, the scope and content of jobs, the rate at which technological changes should be introduced, and preferences of security in employment. The effects of work rules also vary widely with the size of projects and the types of construction operations.

Collective bargaining agreements may contain no provisions described as restrictive practices, but such practices may nonetheless be operative; conversely, agreements may contain restrictive clauses that are not actually enforced. Moreover, these practices vary from one locality to another and may even be enforced differently among different branches of construction and among individual contractors in a given locality. Their application may also vary, usually inversely, with the volume of construction activity. The negotiation of a collective bargaining agreement may involve work rule issues. If contractors make a concession on the wage rate for nonacceptance of a restrictive clause, the contract will show no restrictive practices. Moreover, it should not be presumed that nonunion operations are free of work rules and practices.

Several authors have attempted to study work rules. Most analyses have been hardly more than a list of alleged practices or rules with which the surveyed employers expressed unhappiness. Because of the complexities of the issues involved, such a study would require: (1) prior specification of the problem to be investigated in a clear, unambiguous manner; (2) a scientifically selected sample of jobsites to use as a basis for investigating a given practice; and (3) cost data specifically obtained (perhaps by experimentation with alternative methods) to measure the impact of the practice under study. For example, in order to investigate the impact of a collective bargaining contract provision prohibiting the use of a particular tool on-site, the nature of the provision and the tool involved must be clearly defined; a representative sample of jobsites in the study area must be selected and visited or surveyed by questionnaire; and the cost of the prohibited method of work must be weighed against that of methods in use.

The most interesting serious study of work rules and their impact on costs in housing was made by Mandelstramm in 1965.[35] Mandelstramm studied efficiency differentials in ten specialties involved in residential construction in two Michigan cities, one highly organized by unions, the other nonunion. One aspect of the study involved the use of new construction techniques. His comment was that "in most cases, the more heavily unionized city . . . was

[35] Allan B. Mandelstramm, "The Effects of Unions on Efficiency in the Residential Construction Industry: A Case Study," *Industrial and Labor Relations Review* 18 (July 1965): 503–521.

utilizing the new techniques more fully. . . . It may be concluded that the union's effect on the use of techniques was minor." A further issue was the extent to which union working rules as a whole affected costs. Mandelstramm concluded that "although no reliable quantitative estimate can be made of the effect of these rules on efficiency, their total impact would appear to be very small."[36]

Like other labor-management problems, work practices represent a large cluster of interrelated issues, each of which requires separate analysis. Certainly any policy program designed to deal with this range of questions must be detailed and selective; there is no single problem that can be labeled "restrictive practices," and there is certainly no single solution or formula.

Labor Costs in Housing

Virtually all elements of the housing production process were subject to rapidly rising costs in the 1960s.[37] In consequence, sales prices of new houses and rentals on new apartment units rose steadily. It may be inferred from the depressed housing markets of the 1960s that the upward pressure on housing prices originated in input costs rather than in the demands of buyers.

Labor costs in residential construction rose in the presence of wage increases negotiated in the unionized sectors of construction and the manpower shortages experienced by the full-employment economy. In some areas,

[36]*Ibid.*, pp. 509, 512. Included in Mandelstramm's study of working rules were the following: (1) absolute restrictions on output; (2) organized slowdowns; (3) unnecessary quality; (4) jurisdictional rules and disputes; (5) unnecessary men; (6) hiring and firing; (7) overtime; (8) working contractors; and (9) other rules.

Gordon W. Bertram and Sherman J. Maisel, *Industrial Relations in the Construction Industry* (Berkeley: University of California Institute of Industrial Relations, 1955), p. 66, discussed the impact of work rules on technological change in homebuilding in the highly organized San Francisco area:

"It is significant, however, that in this strongly unionized bargaining area, the housing industry recently has been able to make important changes in the organization of the industry and in methods of erection of houses without appreciable hindrance from the building trade unions. Portable power tools which are now widely used in housing construction undoubtedly reduce the man hour requirements on many operations. The tract housing construction techniques impinge upon the skill position of some trades, particularly carpenters, by reducing certain operations to standardized repetitive tasks performed by one crew of men on successive housing units. Neither of these changes has been impeded by craft union resistance, although the downgrading of wage rates which might have been expected to occur as jobs were performed with less skill has not taken place."

[37]There are no fully adequate indices of new housing prices, but the Census Bureau has published an index since 1965 in which there has been some standardization for changes in the characteristics of houses. Between 1965 and 1969, the selling price (including land) of single-family houses rose some 25 percent. Unfortunately, it is impossible to separate land prices from other prices in this index, but land prices are generally believed to have been increasing at a more rapid rate than those of houses themselves. See Sumichrast and Frankel, *The Builder and His Industry*, pp. 22–25.

union organization of residential building meant that negotiated increases were applied directly to residential work. In other areas, rising union scales exerted upward pressure on the rates paid by homebuilders through competition for men between homebuilders and other contractors. Manpower shortages appeared to become a problem in the late 1960s as residential construction recovered from the decline of 1966 and as nonresidential construction and the remainder of the economy continued to boom.[38] Labor shortages tend to reduce productivity at the jobsite in a variety of ways, and in this way they contribute to rising labor costs (just as wage increases do).

Yet labor costs were not the most rapidly rising element of housing costs. Equally or more important have been increases in costs of financing, materials, and land. In fact, over the postwar period from 1949 to 1969, on-site labor costs fell from 33 percent of the total costs of a new home to only 18 percent. The decline in the importance of labor costs is reflected in the decline of the relative cost of the entire structure, from 70 percent of total housing costs in 1949 to 55 percent in 1969 (including land prices, financing, overhead, and profits, as well as labor and materials).[39]

Industrialized Housing

The Future of Industrialized Housing

The advent of what may be called "industrialized" building techniques in housing adds a new dimension to the labor relations and manpower needs of the industry. Proponents of industrialized housing have stressed that the transference of work off site to the controlled conditions of factory production can stabilize building costs and help the problem of shortages of skilled

---

[38] See, for example, Battelle Memorial Institute, "Recent Developments in the Residential Construction Industry," p. 107:
"Labor costs and lack of skilled labor appear to be significantly affecting small homebuilders. Labor cost was identified as a problem by one-fourth of the builders in 1965; by 1968 one-half of the builders identified it as a problem. Lack of skilled labor was a problem for less than half of the builders in 1965; in 1968 four-fifths identified this lack as one of their three major headaches. Moreover, in both cases the number of builders identifying the two labor areas as their *first* problem rose significantly. Construction costs also appear to be a growing problem; in 1965 and 1966 about one-third of the builders found this to be a major concern. The proportion grew to about three-fifths in 1967, and three-fourths in 1968."
[39] These estimates are quoted by Nathaniel Goldfinger in "The Myth of Housing Costs," *American Federationist* (AFL-CIO) 76 (December 1969): 1–6, from presentations by the Bureau of Labor Statistics and the National Association of Home Builders to Congress. See the *Congressional Record*, October 29, 1969, p. E9113.

craftsmen at the jobsite.[40] In a factory, it is argued, work operations can be designed to be performed by semiskilled personnel, rather than by the craftsmen necessary in on-site construction. Although there is some debate as to what aspects of industrialized technology are really new,[41] there is no doubt that a large increase in the volume of factory-produced housing would substantially affect aggregate labor requirements in residential construction.

In fact, industrialized housing had little impact in the United States during the 1960s except in the sector of single-family houses. Mobile and manufactured houses grew rapidly,[42] both in absolute numbers and as a percentage of total housing starts. By 1969, in a still-depressed market for conventionally financed (that is, mortgage-financed) single-family houses, mobile and manufactured houses captured more than half of the single-family market.[43] In high-rise or garden-type apartment construction, however, there was little utilization of industrialized techniques.[44]

The prospects for industrialized housing are mixed. The recovery of single-family homebuilding with conventional mortgaging is likely to reduce the importance of mobile and manufactured houses. Furthermore, there are several reasons why most of the high-rise construction work is likely to continue to be done on site in this country. The most important factors involve the structure of the housing industry. Two major elements that appear to be essential to the development of large-scale industrialized building are a wide and

[40] See, for example, *Towards Industrialized Building, Third Congress of International Council of Building Research, Studies and Documentation* (New York: Elsevier, 1966); also U.S. Department of Housing and Urban Development, Division of International Affairs, *Industrialized Building — A Comparative Analysis of European Experience* (Washington, D.C., 1968).

[41] See U.S., Building Research Advisory Board, National Academy of Sciences–National Research Council, "Historical Evaluation of Industrialized Housing and Building Systems," in *Report of the President's Committee on Urban Housing: Technical Studies*, vol. 2 (Washington, D.C., 1968), pp. 177–190.

[42] Manufactured houses are prefabricated in a factory and assembled at a homesite. The larger degree of factory prefabrication of the shell of the manufactured house distinguishes it from conventional housing. The final house may or may not contain largely prefabricated mechanical and plumbing systems.

[43] Estimates made by Charles Field, "Industrialized Housing and Building Codes" (Ph.D. thesis, Harvard University, 1971), from data published by the National Association of Home Manufacturers. Field includes among the manufactured houses a very large number of wooden panel houses requiring extensive assembly at the jobsite.

[44] Most industrialized systems, including those in use in Europe, involve prefabricated (precast) concrete panels or boxes. There are also systems in use abroad in which mechanical, electrical, and plumbing systems are prefabricated to a greater degree than is common here. Certainly, precast concrete structural elements are in use in this country and will continue to be. But the large-scale factory production of high-rise systems is less likely. There will continue to be a much cast-in-place concrete and masonry construction as well as steel and glass construction, which is referred to abroad as the American method.

steady market with long-term stability. Large volume and stable demand may justify the big capital investments required by industrialized building. In this country, two major aspects of housing markets prevent the development of such large and stable demand.[45] First, it is unlikely that consumers will accept the high degree of housing standardization required by industrialized methods.[46] Other producers selling less standardized products (even at higher cost, if necessary) will probably compete effectively with industrial builders. Second, in the United States both public and private owners seem unwilling to accept the unresponsiveness to short-run changes in input prices that is a necessary element of industrialized building. In the flexible price system of our economy, variations in relative prices among materials and labor inputs continually alter the least-cost design of buildings. For example, an increase in the price of concrete and in the wages of carpenters can stimulate construction with structural iron in areas in which it has not been used for years. Alternately, an industrialized system designed at a time when prices of concrete are relatively low may become quite expensive if materials or labor prices shift in favor of other materials. Private and public developers in this country are unlikely to be willing to ignore short-term cost reductions that would be made available for a project by designing with least-cost materials and labor, even where systems using certain materials may be alleged to be less expensive in the long run.

In general, high-rise systems techniques are currently too standardized and too inflexible in a variety of ways for the American market. It is likely, therefore, that conventional high-rise construction, with the many rapid alterations in techniques and components that characterize what we call

[45] Demand is used here in the economist's sense of effective demand, that is, available purchasers — not in the sense of persons in need of housing.

[46] How great a degree of standardization is required has been the subject of much dispute. Certainly the external appearance of the systems can be varied widely, and some internal variations are possible. But no one, to my knowledge, has questioned that the degree of standardization would be much greater than what is normally practiced in this country. Whether or not the necessary degree of standardization can be made acceptable to American consumers cannot, of course, be known at this moment.

One aspect of this issue involves the role of government as a developer and owner of housing. It is often pointed out that abroad central governments take a much greater and more direct role in housing construction than in this country. It is then suggested that government involvement is a condition of large-scale industrialization, In fact, what foreign governments have provided is large-scale standardization. See U.S. Department of Housing and Urban Development, *Industrialized Building*, especially pp. 105–107. There is little evidence of a willingness on the part of United States citizens to accept large-scale standardization from the government any more than from private industry. See, for example, Martha Derthick, "Defeat at Fort Lincoln," *The Public Interest*, no. 20 (September 1970).

"conventional" work, will continue to dominate the apartment market.

Industrialization and the Unions

With the development of considerable interest in American industry in further extensions of industrialized fabrication in residential construction, concern was expressed in many quarters that the building trades unions would attempt to restrict the spread of the new techniques. Industrialized building has as a primary purpose the shift of work off site to factories, and proponents normally expect as well that factory wages will be lower than building-site rates. Both these effects of industrialization have been believed to be against the interests of the building trades unions, and their possible resistance is viewed as a particularly important constraint to industrialized housing.[47]

In fact, prefabricated housing is not a new development, and the unions have lived with it in one form or another for years.[48] Currently there are four major types of residential prefabrication operating in this country: mobile homes, sectionalized homes, manufactured homes, and preassembled components. The last is by far the most important element of prefabrication, and even conventional building techniques normally include a large volume of preassembled components. But industrialized techniques are not new. After World War II, the federal government and private sources invested considerable funds in an attempt to market a prefabricated home. The experiment (the Lustron home) was a failure.[49]

The relationship of organized labor to efforts to industrialize building is an uncertain one at the moment, though its broad outlines are clear. Most importantly, there is almost no possibility that labor unions will successfully prohibit or even try to prohibit the utilization of new techniques of construction where they are economically justified on other grounds than low wages. For the most part, the unions have little long-term interest in trying to halt the introduction of building systems; rather, they wish to control the work.[50] Control, of course, implies that the work be done union and under

[47]See, for example, J. Karl Justin, "Can We Rebuild an Industry?" *Technology Review* 72 (May 1970): 22–29.

[48]See Battelle Memorial Institute, "The State of the Art of Prefabrication in the Construction Industry" (report prepared for the Building and Construction Trades Department, AFL-CIO, Columbus, Ohio, 1967).

[49]See Building Research Advisory Board, "Industrialized Housing and Building Systems."

[50]"More and more work formerly done on the construction job site is now prefabricated or manufactured. We cannot stop this trend. It is the evolution of time. It also indicates how our trade is changing and the need to change with the times if we are to keep abreast." Committee on Resolution, *Proceedings* of the Carpenters Convention, 1966, p. 456.

conditions established by collective bargaining contracts. What is now at issue is the degree of organization in the residential industry and the nature of the wages and working conditions to be established in the organized sectors.

There are several forms of technological change involved in industrialized housing, some more acceptable to the unions than others. First, change may involve increasing mechanization of the construction process. Second, systems building may entail increased standardization of components. Third, work traditionally done at the jobsite may be transferred off-site. Fourth, there may be a recombination of job tasks at the work site. Industrialization of residential units primarily involves standardization of components and the transferring of work off-site. For the most part, some building trades unions would resist most strongly the changes in the combination of tasks at the site, because this may directly affect the work jurisdiction of the unions. Shifting of work off-site, where the shift is to lower wage scales, is also a potentially serious problem. The mass production of standardized components and mechanization provide little difficulty except as jurisdiction and wage issues are involved.

There is no doubt that the unions will adamantly resist the construction of factories specific to jobsites in which units or components are "prefabricated" if the wages paid in those factories are less than the on-site rates. There is no problem associated with prefabrication at building trades rates. The unions resist factory work for a specific site at a lower rate for several reasons, but the major concern is that any such arrangement would provide directly for the undermining of on-site rates and conditions. In fact, many operations in virtually all types of construction could easily be shifted to a temporary "factory" near the jobsite if wage differentials made it profitable to the employer.

Where a permanent factory is established to produce units or components for scattered jobsites, there are several relationships possible between the employer and organized labor. Each type of relationship has advantages and disadvantages to the employer. Some examples follow; other relationships that are not now apparent may yet emerge.

1.
A joint agreement with the IBEW (electricians), the UA (plumbers), and the Carpenters was signed by Prestige Structures, Inc., of Charlotte, Michigan. Under this arrangement, local affiliates of the three internationals will represent the employees in the manufacturing plant under an industrial-type labor agreement at industrial wage rates. The company also agreed to employ

at least one journeyman from each of the three trades in the plant at the construction rate.

The unions agreed to work out a composite union label for application to the company's products. Under the union label agreement, the company must furnish the unions with the destination of all shipments, both geographically and by name. The value to the employer of attaching the union label to his product is to facilitate (it does not insure) acceptance and installation of the products by journeymen of the three trades at the erection site. Since these three trades are the most affected by prefabrication, the agreement is potentially a valuable one.

Finally, the company has signed a national agreement with each international union by which it agrees to do and to subcontract all its work union and to meet local construction standards (wages and conditions) at the jobsites. The unions agree, essentially, to furnish on-site labor to the company and to assist it in resolving local labor disputes at construction sites.

2.

In Detroit, LeBon Homes, Inc., signed an agreement with the local Building and Construction Trades Council to represent its employees in a plant manufacturing homes.[51] The agreement recognizes the Detroit Building and Construction Trades Council as the representative of the company's production facility employees. Three classifications of workers are established at industrial wage rates. The company also agreed to have at least one carpenter, one electrician, and one plumber for in-plant work at construction rates. Erection of homes at the jobsite is to be the work of building tradesmen.

3.

Sterling-Homex, an Avon, New York, home manufacturer, signed both local and national agreements with the Carpenters union. The national agreement is a standard-form Carpenters national construction agreement. The local agreement will establish industrial wage scales and conditions for the factory work force.[52] Such agreements will probably protect the company from

---

[51] The agreement is dated June 9, 1969. LeBon Homes apparently went into reorganization in 1971.

[52] The signing of the national agreement on June 17, 1969, was held in Washington, D.C., in the presence of Secretary Romney of the Department of Housing and Urban Development. Because the agreement is a standard-form national agreement, it had already been signed by several hundred general and carpentry contractors. Essentially, the agreement had been available to the company any time, at its discretion. Yet Secretary Romney referred to the agreement as "very significant" and "lauded the union for recognizing the important role that manufactured units play in meeting the nation's housing needs." *Daily Labor Report* (Bureau of National Affairs), no. 116 (June 17, 1969), p. A10.

jobsite disputes with the Carpenters, but they provide no guarantee of assistance if disputes arise with other crafts.

4.

A manufacturer may, of course, find his plant organized by an industrial union (for example, the United Automobile Workers). Such a situation almost guarantees difficulty for the manufacturer if his product must be erected at the jobsite by union building trades mechanics.

5.

Firms producing concrete components that are used for garden-type and high-rise apartment buildings have signed a national agreement with the Laborers International Union for the representation of the in-plant production workers.[53] The agreement provides that wages and fringes will be negotiated locally. Presumably, on-site erection will be by Laborers or by the Laborers and other building tradesmen. There are, of course, potential problems of other crafts' acceptance of the Laborers' label, which will be on the components.

6.

A plant may also remain nonunion. Where this occurs, acceptance of the product at the jobsite may involve difficulties if union building trades mechanics are used. Much jobsite work in residential construction is, however, nonunion. Most home manufacturers now operate nonunion and ship their products into nonunion or weakly unionized areas.

The importance of these various agreements is, in part, that they allowed the building trades to obtain a foothold in the manufactured housing industry during 1969–1970. To do so, the unions adapted their standards and arrangements to the conditions of this developing industry. In the past, building trades unions have often followed the work into the shop to preserve their work jurisdictions, but the organization of industrialized building appears to be proceeding ahead of actual threats to job opportunities at the site. Industrialized housing may even become a major toehold for the unions in the organization of on-site residential work.[54]

[53] See the agreement between the Laborers and Prestressed Concrete of Colorado and Midwest Prestressed Concrete of Springfield, Illinois, signed at HUD headquarters in Washington in March 1970. See "Laborers Sign Contract for Prefab Housing," *AFL-CIO News,* March 21, 1970.

[54] There is little doubt that the federal government has inadvertently facilitated the organization of industrialized housing by the unions. The government largely misunderstood the labor relations situation in homebuilding, believing organization by the unions to be greater than it is, and publicized as critical a somewhat minor problem of union acceptance of prefabricated housing. In order to resolve the supposed dispute, the

Conclusions

The structure of firms in the residential construction industry and the organization of the labor market are both generally efficient responses to the instability of the housing market. The purpose of traditional arrangements is to allow the firm considerable flexibility in adjusting to changing conditions of demand. There are, however, great weaknesses in these arrangements from the point of view of the long-run production of housing. The small size of firms limits the application of advanced management techniques to the organization and operation of production. The casual character of the employment relationship results in a low level of formal training and a substantial underutilization of labor in the industry. Numerous small firms and weak employment relationships jointly result in a poorly developed pattern of industrial relations, with residential builders having little role in the determination of industrial relations policies in construction in most of the United States.

The likelihood of a substantial and prolonged expansion in residential construction in the 1970s provides the opportunity for private parties to seek to stabilize and rationalize production in the industry. Public support will be necessary to achieve substantial improvements in the efficiency of the industry, for public policy is largely the source of the market instability that pervades the industry.

---

government sought labor agreements to facilitate on-site acceptance by the unions. The government, of course, publicized widely the solution achieved. In the process, the building trades obtained further representation in the housing production industry. The industrial unions never really got into the act at all. See "UAW and Teamsters Map Housing Plans," *Engineering News-Record,* June 5, 1967, p. 65. (The Teamsters are not, of course, an industrial union in the same sense as the United Automobile Workers.)

10

Government Policies

Requirements for Effective Policies

Public policy in construction has had a record of both success and failure.
In times of national need, the industry and the government have often cooperated to stabilize conditions in the industry and to permit public construction to proceed unhindered. Among the most significant such instances were
the Wage Adjustment Board of World War II, the Construction Industry
Stabilization Commission of the Korean War, and the Missile Sites Labor
Commission of the mid-1960s. Less significant aspects of the industry's
operation than its wartime, or defense-related, stability have also been the
subject of successful government-industry efforts, including legislative reforms, promotion of apprenticeship, and others. But the list of government
policies that have been largely unsuccessful is also long. There are several
elements that may determine the success or failure of public policy, including
the degree to which it is founded on a correct understanding of the operations
of the private industry, the degree to which it has the consent and the
cooperation of the industry, and, finally, the care with which the government
has worked out not only the objectives of the policy but also the methods
for implementing it.[1]

The list of federal policy ventures in construction that have ended in failure is very long, even when only the recent past is considered. Programs of
the Department of Housing and Urban Development directed at improving

---

[1] ". . . policy does not consist primarily in proclaiming each year the ideal or utopian
world . . . . Policy is to be judged rather in terms of the implementation of those objectives and in the administrative arrangements suitable and practicable to achieve the
goals." John T. Dunlop, "Guideposts, Wages, and Collective Bargaining," in George
P. Shultz and Robert Z. Aliber, eds., *Guidelines, Informal Controls and the Market
Place* (Chicago: University of Chicago Press, 1966), p. 89. Another student of public
policy making makes the same points as follows: "The real test of policymaking is
its effect on real situations . . . . The first question that should be asked about a policy
is 'What are its chances to affect reality?' . . . . how good a policy *looks* may not have
much to do with how good it *is.*" Yehezkel Dror, *Public Policymaking Reexamined*
(San Francisco: Chandler Publishing Company, 1968), pp. 34–35.

In order to make these distinctions clear for the purposes of the present discussion,
public policy is referred to as having two elements, objectives and implementation.
Implementation includes both the instrument(s) by which policy is carried out (for
example, legislation or administrative guidelines) and their administration.

Generally, there is an agent or agency of administration that possesses certain resources and methods for the conduct of the policy. For example, the Congress established in the Davis-Bacon Act a policy of paying prevailing wages in each area in which
federal or federally assisted construction is done. In order to implement this policy, the
act provides for the issuance of an order by the Secretary of Labor setting wages to be
paid on each project. Agencies within the Department of Labor administer the act,
preparing determinations and overseeing their enforcement.

the productive capacity of the housing industry (for example, the In-City Project) have sputtered and all but expired.[2] The requirement of the Model Cities Act to provide "maximum feasible participation" of residents of the area in the design and renewal of their neighborhoods became a reality in only a few cities, in part owing to the incapacity of local and national authorities in the programs to develop and implement effective guidelines for this purpose (and in part owing to failure of the program to generate significant volumes of construction in the Model Cities areas). Housing rehabilitation programs funded by HUD in the center cities have been repeatedly delayed, the work of low quality, and employment possibilities for the community limited and short-term. There are no reasons inherent to the objectives of the programs for these failures or near failures — rather the implementation and administration have been at fault.

Many efforts of the federal government to affect manpower practices in the industry have been beset by similar problems. First, repeated attempts by federal agencies to increase the number of men in training in construction have met with very limited success, primarily because the federal proposals have not, in many cases, been developed in conjunction with the industry or designed to include any practical means of implementation. Often, specific federal suggestions, if implemented, would not even have supported the stated objectives of the government. The industry rightly resisted such schemes. Second, many efforts of the federal government to improve minority participation in the industry have also been without success. Both Philadelphia Plans have been falsely conceived as a major means of increasing nonwhite participation in the crafts and would have proved — had they been widely imposed — impossible to enforce or administer. Third, federal training contracts with *individual* employers in construction to train craftsmen have not had much success. Most such projects, despite whatever careful procedures are written into the contract, have resulted only in a wage subsidy to the employer for his unskilled labor, and little training has taken place. Contracts with individual employers cannot ordinarily provide continuity or breadth of training, and the government lacks the capacity to oversee the standards of these contracts.

Nor have federal wage guidelines, whether publicly or privately suggested, affected wage or price behavior in construction. Ineffective in most industries, wage guidelines tend to operate perversely in construction. Settlements vary greatly among crafts and areas. A guidelines figure reflecting the average

[2]See pp. 280 ff.

settlement simply becomes a floor to wage increases without restraining higher settlements. A guidelines wage policy in construction cannot restrain major settlements without public intervention in individual disputes. However, the decentralized bargaining structure of the industry would require intervention in a great number of disputes, often simultaneously, and success in one such intervention would not be likely to affect other negotiations. In consequence, overt, ad hoc intervention in local disputes is largely futile. In construction, wage stabilization requires extensive public intervention, like that provided through the establishment of the Construction Industry Stabilization Commission in 1971.[3]

The objectives of government policy — such as wage and price stability, racial integration, economic growth, and high employment — are not an issue here. Most citizens support these objectives, as do most contractors, unions, and workers in construction. But the government has devoted far too little attention to aspects of policy other than the choice of objectives and for this reason often failed to progress toward its goals.

The implementation of policy through careful design of mechanisms and their administration has been the greatest weakness of government policy toward construction. Knowledge of the operations of the industry and cooperation with its constituent groups are necessary to effective design and implementation. Too often federal policies directed toward the economic and industrial relations behavior of construction have been limited to statements of worthwhile objectives. Public policymaking affecting construction has often followed an irrational course in which public authorities, unfamiliar with the industry, designed programs to appear as if they would meet public objectives and then tried to impose the programs on an industry whose institutional and economic situation made the programs unworkable. These efforts were generally accompanied by considerable publicity, often concealing from the public the inadequacy of the programs. Unfortunately, the government has not always learned from its mistakes. Where public

[3]See Dunlop, "Guideposts, Wages, and Collective Bargaining," pp. 95–96. The creation of the Construction Industry Stabilization Committee by President Nixon on March 29, 1971, by Executive Order, was a substantial step beyond the guidelines concept. The committee, provided by the President with legal authority to involve itself in negotiations in an orderly manner, held out the hope of moderating the rates of negotiated wage increases short of a wage freeze and formal controls. The long-term contribution of such a policy as that suggested by the establishment of the Stabilization Committee will depend on the degree to which it can combine short-term actions with steps toward long-term reforms in the structure and operation of collective bargaining in the industry.

policies were effective, they invariably resulted from a devotion to methods of implementation as well as to goals.

Several examples of public initiatives accompanied by concern for implementation that have had a large degree of success have been touched on in earlier chapters. Two may be repeated here for emphasis, First, while the Taft-Hartley Act in 1947 outlawed jurisdictional strikes, the government, recognizing the unusual character and circumstances of such disputes in construction, provided that a private industry board may resolve disputes in lieu of litigation in most situations. Second, in the early 1960s the Labor Department, working with the industry, developed procedures to insure nondiscrimination in the selection of apprentices and later provided financial support to organizations (including local building and construction trades councils, local chapters of the Urban League, and branches of the Workers Defense League) for the recruitment and tutoring of minority youth for acceptance into apprenticeship. These two efforts, while neither eliminating jurisdictional disputes nor providing immediate full integration of all the skilled trades, have nonetheless been the most effective means developed to make progress in these areas. In both cases, the government sought out the best method of implementating its policies and cooperated with the affected parties (employers, unions, and civil rights groups) to carry them out.

Public officials must consider, to a far greater degree than is often the case, the following aspects of policy in addition to general goals: (1) realization of what it is practicable to accomplish within the time period available and within whatever constraints are imposed; (2) the limitation of immediate objectives to what is practicable; (3) the development of mechanisms for implementing policy that can actually achieve the objectives established; and (4) concern for the methods and feasibility of administration and enforcement of the proposed programs. The waste of public and private effort in construction resulting from conflict between well-intentioned but inept public initiatives and the resistance of the industry has been very great.[4]

In general, where public policy confronts a private industrial relations system of considerable strength and complexity, as in construction, public

[4] There are those who accuse the industry of creating this situation by refusing to advise public officials on more effective means of implementing policy. (For example, Michael J. Piore spoke of public policy regarding minority training in construction as "a kind of blind pressure" and attributed it largely to the secrecy of the operations of the industry. See Industrial Relations Research Association, *Proceedings of the Twentieth Annual Winter Meeting* [Madison, Wisc., 1969], p. 79). Yet, for the most part, high public officials need not be without public or private assistance in developing policy if they wish to avail themselves of these resources.

initiatives must, if they are to be successful, adapt themselves to the mode of operation of the private system. Successful implementation of policy requires cooperation of important parties in the private sector. Without a degree of cooperation, there can be only the most limited success, if not actual failure. This offends some persons who prefer to imagine that public policy may be designed independently of those it is intended to affect and that it may then best be implemented by imposition (for example, by enactment of the objectives into law or by order of the public executive). But government legislation or decree, without the consent of the affected parties, is often ineffectual. In fact, following such a pattern of policy in construction is almost certain to lead to considerable conflict and to the continual frustration of public purposes.

Directions for the Future

Reducing Instability of Demand

Many aspects of the industrial organization of construction and its industrial relations are a result of the characteristics of the product market and technology of the industry. Fundamental alterations in industrial structure and industrial relations can occur only as a result of changes in underlying causes. Particularly important are the characteristics of market demand for construction products. A construction world of stable output at fixed locations (itself an impossibility) would be associated with a very different size of labor force and different occupational and craft categories, relative wage rates, and training procedures. The size of enterprises, the characteristics of management, and capital structure would also be quite different.

While stability in product markets and production techniques of the type that characterizes the manufacturing, sales, and services sectors of the economy can never be obtained in construction, it is still possible to lessen the market instability that has been the dominant influence on construction. In large part instability is a direct result of government policies and can be affected through changes in those policies. Business spending on industrial plants responds to the direction of the aggregate economy and expectations regarding future sales, as well as to the availability of earnings for investment. Housing expenditures respond to monetary conditions. Public highway and heavy construction are the direct consequence of expenditure decisions by public authorities. It is under these aspects of public policy that improvements in the general stability of the industry may be most directly achieved.

Still, it is too much to expect that more than marginal improvements can occur in the manner in which government economic policy affects construction. The government cannot abandom discretionary economic policy simply to provide additional stability to construction. Rather, public policy must also seek to assist the industry in improving its adaptations to shifting demand. Earlier chapters have suggested what would be potentially valuable adjustments in the operation of the industry. Here it is best to summarize the most important general areas of public concern and then to examine in greater detail certain aspects of public policy toward the industry.

First, public authorities must be willing to assist the industry in efforts to lessen the impact of changing demand conditions on employment, wages, and other costs, and on the operations of firms generally. Federal authorities should seek to provide, in a manner consistent with other objectives, an economic climate in which the variability of demand is minimized. Each level of government may contribute to the stabilization of construction activity over time by (a) initiating comprehensive local planning for construction; (b) establishing priorities for public, and perhaps all, construction in areas in which construction demand is especially strong; and (c) undertaking programs in cooperation with the industry to reduce the seasonality of construction activity.

Second, Congress and the federal executive branch should cooperate with industry groups in restructuring collective bargaining in the industry in ways that will allow an increased capacity to adjust to changing economic conditions. This may involve modifications of federal labor laws to encourage greater involvement of national union and contractors' association officials in the activities of local unions and associations. Further, legislation may be necessary to strengthen employer bargaining units by reducing their fragmentation and increasing the capacity of the associations to undertake industrial relations activities.[5]

Third, the influence of federal and state authorities should be used to encourage (a) the creation and operation of joint labor-contractor-public forums for discussion and resolution of mutual problems; (b) a greater degree

[5] During the late 1960s, several suggested programs for legislative action regarding employers' associations and collective bargaining in construction were introduced to Congress. In some cases, these proposals called for certification by a government agency of employer bargaining units on a craft and area basis (to the policies of which all contractors in an area would be required to conform). Other proposals sought to widen the geographic scope of bargaining. There was, however, great division among employers over the merits of different proposals, and as a result the likelihood of congressional action seemed small.

of cooperation among the many private parties in the industry; (c) development of proposals for improvements in bargaining structures and manpower programs; and (d) greater communication among public authorities in the many agencies and levels of government and industry leaders.

Fourth, public monies should continue to be used for subsidies and other assistance in (a) the development of labor and product market information systems in the industry; (b) improvement of training mechanisms, including planning, recruitment, promotion, and methods of training (although public funds should not ordinarily be used to pay for on-site training); and (c) supporting technological innovations and diffusion in the industry.

Controlling Inflation

During the late 1960s the American economy moved out of its historic sluggishness into a full-employment period. In this century, full employment had previously been reached only in wartime and was always accompanied by wage and price controls. In the late 1960s, full employment was again associated with wartime, but two national administrations refused for an extensive period to impose wage and price controls. Thus, a brief period of full employment ensued without controls. Wages and prices rose rapidly, and their rates of increase reached historic highs for the United States in this century. The inflation was particularly pronounced in certain sectors, among them construction. Failing to find a method to limit inflationary tendencies short of control, in 1969–1970 the national administration employed fiscal and monetary restraint to cool off the economy. [6]

Economists had suggested other means than recession to control inflation. One repeated suggestion was for voluntary controls, or guidelines.[7] Guidelines were believed to have been at least partially successful in the 1962–1966 period,[8] though they were rapidly abandoned as the inflation accelerated in the late 1960s.[9]

Yet no evidence had ever been produced of the success of guideposts in

[6] Paul W. McCracken, chairman of President Nixon's Council of Economic Advisors, testified before a Senate Committee that in 1971, despite an expansive federal budget, unemployment would remain high and that therefore "throughout the year there would be restraining pressure of excess supply on the price and wage levels."*New York Times*, February 6, 1971.
[7] See, for example, John M. Blair, "Economic Concentration," *Washington Post*, January 31, 1971.
[8] George L. Perry, "Wages and the Guideposts," *American Economic Review* 57 (September 1967): 897–904.
[9] See Derek C. Bok and John T. Dunlop, *Labor and the American Community* (New York: Simon & Schuster, 1970), pp. 298–299.

limiting wage or price increases in decentralized sectors of the economy such as construction.[10] As the boom of the late 1960s continued, construction became perhaps the most inflationary of all sectors of the economy. Because of its great size, its geographic dispersion, and its high proportion of skilled workers, construction became a very difficult sector for economic policy makers.[11]

Construction is in a sense a service industry. Construction prices are established for each project separately. Costs in construction include wages and other compensation, material costs, profits, overhead, and machinery costs. By far the most important costs in most branches of the industry are materials, labor, and overhead-profits costs. Materials costs are not established in construction but in supplying industries and are necessarily the object of policies directed at those industries. Labor costs and profits originate in the industry.

The organization of construction projects, their location, management, and design, the type of pricing of a project (for example, by competitive bidding or negotiation), and other factors are the determinants of the size of profits and, to a large degree, of labor costs, for these aspects of a project affect the productivity of labor on a job. Unfortunately, there is no space here for a thorough examination of the effects of these factors on total project costs. Wages, however, are determined through collective bargaining and are the subject of economic and institutional influences. Chapter 3 provided an analysis of the determinants of wage increases in construction in the late 1960s. It also suggested means to reduce the impact of inflationary demand conditions on strikes, wage settlements, and other aspects of industrial relations in the industry. Structural reforms in collective bargaining and means for reducing the pressure of demand in limited areas at certain times are among the most important methods of reducing the inflationary potential of the industry at full employment. But structural reforms cannot be made instantly, nor can the processes of manpower recruitment, training, and allocation be improved at will. Instead, a sustained effort by private authorities with public assistance is required.

Needed structural modifications in construction are many, but in the short run they promise to have only a limited impact on inflationary tendencies. In consequence, controls may be necessary to restrain increases over

[10]See, for example, John Sheahan, *The Wage-Price Guideposts* (Washington, D.C.: Brookings Institution, 1969), pp. 52–54.
[11]See *The Economic Report of the President and Council of Economic Advisors*, issued annually since 1965.

the immediate future. Yet short-term controls can be of no value in the long run unless accompanied by basic reforms. The list of reforms should begin with improvements in the capacity of employers' associations to conduct collective bargaining and should also include greater involvement by international unions in local bargaining, the merger of small and competing international unions, and the encouragement of multicraft bargaining.

Some reduction in unit cost increases, if not in wages or other input prices, could be achieved through a more effective manpower policy in construction. Manpower (and other input) bottlenecks contribute significantly in some cases to cost increases. But bottlenecks normally occur in specialties or certain skills, so that response must be in terms of those requirements, not in the aggregate supply of labor. Public policy should seek to identify coming bottlenecks and to work with the appropriate parties in the industry to avoid or limit the occurrence of shortages.

A Manpower Program

The government might usefully play a larger role in the operation of the labor market in construction without engaging itself any more deeply in the operation of the training or referral processes themselves. For a variety of reasons, the operation of training and referral programs is an important element of collective bargaining in construction, and government intervention into these functions would be resisted (and probably thwarted) unless the federal role were strictly limited to what would be acceptable to the industry.[12] However, public action to assist the industry in manpower planning, in formal training, in improving the utilization of the existing labor force, and in increasing minority group entry may well be welcomed.

Public agencies should provide data, technical assistance, and funds to improve manpower projections and planning mechanisms both on a national and on a local basis. A full range of functions in the industry needs support, extending from the allocation of available manpower among projects in a local labor market to long-run planning that considers both formal training and informal entry. Federal participation in forecasting manpower demand, in foreseeing the impact of changing technology, and in assisting national union leadership and contractors' associations to exert greater influence over local manpower planning would be valuable to the industry. Better manpower information could make an important contribution to the manpower plan-

[12] This includes, of course, the role of the government as a regulator of the manner in which recruitment, training, and referral are conducted where questions of racial discrimination or other such matters are involved.

ning process, and the federal government is uniquely situated to improve the information system in the industry, since it is the prime source of employ- ment and unemployment data, of expenditures data, and of activity fore- casts for construction. Carefully researched manpower studies, prepared in association with industry representatives, are likely to be widely used through- out the country and to provide a bench mark against which industry leaders may measure the adequacy of their programs.[13]

Formal manpower training can best be supported in three ways. First, the current planning mechanisms require extensive development. The most important contributions to increasing the capacity of apprenticeship and other formal training programs to meet national manpower needs would be to expand the role of national authorities in the local planning process and to refine considerably the technology of planning. Second, individual formal programs should be encouraged to modify their practices with regard to admission standards, rates of compensation, length of compensation, length of training, and quality and content of training, as necessary to attract and retain trainees. Third, the financing of training programs by the industry should be expanded greatly. The government could usefully encourage con- tractors and unions to divert some small portion of the large hourly wage increases now being negotiated in construction into training funds to support entry-level and upgrading programs.

The continued underutilization of construction manpower is a waste of resources the country can ill afford in an inflationary period. Meeting in- creased manpower demand through additional purpose is very difficult in the high-employment economy. However, better allocation of the existing labor force among jobs, greater stability in the industry in volume of work, and reduced seasonality each promise considerable increases in productive labor available to the industry without unduly straining the sources of man- power supply. Governments at the federal and state level could do much to promote better utilization of labor in the industry.

Finally, all levels of government can do more to promote and facilitate entrance of minority group members to construction. The most important means by which increased minority participation can be furthered are (1)

[13] For example, the Office of Education provided financial support to academic and industry personnel in developing the "World of Construction" program for the public schools (see Chapter 7). Also, the Manpower Administration of the Department of Labor funded the Purdue University study that attempted to establish models of more effective apprenticeship programs; see Purdue Research foundation, "A Study of the Need for Educational and Training Adjustments in the Apprenticeship Programs for Selected Craft Occupations," xerox, report prepared for the U.S. Department of Labor, Manpower Administration, by Alfred S. Drew (Lafayette, Ind., 1970).

expansion of areawide training programs in all crafts; (2) increased recruitment of nonwhite high school students for construction; (3) improved vocational and academic preparation of nonwhite youth in the schools; and (4)
adjustments in apprenticeship and other formal training programs to the low
academic performance of some minority group members through basic education, supplementary courses, and other means. Governments must, if
these purposes are to be achieved, stop playing politics with the entry of
nonwhites to the craft unions and stop funding imaginary training programs
(for example, many of those in construction with individual employers). In
crafts and areas where, for political or other reasons, the government supports
programs ostensibly directed at training nonwhite mechanics but that actually
provide second-rate or illusory training, it is exceedingly difficult to develop
substantive and effective programs.

Assisting Residential Construction

Federal economic policy in the late 1960s was a major contributor to the
poor performance of the housing industry. Rather than attempting to reverse
the decline of housing construction, the federal government for several years
acted through different agencies with different purposes, the net effect of
which was to restrict housing production substantially during 1966–1970.
Housing served during this period as the major stabilizer of the American
economy. Restrictive monetary policy held down the rate of housing starts
as a means of reducing aggregate demand in the economy (thereby mitigating
to a degree the rise of prices). After monetary restraint was relaxed in 1970,
housing starts began to rise and within a few months reached rates not
known in the country since the 1950s. This pattern of monetary restraint
and release, with its consequent effects on housing construction, is familiar
in the United States and is unlikely to be altered in the near future.[14]

During the period of monetary restraint, several other actions were taken
by the federal government with regard to housing production. In concert with
the private residential construction industry, the government enacted into
law and began to operate several new programs designed to bring mortgage
money into the housing market. Other programs provided federal subsidies
for construction and rehabilitation of housing units for special groups in the
population, including especially the poor and elderly.[15] Furthermore, in the

[14]See Chapter 9.
[15]These programs were often marred by inadequate administration by the federal
government. See, for example, the report to the Congress by the Comptroller General
of the United States, "Improvements Needed in the Management of the Urban
Renewal Rehabilitation Program" (April 25, 1969). In 1970, the operation of the
rehabilitation programs was suspended for reorganization and reform.

Housing Act of 1968 the Congress committed the nation to an explicit quantitative goal for new housing construction over the next decade and directed
the President to report to Congress annually on progress toward this goal.[16]
These and several other actions of the government were on the whole constructive efforts to support the volume of housing production under generally
restrictive monetary policy.

The government also sought during this period to initiate far-reaching
changes in housing production methods.[17] The Department of Housing and
Urban Development (HUD), unable to effect changes in monetary policy
(adopted by the board of governors of the Federal Reserve System) began to
devote considerable attention to special programs intended to alter the structure and technology of the residential construction industry. Adopting the
view that the industry was characterized by ineffective management and inefficient technology and that productivity was strangled by the building trades
unions, HUD sought means to radically restructure the industry in a short period. Changes in technology and organization would, HUD agreed, stabilize construction costs and stimulate greatly increased volumes of housing construction.[18] In 1968, the department conducted a nationwide competition (the
In-City Project) among firms and consortia of firms for a major research and
development contract to construct in at least 20 cities prototypes of industrialized housing systems. Kaiser Engineers emerged as the successful applicant.
Thereafter, the size of the undertaking was steadily reduced, until all that
remained was the construction of some 48 units on 6 scattered sites in the
Miami area.[19] In 1969, HUD conducted a second competition (Operation
Breakthrough) for contracts to develop and build new housing units utilizing
new technological developments. In early 1970, several consortia of firms
were selected under Operation Breakthrough for the negotiation of construction contracts. Under Breakthrough some 3000 units were planned for construction at various sites around the country.[20]

There is no doubt that these federal competitions and their accompanying

[16]See the President's annual reports on national housing goals for 1969 and 1970.
[17]See, for example, "Cities' Plight Spurs Quest for New Techniques," *Engineering News-
Record,* January 25, 1968, pp. 92–94. See also Chapter 9.
[18]See, for example, "Operation Breakthrough," in U.S. President, *Second Annual
Report on National Housing Goals* (Washington, D.C., 1970).
[19]For other reasons, the Miami area was at the time experiencing the biggest housing
boom in the nation. See "Bids Called . . . ," *Engineering News-Record,* January 8, 1970,
p.15.
[20]U.S. Department of Housing and Urban Development, *This is Operation Breakthrough*
(Washington, D.C., 1969).

publicity have created tremendous interest in American industry in the housing field. Further, these competitions have been accompanied by large expenditures by business on research and development of new housing technologies. In consequence, it is likely that some significant advances in materials and design may emerge from these efforts.

Unfortunately, public policy of the type represented by the In-City Project and Operation Breakthrough also has its costs. To a large degree those costs are the lost opportunity to do more constructive things. There have always been many problems in the residential construction industry that federal support and assistance might be of great use in relieving. Among them are the extreme variability of market demand (resulting mainly from monetary factors), the seasonality of work, the small degree of formal training provided to the work force, the allocation of the labor force among sites and builders, the difficulty of management training in small firms, and the diffusion of information regarding technological advances. In these areas, the contribution of HUD has been very limited, although other federal agencies have provided some support to the industry.[21] Furthermore, in publicizing the rhetoric of revolutionary technological change, HUD failed to investigate, to understand, and to inform the nation and its leaders of the realities surrounding housing production. In consequence, public and governmental discussions regarding housing and housing policies acquired an aura of unreality, in which the problems and processes understood by the industry to be important were of no interest to the government, while the government, for its part, conducted negotiations with large firms in other industries regarding housing production. In this atmosphere, the private housing industry continued production largely unaffected by the government except through the traditional means of the availability and cost of financing.

Epilogue

The preceding pages have described a program for public policy that might be carried out over a period of years, with adjustments as necessary. This long-term program promises a considerable degree of success in reconciling high-employment conditions with price and wage stability in construction. Only such a comprehensive and well-thought-out program offers real hope

---

[21] For example, the Department of Labor has provided support for manpower training programs in homebuilding, and the Department of Commerce has sought to improve methods of transfer of technological information.

of significant and lasting accomplishments. Limited programs, involving make-shift adjustments in current practices (for example, attempts to amend or change the administration of the Davis-Bacon Act) generate intensive and exhausting disputes and, even if successful, hold out small hope of contrib-uting to public objectives. Programs that are too ambitious (for example, attempts to impose open-shop conditions nationally or in other ways to shift dramatically the locus of power in the industry) will also lead to ex-tensive conflicts, chaos, and, ultimately, very meager results.

Selected Bibliography

Avid, David C. *Manpower Utilization in the Canadian Construction Industry.* National Research Council Technical Paper no. 156. Ottawa, 1963.

Barbash, Jack. Union Interests in Apprenticeship and Other Training Forms. *Journal of Human Resources* 3 (Winter 1968): 63–85.

Battelle Memorial Institute. Final Report on an Evaluation of the United Association's Training Program. Prepared for the United Association by D. N. McFadden et al. Columbus, Ohio, 1968.

_____. Final Report on a Study of Recent Developments in the Residential Construction Industry and Their Effects on Small Homebuilders. Prepared for the Small Business Administration by Edward E. Laitila et al. Columbus, Ohio, 1969.

Belitsky, Abraham Harvey. Hiring Problems in the Building Trades, with Special Reference to the Boston Area. Ph.D. thesis, Harvard University, 1960.

Berliner, Joseph S. The USSR Construction Industry. Report prepared for the Council for Economic and Industrial Research. Washington, D.C., 1955.

Bertram, Gordon W. *Consolidated Bargaining in California Construction.* Los Angeles: University of California Institute of Industrial Relations, 1966.

Bertram, Gordon W., and Maisel, Sherman J. *Industrial Relations in the Construction Industry.* Berkeley: University of California Institute of Industrial Relations, 1955.

Bok, Derek C., and Dunlop, John T. *Labor and the American Community.* New York: Simon & Schuster, 1970.

Bonadio, Frank, et al. *The Resolution of Jurisdictional Disputes.* Detroit: University of Michigan–Wayne State University Institute of Labor and Industrial Relations, 1958.

Briggs, Vernon M., Jr., and Marshall, F. Ray. *The Negro and Apprenticeship.* Baltimore: Johns Hopkins Press, 1967.

Brownlee, Oswald. The Effects of Monetary and Credit Policies on the Structure of the Economy. *Journal of Political Economy* 76. no. 4, pt. 2 (July–August 1968): 786–795.

Burt, Samuel M. *Industry and Vocational-Technical Education.* New York: McGraw-Hill, 1967.

Cassimates, Peter J. *Economics of the Construction Industry.* National Industrial Conference Board Studies in Business Economics no. 111. New York, 1969.

Chao, Kang. *The Construction Industry in Communist China.* Chicago: Aldine, 1968.

Christie, Robert A. *Empire in Wood: A History of the Carpenters Union.* Ithaca, N.Y.: Cornell University Press, 1956.

Clough, Richard H. *Construction Contracting.* New York: John Wiley & Sons, 1969.

Cohen, Henry A. *Public Construction Contracts and the Law.* New York: McGraw-Hill, 1965.

Colean, Miles L. *American Housing.* New York: Twentieth Century Fund, 1944.

Council on Industrial Relations of the Electrical Contracting Industry. *Rules and Procedures.* 9th ed. Washington, D.C., 1968.

Cullen, Donald E. Union Wage Policy in Heavy Construction: The St. Lawrence Seaway. *American Economic Review* 49 (March 1959): 69-84.

Douglas, Paul. *American Apprenticeship and Industrial Education.* New York: Columbia University Press, 1921.

Dunlop, John T. Guideposts, Wages, and Collective Bargaining. In George P. Shultz and Robert Z. Aliber, eds., *Guidelines: Informal Controls and the Market Place.* Chicago: University of Chicago Press, 1966, pp. 81-96.

——. The Industrial Relations System in Construction. In Arnold R. Weber, ed., *The Structure of Collective Bargaining.* Chicago: University of Chicago Graduate School of Business, 1961, pp. 255-278.

——. *Industrial Relations Systems.* New York: Holt, Rinehart & Winston, 1957.

——. Jurisdictional Disputes: 10 Types. *The Constructor* (journal of the Associated General Contractors), July 1953, p. 165.

——. *Wage Determination under Trade Unions.* New York: Macmillan, 1944.

Dunlop, John T., and Mills, D. Q. Manpower in Construction. In *Report of the President's Committee on Urban Housing: Technical Studies.* Vol. 2. Washington, D.C., 1968, pp. 241-286a.

Estimating Future Occupational Labor Requirements for Private Construction. *Monthly Labor Review* 65 (July 1947): 73-75.

Farber, David A. Apprenticeship in the United States: Labor Market Forces and Social Policy. *Journal of Human Resources* 2 (Winter 1969): 70-90.

——. Construction Apprentices and Construction Workers: A Study of Worker Mobility. Mimeo, 1968.

Field, Charles. "Industrialized Housing and Building Codes." Ph.D. thesis, Harvard University, 1971.

Fisher, Robert W. Labor and the Economy in 1969. *Monthly Labor Review* 93 (January 1970): 30–43.

Foster, Howard G. Labor Supply in the Construction Industry: A Case Study of Upstate New York. Ph.D. thesis, Cornell University, 1968.

Goldfinger, Nathaniel. The Myth of Housing Costs. *American Federationist* (journal of the AFL-CIO) 76 (December 1969): 1–6.

Gordon, R. J. $45 Billion of U.S. Private Investment Has Been Mislaid. *American Economic Review* 112 (June 1969): 221–238.

———. A New View of Real Investment in Structures, 1919–1966. *Review of Economics and Statistics* 50 (November 1968): 417–428.

Graves, Bernie. Breaking Out: An Apprenticeship System among Pipeline Construction Workers. *Human Organization* 17 (Fall 1958): 9–13.

Grebler, Leo. *Housing Issues in Economic Stabilization Policy.* Los Angeles: National Bureau of Economic Research, 1960.

———. Stabilizing Residential Construction. *American Economic Review* 39 (September 1959): 898–910.

Groom, Phyllis. Statistics and Their Limitations, Part 3 of An Assessment of Apprenticeship. *Monthly Labor Review* 87 (April 1964): 391–395.

Haber, William. *Industrial Relations in the Building Industry.* Cambridge: Harvard University Press, 1930.

Haber, William, and Levinson, Harold. *Labor Relations and Productivity in the Building Trades.* Ann Arbor: University of Michigan Bureau of Industrial Relations, 1956.

Herzog, John P. *An Analysis of the Dynamics of Large Scale Home Building* Berkeley: University of California Press, 1962.

Hicks, J. R. *The Theory of Wages.* 2nd ed. New York: St. Martin's Press, 1964.

Hodge, C. C. The Negro Job Situation: Has It Improved? *Monthly Labor Review* 92 (January 1969): 20–28.

Holland, D. M. *Private Pension Funds: Projected Growth.* National Bureau of Economic Research Occasional Paper no. 97. New York, 1966.

Holshouser, Eugene C. *Construction Budgeting in State Highway Departments.* Lexington: University of Kentucky Bureau of Business Research, 1962.

Hoskings, William. A Study of Area Wage Structure and Wage Determination in the Building and Construction Industry of Central New York State, 1942–51. Ph.D. thesis, Cornell University, 1955.

Housing: More Industrialization. Thirteenth Urban Design Conference, Harvard Graduate School of Design and the National Urban Coalition, May 1970.

International Labor Organization. *Construction Skills.* Geneva: CIRF Publications, 1969.

Jung, Allen F. Price Variations among Home-Remodeling Contractors. *Journal of Business* 34 (January 1961): 52-56.

Justin, J. Karl. Can We Rebuild an Industry? *Technology Review* 72 (May 1970): 22-29.

Kalachek, Edward D. The Composition of Unemployment and Public Policy. In R. A. Gordon and M. S. Gordon, eds., *Prosperity and Unemployment.* New York: John Wiley & Sons, 1966, pp. 227-245.

Kaufman, J. J. The Role of Vocational Education in the Transition from School to Work. In Arnold R. Weber et al., eds., *Public-Private Manpower Policies.* Industrial Relations Research Association Series. Madison, Wisc., 1969, pp. 191-288.

Kheel, Theodore W. Increasing Employment Opportunity in the Printing and Electrical Trades. In H. R. Northrup and R. L. Rowan, eds., *The Negro and Employment Opportunity.* Ann Arbor: University of Michigan Press, 1964. pp. 193-198.

Klaman, Saul B. Public/Private Approaches to Housing. *Law and Contemporary Problems* 32 (Spring 1964): 250-265.

Lefkoe, M. R. *The Crisis in Construction: There Is an Answer.* Washington, D.C.: Bureau of National Affairs Books, 1970.

Lester, Richard A. Negotiated Wage Settlements, 1951-1967. *Review of Economics and Statistics* 50 (May 1968): 173-181.

_____. The Role of Organized Labor. In R. A. Gordon, ed., *Toward a Manpower Policy.* New York: John Wiley & Sons, 1967; pp. 317-332.

McCaffree, Kenneth M. Regional Labor Agreements in the Construction Industry. *Industrial and Labor Relations Review* 9 (July 1956): 595-609.

MacKall, Luther E. *Surety Underwriting Manual.* Indianapolis: Rough Notes Co., 1963.

Maisel, Sherman J. The Effects of Monetary Policy on Expenditures in Specific Sectors of the Economy. *Journal of Political Economy* 76, no. 4, pt. 2 (July–August 1968): 796–814.

——. *Homebuilding in Transition.* Berkeley: University of California Press, 1953.

Mandelstramm, Allan B. The Effects of Unions on Efficiency in the Residential Construction Industry: A Case Study. *Industrial and Labor Relations Review* 18 (July 1965): 503–521.

Mangum, Garth. *The Operating Engineers: The Economic History of a Trade Union.* Cambridge: Harvard University Press, 1964.

Marshall, F. Ray. *The Negro and Organized Labor.* New York: John Wiley & Sons, 1965.

——. Union Racial Practices. Hearings before the U.S. Senate Committee on Labor and Public Welfare, Subcommittee on Employment and Manpower, September 10, 1963. Reprinted in H. R. Northrup and R. L. Rowan, eds., *The Negro and Employment Opportunity.* Ann Arbor: University of Michigan Press, 1964, pp. 167–185.

Mills, D. Q. Factors Affecting Patterns of Employment and Unemployment in the Construction Industry. Ph.D. thesis, Harvard University, 1967.

——. Housing and Manpower in the 1970's. In Papers Submitted to the House Committee on Banking and Currency, Subcommittee on Housing Panels on Housing Production, Housing Demand, and Developing a Suitable Living Environment, Part 1. 92nd Cong., 1st sess., 1971, pp. 287–314.

——. Manpower in Construction: New Methods and Measures. In Industrial Relations Research Association, *Proceedings of the Twentieth Annual Winter Meeting: The Development and Use of Manpower.* Madison, Wisc., 1967, pp. 269–276.

Mooney, Booth. *Builders for Progress.* New York: McGraw-Hill, 1965.

Myers, Robert J., and Swerdloff, Sol. Seasonality in Construction. *Monthly Labor Review* 90 (September 1967): 1–8.

National Constructors' Association and AFL-CIO Building and Construction Trades Department. *National Disputes Adjustment Plan.* Rev. ed. Washington, D.C., 1968.

Negroes in Apprenticeship. *Monthly Labor Review* 83 (September 1960): 955.

Nellum, A. L., and Associates. Manpower and Rebuilding. Report prepared for the U.S. Department of Housing and Urban Development. Washington, D.C., 1969.

Newcomb, Robinson, and Colean, Miles L. *Stabilizing Construction: The Record and the Potential.* New York: McGraw-Hill, 1952.

Northrup, Herbert R. *The Negro in the Automobile Industry.* Philadelphia: Wharton School of Finance Industrial Research Unit, 1968.

Northrup, Herbert R., and Rowan, R. L., eds. *The Negro and Employment Opportunity.* Ann Arbor: University of Michigan Press, 1964.

Parodi, Maurice. Wage Drift and Wage Bargaining: A Case Study of the Building Industry in Marseilles. *British Journal of Industrial Relations* 1 (June 1963): 213–227.

Perlman, Selig. *A Theory of the Labor Movement.* New York: Macmillan, 1928.

Petro, Sylvester. Unions, Housing Costs and the National Labor Policy. *Law and Contemporary Problems* 32 (Spring 1967): 319–348.

Pierson, Frank. Master Labor Plan. *Monthly Labor Review* 70 (January 1950): 14–18.

Pinkus, Edward C. The Workers Defense League. In P. B. Doeringer, ed., *Programs to Employ the Disadvantaged.* Englewood Cliffs, N.J.: Prentice-Hall, 1969, pp. 168–200.

Piore, Michael J. On-the-Job Training in the Dual Labor Market: Public and Private Responsibilities in On-the-Job Training of Disadvantaged Workers. Mimeo. M.I.T. Department of Economics Working Paper no. 23. Cambridge, 1968.

Purdue Research Foundation. A Study of the Need for Educational and Training Adjustments in Selected Apprenticeable Trades. Xerox. Prepared for the U.S. Department of Labor, Manpower Administration, by Alfred S. Drew. Lafayette, Ind., 1969.

Rajan, G. Soundara. *A Study of the Registered Apprenticeship Programs in Wisconsin.* Madison: University of Wisconsin Center for Studies in Vocational and Technical Education, 1966.

Rensselaer Polytechnic Institute Center for Architectural Research. A Construction Information and Analysis System for the State of New York. Reports nos. 1 and 2. Prepared for the State University Construction Fund. Troy, N.Y., 1969.

Research in Apprenticeship Training. Madison: University of Wisconsin Center for Studies in Vocational and Technical Education, 1967.

Ross, Arthur M. *Trade Union Wage Policy.* Berkeley: University of California Press, 1948.

Rottenberg, Simon. The Irrelevance of Union Apprenticeship/Journeyman Ratios. *Journal of Business* 34 (July 1961): 384–386.

Rowley, Raymond K., and Sabbatini, J. Labor Unions' Encroachment on Contractors' Right to Manage. Stanford University, Department of Civil Engineering, Construction Institute Technological Memo no. 1. Stanford, Calif., 1969.

Ryan, Frederick L. *Industrial Relations and the San Francisco Building Trades.* Norman: University of Oklahoma Press, 1936.

Salt, Alan F. Estimated Need for Skilled Workers, 1965–76. *Monthly Labor Review* 89 (April 1966): 365–371.

Scheuch, Richard. The Labor Factor in Residential Construction. Ph.D. thesis, Princeton University, 1951.

Scoville, James G. Concepts and Measurements of Manpower and Occupational Analysis. Mimeo. Prepared for the U.S. Department of Labor, Office of Manpower Research. Washington, D.C., 1969.

Seasonal Unemployment in the Construction Industry: Report and Recommendations of the Secretary of Labor and the Secretary of Commerce. Mimeo. Washington, D.C., 1969.

Segal, Martin. *The Rise of the United Association.* Cambridge: Harvard University Press, 1969.

Simons, Henry. Some Reflections on Syndicalism. *Journal of Political Economy* 52 (March 1944): 1–19.

Slatzman, Arthur W. Manpower Planning in Private Industry. In Arnold R. Weber et al., eds., *Public-Private Manpower Policies.* Industrial Relations Research Association Series. Madison, Wisc., 1969, pp. 79–100.

Slichter, Sumner H., Healy, J. J., and Livernash, E. R. *The Impact of Collective Bargaining on Management.* Washington, D.C.: Brookings Institution, 1960.

Stinchcombe, A. L. Bureaucratic and Craft Administration of Production: A Comparative Study. *Administrative Science Quarterly* 4 (1959): 168–187.

Stone, Joseph, and Brunozzi, J. R. *The Construction Worker under Federal Wage Laws.* Washington, D.C.: Livingston Press, 1959.

Strand, Kenneth T. *Jurisdictional Disputes in Construction.* N.p.: Washington State University Press, 1961.

Strauss, George. Controls by the Membership in Building Trades Unions. *American Journal of Sociology* 61 (May 1956): 527–535.

_____. Union Policies toward the Admission of Apprentices. In Stanley M. Jacks, ed., *Issues in Labor Policy.* Cambridge: MIT Press, 1971, pp. 71–108.

Strauss, George, and Ingerman, Sidney. Public Policy and Discrimination in Apprenticeship. In L. A. Ferman et al., *Negroes and Jobs.* Ann Arbor: University of Michigan Press, 1968, pp. 314–315.

Structural Clay Products Institute. Cold Weather Construction Techniques. Washington, D.C., 1967.

Stucke, A. L., and Gordon, E. M. Manpower Impact of the Proposed $101 Billion Highway Program. *Construction Review* 1 (February 1965): 5–8.

Sumichrast, Michael, and Frankel, Sara A. *Profile of the Builder and His Industry.* Washington, D.C.: National Association of Home Builders, 1970.

Taft, Philip. *The AFL in the Time of Gompers.* New York: Harper & Brothers, 1957.

Thurow, Lester C. Adequate Housing Policies. In U.S. Congress, House, Committee on Banking and Currency, *Emergency Home Financing: Hearings on H.R. 136964, H.R. 14639, H.R. 15402, and H.R. 11.* 91st Cong., 2nd sess., February 3, 1970, pp. 61–67.

Towards Industrialized Building, Third Congress of International Council of Building Research, Studies and Documentation. New York: Elsevier, 1966.

Tyler, Gus. Contemporary Labor's Attitude toward the Negro. In J. Jacobson, *The Negro and the American Labor Movement.* New York: Doubleday, 1968. pp. 363–364.

Ulman, Lloyd. *The Rise of the National Trade Union.* 2nd ed. Cambridge: Harvard University Press, 1966.

United Nations Economic Commission for Europe. *Effect of Repetition on Building Operations and Processes on Site.* Report of an inquiry by the Committee on Housing, Building and Planning. New York, 1965.

U.S., Building Research Advisory Board, National Academy of Sciences–National Research Council. Historical Evaluation of Industrialized Housing and Building Systems. In *Report of the President's Committee on Urban Housing: Technical Studies.* Vol. 2. Washington, D.C., 1968, pp. 177–190.

U.S. Bureau of Apprenticeship and Training. *Career Patterns of Former Apprentices.* Bulletin no. T-147. Washington, D.C., 1959.

———. *Dropouts from Apprenticeship.* Washington, D.C. 1960.

U.S. Bureau of Labor Statistics. *Compensation in the Construction Industry.* Bulletin no. 1656. Washington, D.C., 1970.

———. *Employee Compensation and Payroll Hours: Building Construction, 1965.* Report no. 335-9. Washington, D.C., 1968.

———. *Patterns of U.S. Economic Growth.* Bulletin no. 1672. Washington, D.C., 1970.

———. *Projections 1970.* Bulletin no. 1536. Washington D.C., 1966.

———. *Seasonality and Manpower in Construction.* Bulletin no. 1642. Washington, D.C., 1970.

———. *Tomorrow's Manpower Needs.* Washington, D.C., 1969.

U.S. Bureau of the Census. *1967 Census of Construction Industries.* Washington, D.C., 1970.

U.S. Chamber of Commerce. *Chaos in the Construction Industry.* Washington, D.C., 1969.

U.S. Commission on Civil Rights Advisory Committee. *Reports on Apprenticeship.* Washington, D.C., 1964.

U.S. Congress, House, Committee on Education and Labor, Select Subcommittee on Labor. *Seasonal Unemployment in the Construction Industry: Hearings on H.R. 15990.* 90th Cong., 2nd sess., July 1968.

U.S. Congress, Joint Economic Committee, Subcommittee on Economic Progress. *State and Local Public Facility Needs and Financing.* Vol. 1. 89th Cong., 2nd sess., 1966.

U.S. Congress, Senate, Committee on Labor and Public Welfare, Subcommittee on Employment and Manpower. *Selected Readings in Employment and Manpower,* vol. 3, *The Role of Apprenticeship in Manpower Development.* 88th Cong., 2nd sess., 1964.

U.S. Department of Commerce. *Second Homes in the United States.* Series H-121, no. 16. Washington, D.C., 1969.

U.S. Department of Housing and Urban Development. *Action against Seasonal Unemployment in the Construction Industry: Lessons from Foreign Experience.* Washington, D.C., forthcoming.

U.S. Department of Housing and Urban Development, Division of International Affairs. *Industrialized Building: A Comparative Analysis of European Experience.* Washington, D.C., 1968.

U.S. Department of Labor. *Apprenticeship: Past and Present.* Rev. ed. Washington, D.C., 1969.

———. *Formal Occupational Training of Adult Workers.* Manpower/Automation Research Monograph no. 2. Washington, D.C., 1964.

U.S. Department of Labor, Labor Management Services Administration. *Exclusive Union Work Referral Systems in the Building Trades.* Washington, D.C., 1970.

U.S., National Advisory Commission on Vocational Education. *Annual Report: Vocational Education Amendments of 1968, Public Law 90-576.* Washington, D.C., 1969.

———. *Second Report.* Washington, D.C., 1969.

U.S. President. *First Annual Report on National Housing Goals.* Washington, D.C., 1969.

———. *Second Annual Report on National Housing Goals.* Washington, D.C. 1970.

Wittrock, Jan. *Reducing Seasonal Unemployment in the Construction Industry.* Paris: Organization for Economic Cooperation and Development, 1967.

The World of Construction. Bloomington, III.: McKnight and McKnight, 1970.

Index